WHAT IS SQL?

WHAT IS SQL?

FUNDAMENTALS OF SQL, T-SQL, PL/SQL AND DATAWAREHOUSING.

Victor Ebai

authorHOUSE®

AuthorHouse™
1663 Liberty Drive
Bloomington, IN 47403
www.authorhouse.com
Phone: 1-800-839-8640

www.whatissqlquery.com

Published by AuthorHouse   12/21/2012

ISBN: 978-1-4772-4644-3 (sc)
ISBN: 978-1-4772-4645-0 (e)

Contents

Part One

Part Two

Acknowledgments

I want to thank the various authors who have written valuable books on SQL and Business Intelligence. My research for this book included works by Ben Forta, Itzik Ben-Gan, Jason Price, Ralf Kimball and Cindi Howson.

I am also very grateful to Microsoft and Oracle for providing free development tools for aspiring developers.

Dedication

This book is dedicated to my mum Helen who has always been there in all situations. Thanks for the smiles mum.

Introduction

The SQL programming language is the most widely used database programming language. It is used either directly or embedded within other languages to manage business information assets. Though this language has been standardised by international standards bodies (ISO and ANSI), there are still significant deviations in its implementation by the combined market leaders, namely Microsoft and Oracle Corporation. Larger companies operate heterogeneous database environments which generally include oracle and SQL server databases thus there is a high demand of SQL expertise for both. Moreover, with the increase in demand for business intelligence applications, there is also an increasing demand for SQL datawarehousing expertise. The book covers all of these and is based on the latest database releases (oracle 11g and SQL Server 2012). To get the best out of *What Is SQL* go to the appendix and download and install the free sample databases so that you can experiment with the examples.

Part One of this book practically wrote itself through my own misconceptions about SQL at the start of my Business Intelligence career. It was hard to find any book which met the demands of the ever changing business world. Most good SQL books simply state how to use SQL statements without including the business context thus the user will be at a loss on when and why the statements should be applied in the business environment. There are also several critical nonstandard business intelligence requirements which are ignored by most books. Some of these omissions include data verification, validation and correction concerns or the manipulation of duplicate rows. With all this in mind I decided to write this book to add to and update the wealth of SQL knowledge already in the public domain. Part One will teach you the most important aspects of SQL from database design, data retrieval and modification to more complex concepts such as triggers and performance tuning. All concepts are clearly demonstrated with repeatable practical examples.

Part Two of this book extends the knowledge already gained in Part One. It extends the power of SQL by using its procedural extensions by oracle (PL/SQL) and SQL server (programmable T-SQL). It enables the user to execute complex business processes using these extensions. These extensions are particularly important for complex transactional processing, where a set of mutually dependent SQL statements are executed together. It also teaches the reader how to automate business processes using functions and procedures. The elementary components of these extensions are clearly stated and the business context is also clearly illustrated using repeatable practical examples. The reader will learn how to write functions, procedures, and recoverable transactions which will enable them to develop useful business applications.

Who is What IS SQL for? And how should it be used?

My advice to anyone who uses this book is to be courageous and keep going. If a concept seems out of reach then try the examples. If this does not help, just move on to the next topic and revisit the tricky ones at a later time. The first two chapters are very theoretical and set the foundations of SQL. They can be used as a reference for advanced readers. For those who want to learn by example and hit the road running chapter three is a good starting point. All the examples have been thoroughly tested and are error free. Feel free to copy and paste each example into the SQL editors to replicate the results. The code can also be downloaded from the support website.

- The absolute beginner. All the elementary components are stated and simple repeatable examples are used for clarity.

- The experts and intermediate users. Most standard and nonstandard constructs are illustrated thus this book can be used as a reference. The procedural extensions are also fully covered.

- Business Users. The business context of SQL is clearly explained and the transformation of business requirements to SQL statements is demonstrated.

- Students. This book prepares students for the challenges they will face in the ever changing business environment. Most examples are based on everyday business requirements.

PART ONE

Chapter One

Overview

This chapter introduces relational Database Management Systems (DBMS) and databases. A brief overview of E-R modelling and normalisation is also introduced. By the end of this chapter, the user should be able to design and document simple databases based on clear business requirements. The details regarding how to obtain and install Oracle11g and Microsoft SQL server 2012 databases can be found in the appendix.

Database Management Systems (DBMS) and Databases

Everyday activities such as using the Internet, the ATM machine, buying groceries and paying bills all produce vast amounts of data. With this exponential increase of data from numerous sources, a system is needed to harness its potential and deliver useful information to organisations and people. Thus, DBMSs are used.

A DBMS is software used to manage and control the capture, access, maintenance, storage, organization, and delivery of data in a secure and consistent manner.

DBMS becomes available once the software is installed and provides tools for the creation, maintenance, and administration of databases. The data DBMSs manage is stored in databases. Most database operations are executed using SQL statements. These statements are ether issued through application software such as SAP Hr, Oracle applications, or Maximo or through an SQL editor.

DBMS Tools

During installation, the software creates log files and a system database known as the 'data dictionary', which stores and maintains information about all current and future database objects. The DBMS also provides security tools to create and manage users and other database objects using privileges. Built-in functions, procedures, tablespaces, SQL engines/editors, connection packages, and system views are also created and enabled for future use by database administrators and developers.

The Database

The database is primarily made up of tables. Tables are made up of rows and columns that are used to structure and organise data. The database is designed through a process known as entity relationship modelling and/or normalisation. The end product of this process is a logical database model that details which tables are to be created and what the relationships between them are. Once this model is available, the physical database can be created using SQL by the database developer/administrator. Other useful database objects that could be created include views, stored procedures, triggers, sequences, synonyms, schemas, constraints, and so forth. The description and creation of all these objects is covered in the advanced chapters of this book.

Schemas and Tables

Schemas are logical partitions of databases created to facilitate the management of other database objects. They group relational objects into logical units based on their business function. For example, a database that contains human resources and production tables will have human resources and production schemas. In this way, all tables (objects) in a schema can be backed up or deleted as a group. To access a schema object, the object name must be prefix with the schema name separated by a dot. This is referred to as the fully qualified name of the object. For example, the best way to access the employee table in the HumanResources schema of the SQL server AdventureWorks2012 database is to use the following fully qualified name: **HumanResources. Employee**. Note that the oracle examples do not include the schema name because the user is already connected to the HR shema thus its application is implicit.

Database Tables

Tables are made up of horizontal rows that are divided into vertical columns, such as in an Excel spreadsheet. A row represents an instance of your table data. Each column holds one detail about the data in a row. For example, in an employee table, each row will hold a set of values in each column particular to an employee. Each column holds a detail value of that employee, such as his or her last name, hire date, and first name.

The database accesses table data only through rows. Thus, if data from a column is required, the database first finds the row that contains the column and then retrieves the column value. Every column has a defined data type that dictates the type of data it can contain. For example, the employee_id column will only accept number data types. If an attempt is made to insert a date data type into this column, an error will occur and the data will be rejected. Every table is owned by a schema and the schema name should always prefix table names in SQL statements. Following is an example of an employee table:

EMPLOYEE_ID	FIRST_NAME	LAST_NAME	E-MAIL
100	Steven	King	SKING
101	Neena	Kochhar	NKOCHHAR

Row

Column

Fig 1.1 Example of a Table

Database Design with Entity Relationship (E-R) Modeling and Normalisation

Entity relationship modelling is used to design databases from scratch. The outputs from this process are a data model and a data dictionary. The model is a pictoral entity relationship conceptual representation of what data is needed to support business processes. The model and data dictionary also includes the relationships between the data entities and the business rules that govern their lifecycle. The model is independent of any DBMS and their simplicity serves as a perfect communication tool between business and IT. A common analogy used to describe the final model is an architects side plan of a building. Just as the walls and rooms detailed in the plan are eventualy constructed into physical walls and rooms, the entities attributes and their business rules are eventually created as physical database tables, columns, and constraints. E-R mdelling will generally produce a normalised database stucture. However, during or after E-R modeling, normalisation can be used to ensure that the designed database tables are in 3rd normal form. Note that there is no absolutely correct design but some designs are more efficient than others, and with enough experience simple databases can be designed by intuition without going throught the modelling process.

Overview of Entity Relationship Modeling (E-R Models)

The E-R modelling process generally goes through four stages, with each stage adding more detail to models produced from the previous stage. This process is known as decomposition. The models in each stage are developed based on expanding data perspectives of the different business stakeholders. For example, a business owner perceives data as a set of discreet entities while the database designer understands that these entities are in fact related. The modelling stages include contextual, conceptual, logical, and physical modelling, and then the physical model is implemented. These different models implicitly document the database at different levels, facilitating its integration into the corporate computing architecture models. It also facilitates communication between IT and different levels of management and support staff.

Basic Constructs of E-R Modelling

Entities: These are the principal data objects about which a business is interested in. They are both tangible and intangible objects that are important to the business. Examples of tangible entities include employees and offices, while intangible entities include jobs, projects, and addresses. Entities are transformed to tables in the physical model. An entity can be classified as either being dependent or independent. A dependent entity is one that requires another entity for its identification, while an independent entity identifies itself.

Attributes: Attributes describe the entity they are assigned to. For example, the attribute first_name of the employee entity describes the first name of an employee. Attributes are transformed into columns in the physical model. A set of attributes form a table row in the physical model. A row represent an instance of an entity. Attributes called identifiers are used to uniquely identify each instance of an entity. They are represented in the physical models as primary keys.

Relationships: Relationships are derived from business rules. For example, a business rule can state that an employee must only have one postal address. This rule will dictate the relationship between the employee entity and the address entity. Relationships describe associations between entities. There are several types and categories of relationships, but only binary relationships between two entities are explored. The cardinality of a relationship states the number of occurrences of an instance of one entity relates to another entity instance(s).

There are three types of cardinalities in relationships: one-to-one (1:1), one-to-many (1:N) and many-to-many (M:N). Relationships are implemented using database constraints. Constraints are explained in the advanced chapters of this book (see chapter eleven).

One-to-one (1:1): In this relationship, one instance of entity A can only be related to one instance of entity B. For example, an employee has only one address, and each address can only be associated with one employee.

One-to-many (1:N): In this relationship, one instance of entity A can be related to zero or more instances of entity B, but for each instance of entity B there can only be one instance of entity A. For example, if department is entity A and employees is entity B, each department can have zero or more employees while each employee can only work in one department.

Many-to-many (M:N): In this relationship, one or many occurrences of entity A are related to zero or many instances of entity B and vice versa.

Contextual Modeling

These are the highest and least detailed models. They identifiy the data entities that are important from a business owner's pespective for a particular business area. They are documented in a table that will include the entity number, name, and a brief desription. This table becomes the data dictionary at the end of the modelling process. For example, a subset of the contextual entities for a human resources database will be represented as follows (note that each entity must have a unique name):

Entity Number	Entity Name	Entity Description
1	Employees	Any person working for the company.
2	Candidates	Any person who wants to work for the company
3	Jobs	Available jobs in the company
4	Countries	Countries where business is conducted
5	Job_history	History of Job changes by employees

Table 1.2: E-R Contextual Data Dictionary

Conceptual Modeling

Conceptual models add more detail to the entities identified from contextual stage. It models each entity and defines the relationships between them from a business perspective. Business rules such as security and data validation requirements for each entity can also be identified and recorded. At this stage the pictorial graphical representations of the entities is also produced. The relationships between the entities are also defined. The key rule here is that each entity must be related to at least one other entity. The data dictionary from the previous stage is also enhanced as follows:

Entity Number	Entity Name	Entity Description	Security	Business rule
1	Employees	Any person working for the company	Confidential	The first name of an employee is never null
2	Candidates	Any person who wants to work for the company	secured	Only candidates can become employees
3	Jobs	Available jobs in the company	Shared	Each employee must have only one job. Salary must be between 20 and 50.
4	Countries	Countries where business is conducted	Shared	Each country must belong to one region
5	Regions	Regions where business is conducted	Shared	Each region must have a name.

Table 1.3: E-R Conceptual Data Dictionary

There is no standard notation for entity relationship diagrams but the crow's foot notation is preferred. A simplified subset of the E-R diagram for the human resources database is as follows:

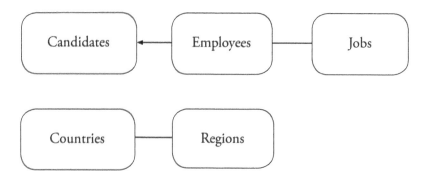

Fig 1.1 Conceptual E-R Model

The simplified entity relationship diagram shows bidirectional relationships between each entity. The existence relationship indicates that each employee must first be a candidate.

Logical Modelling

The logical model adds more details to the conceptual model. It is can be regarded as the data model from a database designer's perspective. On this model, the attributes of each entity are identified and included. The three types of attributes are primary, non-primary, and foreign key attributes. The primary key (PK) enforces entity integrity by uniquely identifying each instance (row) of the entity (table). The non-key attributes describe the entity. The foreign key (FK) enforces referential integrity between two entities. Most foreign keys are primary keys in other tables. Each attribute name must also be unique for each entity. The new logical E-R diagram for the HR database can be represented as follows:

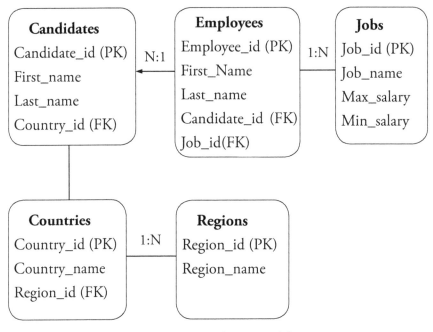

Fig 1.2 Logical E-R Model

The logical model shows the attributes of each entity. This model is independent of any DBMS. Notice that the cardinalities of each relationship have also been specified. It is also important to have a navigational path from each entity to the other through foreign and primary keys.

The Physical Model

This model adds more details to the logical model. The database-specific information such as data types are added to the model. The entities are transformed into tables and the attributes are transformed into columns. The business rules, foreign key, and primary keys are also transformed into database constraints, error handlers and triggers in the physical model. There are certain rules to observe when transforming entities to tables. The rules are there so that the final database tables are normalised to the third normal form. Some of these rules can be ignored if the business requirement invalidates them. For example, if there is a requirement to store a full address in a column, the atomicity rule which states that each column must only contain a single value can be ignored for that table column.

The key rules to transforming the entities into tables include: each value in a column must be atomic (single), and all the values in the column must be of the same data type. For example, the full name of an employee is not stored in one column. The full name is divided and stored in two columns: First_name and Last_name:

The primary key must always exist in each table so that each row is unique. Note that the sequence of columns and rows are also insignificant in the model specification. The DBMS handles the exact physical storage properties of individual rows and columns. The final physical data model that depicts tables and columns can be represented as follows.

Candidates (Candidate_id (PK), First_name, Last_name)
Employees (Employee_id (PK), First_Name, Last_name,
    Candidate_id (FK), Job_id (FK))
Jobs (Job_id (PK), Job_name, Max_salary, Min_salary)
Countries (Country_id (PK), Country_name, Region_id (FK))
Regions (Region_id (PK), Region_name)

Fig 1.3 Common Physical Table Descriptions

The final data dictionary for the human resources database is represented as follows:

Table Number	Table Name	Security	Business rule/constraint
1	Employees	Confidential	NOT NULL on First_name, PRIMARY on Employee_id, FOREIGN on Candidate_id, Job_id
2	Candidates	Secured	PRIMARY on Candidate_id
3	Jobs	Shared	PRIMARY on Job_id, CHECK on Max_salary,_Min_salary
4	Countries	Shared	PPRIMARY on Country_id FOREIGN on Region_id
5	Regions	Shared	PPRIMARY on Region_id

Table 1.4: Physical Data Dictionary

This final physical model can be used by the database administrator or developer to create the tables and their constraints. This physical model is DBMS specific. The columns and their data types are also specified at this point. The details of table creation and maintenance are covered in chapter eleven.

Normalisation

There are two types of relational databases. They are OLAP (On-Line Analytical Processing) and OLTP (On-Line Transactional Processing) databases. OLAP databases are designed for optimised reporting. They are usually implemented as data warehouses and are optimised to efficiently process SELECT statements. These reporting statements are highly efficient because of the small number of tables required for these queries. They are referred to as denormalised databases. OLTP databases are designed to process a large number of discreet transactions. For example, an ATM uses an OLTP database to process millions of cash transactions every week. These types of databases are efficient at executing INSERT, DELETE, and UPDATE SQL statements, but they are inefficient for reporting using SELECT statements because of the large number of tables involved. During or after entity relation modelling of OLTP databases, normalisation could be used to confirm that the tables in the model are optimised to facilitate intensive business data processing.

Database normalisation prevents data redundancy and update anomalies and makes the best possible usage of storage. It also structures the data for optimal analysis. To understand these undesirable characteristics of databases that are not normalised, consider the following employees and department tables.

Employee_id	Full_name	Department Name
100	Steven King	Programming
101	Victor Ebai	Sales

Table 1.5 Employee Table

Department Name	Full_name	Location
Programming	Steven King	England
Sales	Victor Ebai	Germany

Table 1.6 Department Table

Notice that the employee full_name is unnecessarily repeated in both tables, creating data redundancy and wasting disk space. If the employee full_name changes, the name will have to be changed in both tables, which might create update anomalies. Finally, if there is a business requirement to retrieve all employees whose last name is, for example, Ebai, it becomes tricky because the employee's first and last name are stored together as full_name. Normalization eradicates these undesirable properties.

Normalization is the process of continually dividing large tables into smaller ones and redefining their relationships. In this way, data is sufficiently isolated where a modification in one table is propagated to the other related tables. Normalization is based on the concept of normal forms as defined by computer scientist, E. F. Codd. There are five normal forms, but we will only cover the first three. A table is considered to be in a particular form if it conforms to a set of rules.

Most OLTP database tables should be in the third normal form (3NF). For a table to exist in 3NF, it must also conform to the rules of the first normal form (1NF) and second normal form (2NF).

First Normal Form (1NF)

A table is considered to be in the first normal form if the rows are all unique and each column data is atomic. The uniqueness is achieved by having a unique primary key. To make column values atomic, some columns will have to be split up. For example, the following employees table is not in the 1NF. To render it into the 1NF, an employee_id primary key is added to guarantee uniqueness and the full_name column is split into First_name and Last_name to guarantee column atomicity.

E-mail	Full_name	Department_Name
sking@hotmail.com	Steven King	Programming
ve@yahoo.com	Victor Ebai	Sales

Table 1.7 Employees Table

Employee_id	First_name	Last_name	E-mail	Department_Name
100	Steven	King	sking@hotmail.com	Programming
101	Victor	Ebai	ve@yahoo.com	Sales

Table 1.8 1NF Employees Table

Second Normal Form (2NF)

A table is considered to be in 2NF when it conforms to the first normal form and when the non-key attributes are totally functionally dependent on the primary key (candidate key). This means that to retrieve any non-key column value, the full value of the primary key must be used. This situation arises when a table has a composite primary key. Composite primary keys are primary keys that are made up of more than one column. This leads to the splitting of tables so that all the attributes in each table are totally dependent on the primary key.

For example, using our 1NF employees table, if a composite primary key is defined on the employee_id and department_name columns, the non-key attribute First_name can be obtained by only specifying department_name and ignoring the employee_id. This violates the 2NF rules. This situation is resolved by splitting the table into an employees and departments table and then eliminates the department_name column from the employees table primary key.

Employee_id	First_name	Last_name	E-mail	Department_ID
100	Steven	King	sking@hotmail.com	1
101	Victor	Ebai	ve@yahoo.com	2

Table 1.9 2NF employees table

DEPARTMENT_ID	Department_name	Location
1	Programming	England
2	Sales	Germany

Table 1.10 2NF Departments Table

After splitting the table, each non-key employee attribute can only be retrieved from the full employee_id primary key.

Third Normal Form 3NF

A table is considered to be in the 3N when it conforms to the 2NF and all non-key attributes are totally independent of each other. For example, in the 2NF departments table, the non-key attribute location can be used to determine the other non-key attribute department name. This violates the 3NF. This can be resolved by creating a new locations table resulting in three 3NF tables.

LOCATION_ID(PK)	Location_Name	Department_id(FK)
1	England	1
2	Germany	2

Table 1.11 3NF Locations

DEPARTMENT_ID(PK)	Department_name	Location
1	Programming	England
2	Sales	Germany

Table 1.12 3NF Departments

EMPLOYEE_ID(PK)	First_name	Last_name	E-mail	Department_ID(FK)
100	Steven	King	sking@hotmail.com	1
101	Neena	Kochhar	sking@yahoo.com	2

Table 1.12 3NF Employees

Notice that the data redundancy and update anomalies have been eliminated as data about each entity is stored only in a single table. Changes to any entity are logically projected to the other entities through their foreign and primary key constraints. For example, if the last_name of employee 100 changes from King to Fontain, a query that needs to return the names of employees who work in department 1 will simply return the names of all employees whose foreign keys is equal to 1. This will include employee 100 with the changed name implicitly propagating the change to the department table. Note that these update anomalies are slightly more complicated in data warehouse environments where they are treated as slowly changing dimensions (SCD).

Design Completeness and Table Navigation

A simple test for the completeness of the database design is to verify if it is possible to navigate from one table to every other table. These relationships are maintained through primary and foreign key relationships. This is logical because the database is modelled to represent a complete business process thus most of the entities will have both direct and indirect relationships. This is important when queries are required to access multiple tables.

For example, in the database designed in this chapter it is possible to navigate from the locations table to the employees table through the departments table as follows:

Locations.Department_id (FK) → Departments.DEPARTMENT_ ID(PK) → Employees. Department_ID(FK).

Conclusion

The chapter introduced the key concepts of E-R modelling. Though this is not an exhaustive exploration of E-R modelling, the reader should be able to design and document simple databases. One key principle to consider during E-R modelling is not to be constrained by the rigours of the methodology. The designer should focus more on the desired business outcomes derived from the database.

Chapter Two

Overview

This chapter introduces the key building components of SQL statements. These components are applicable to both SQL server 2012 and Oracle 11g. For readers who would rather learn by example this chapter can be ignored and used only for referencing.

SQL Overview

SQL stands for Structured Query Language. Sometimes SQL is referred to as 'sequel'. It is a non-procedural language that is used by all programs and users to access databases. It is non-procedural because it describes what needs to be done rather than how it should be done. The programmer need not worry about how the data is stored or how the processing is handled. The entire processing logic is managed by the DBMS. This property of SQL makes it one of the easiest programming languages to learn.

SQL is both an ISO (International Standards Organisation) and ANSI (American National Standards Institute) standardized language. It was initially developed by IBM. Since the mid-eighties several revisions of SQL standards have been released by these organisations. Though these standards bodies promote SQL uniformity, the SQL standard implemented by commercial Database Management Systems (DBMS) differ to some degree. This book covers the SQL implemented in the Oracle 11g and SQL server 2012 DBMSs produced by Oracle and

Microsoft respectively. Most of the statements used in both DBMS are equivalent and they both conform to international standards. Only the major SQL implementation differences are highlighted. The second part of this book covers the procedural extensions of SQL by Oracle (PL/SQL) and Microsoft (Programmable T-SQL).

There are four general groups of SQL statements, each performing different database maintenance and querying functions:

- *Data Control Language* (DCL): These statements are used to manage access to database objects. Typical commands include GRANT and REVOKE permission to access an object. Mostly used by database administrators (DBAs).

- *Data Definition Language* (DDL): These statements are used to create and maintain database objects such as tables, constraints, views, and indexes. Typical commands include *ALTER, CREATE,* and *DROP* objects.

- *Transaction Control*: These statements are used to manage groups of DML statements. They help ensure data and process consistency when complex interdependent transactions are executed. The statements include *ROLLBACK, SAVEPOINT, AND COMMIT.*

- *Data Manipulation Language* (DML): These statements are used to query and maintain table data. Typical commands include *SELECT, MERGE, UPDATE,* and *INSERT* statements. This book will focus on DML, Transaction control and DDL statements.

The Oracle queries in this book will be based on the Oracle HR sample database that is created when the free Oracle 11gexpress DBMS is installed. The SQL server queries are based on SQL server 2012 AdventureWorks2012 sample database. The details of how to download and install these databases can be found in the Getting Started section of this book (see Appendix).

The Oracle SQL developer, the SQL command editor, Toad, or SQL*Plus editor are the SQL development environments for Oracle.

SQL server uses the SQL server management studio query editor. All these tools are used to create a connection to the database and to provide an SQL worksheet where queries can be written and executed.

Basic Components of SQL

The Oracle implementation of SQL is simply called SQL, while the SQL server implementation is called Transact-SQL (T-SQL). Most SQL statements are called queries. The syntax of SQL statements is made up of a combination of English keywords and two or more clauses. Clauses are individual sections of the statement. Clauses are used to introduce other basic components such as table names, expressions, and literals (see below) into an SQL statement. Each clause is defined by a keyword. For example, the SELECT keyword is used to define the SELECT clause that lists required columns, the FROM keyword is used to define the FROM clause that lists the originating tables, and the WHERE keyword is used to define the WHERE clause that defines the filtering conditions. Queries are always terminated with a semicolon. A simple query composed of two clauses can be written as follows:

```
SELECT first_name, last_name, salary +100
FROM employees;
```

The query uses the SELECT keyword to define the SELECT clause that introduces two columns (first_name and last_name) and an expression (salary +100). The FROM keyword is used to define the FROM clause that specifies the originating table of the columns. The basic components that can be introduced in clauses are defined below.

Literals: Literals are constant fixed data values. They are frequently used for data filtering and calculations. There are three general types of literals: string, numerical, and date time.

Sting literals are alphanumeric constants. They are always enclosed in single quotes. Examples are 'laptop', '2000', and 'Book'. These literals are case sensitive. Thus, 'Book' is different than 'book'. Note that a number enclosed in single quotes becomes a string literal.

Numerical literals are numerical constants. These could be integers, real numbers, or floating point numbers. They stand alone without any special symbols. Examples include 1,500; 7000; 3.76; and 25F.

Date time literals are date constants. They are expressed as a string literal. An example is '12-12-2012'. In chapter eight functions and format models will be used to inform the database that the date represented as a string literal is indeed a date data type.

Comments

Comments are optional but should be included to document the SQL code. This facilitates maintenance. Comments are ignored by the compilers. Comments can be included as a single line or they might span more than one line. Single line comments are declares with a double minus sign (--) while multiline comments are decleared using the following symbols /* */.Following is an example of how to add both types of comments in a statement:

```
SELECT first_name, last_name, salary, rownum FROM employees
--This is a single line comment.
/* This is a multi line comment which spans more than one line.
*/
WHERE employee_id <102;
```

Nulls

Columns with no values are refered to as null values. Null values are not 0 (zero), nor are they an empty string (' ') they simply do not exist. Nulls can appear for any data type, and to test for nulls, always use the NULL operators such as IS NULL and IS NOT NULL. The equality (=) operator cannot be used to test for nulls. When NULLS are combined with other values in expressions, the results are generally NULL. The following SQL server examples demonstrate the behaviour of NULLs :

```
SELECT 'SQL' +' ';--an empty string is not a null thus 'SQL' is
    returned from this query.
```

SELECT 'SQL' + NULL;--a string combined with a null returns null

SELECT 1 + 0;--a zero is not a null thus one is returned.

SELECT 1 + NULL;--a number added to a null returns null.

Oracle NULL examples:

SELECT 1 + NULL FROM DUAL;--a number added to a null returns null.

SELECT 1 + 0 FROM DUAL--a zero is not a null thus one is returned.

SELECT 'SQL' || '' FROM DUAL;--an empty string is not a null thus 'SQL' is returned from this query.

SELECT 'SQL' || NULL FROM DUAL;--a string combined with a null returns null

These examples show how NULLs are handled by databases. The syntax of these statements is treated in later chapters. The one thing to note is that SQL server displays nulls in tables as NULL while oracle displays them as '−'.SQL server displays empty strings (") as an empty cell while oracle still displays them as '−'. These representations of NULLs can be influenced by the SQL editor being used.

Format Models

Format models are used to instruct the DBMS on how to interpret strings so they can be used correctly in queries. They are mostly used with data conversion functions.

Operators and Operands

An SQL operator manipulates individual data items and returns a result. The data items are called 'operands', or arguments. Generally, an operator is used before or after an operand or between two operands.

Operators fall into six groups: arithmetic, comparison, character, logical, set, and miscellaneous. Operators can either be unary or binary. Unary operators evaluate only one operand, while binary operators evaluate two operands.

Arithmetic Operators. The main arithmetic operators used in SQL are plus (+), minus (-), divide (/), and multiply (*). They function as used in mathematics.

Comparison Operators. Comparison operators compare expressions and return one of three values: TRUE, FALSE, or UNKNOWN. Unknown is returned when one of the arguments in the expression is null. Most databases will turn an unknown result into false. Comparison operators include single row operators, which are: equality (=), nonequality (<>), nonequality (!=), less than (<), less than or equal to (<=), not less than (!<), greater than (>), greater than or equal to (>=), not greater than (!>). Multiple-row Comparison operators include ANY, EXISTS, ALL, and IN.

Character Operators. Character operators are used to manipulate character strings. They include the concatenation (|| for Oracle) (+ for SQL server) and LIKE operator.

Logical Operators. Logical operators are used to connect two expressions in the WHERE clause. They include AND, OR, and NOT. *AND* means the expressions on both sides must be true to return *TRUE. OR* means that the expressions on one or both sides must be true to return TRUE. NOT reverses the result of an expression. True becomes False and False becomes True.

Set Operators. Set operators are used to apply set theory in SQL. They include UNION, UNION All, INTERSECT, and Set difference (MINUS for Oracle) (EXCEPT for SQL server). Union is used to combine the results of two or more queries while intersection is used to return common rows from the results of two or more queries.

Miscellaneous Operator. This operator includes BETWEEN. The between operator limits your results to a known target range of values.

Built-in Functions. Built-in functions are installed and are ready for use once the DBMS is installed. They manipulate operands and return a result. They are used in queries to automatically transform data. The greatest difference between T-SQL and Oracle SQL is in the implementation of functions.

SQL Expressions. SQL expressions are used to evaluate combinations of operands, literals, and functions. They always return a value that always assumes the data type of its operands. Thus if an expression evaluates numerical operands the return data type will always be numerical. An example of an expression is: SELECT 1 + 1; which returns 2.

SQL Conditions. SQL conditions are used to filter queries. They evaluate a combination of expressions and return a value of TRUE, FALSE, or UNKNOWN. Conditions are typically used in the WHERE clause of a DML statement. Rows are returned when they satisfy the condition in the WHERE clause. Each time a condition evaluates to TRUE the tested rows are returned.

Column Data Types

Each column in a table has a specified data type. The data type is a constraint to the column as they restrict the values that can be inserted into that column to a particular data type. Oracle and SQL server database tables use data types with similar properties but are called different names. Below is a subset of common database data types.

Oracle Data Type	SQL Server Data Type	Description
Nchar, Varchar2, Nvarchar2	Char, Nchar, Nvarchar, Varchar	Stores fixed length and variable length strings
Date, Timestamp	Date, Datetime	Stores date and time values
Integer, Decimal	Integer, Decimal	Stores numbers

It is important to note that some data types are implicitly converted from one data type to the other by databases. For example, if an attempt is made to insert the character string '01110' into an integer column, the database will implicitly convert it into the number 111 and the INSERT statement will succeed.

Table and Column Aliases

Aliases are names given to database tables and columns in SQL statements. Their use is mostly cosmetic. Not using them will not trigger errors. A column might be aliased in a statement if the alias name is more meaningful than the column name to the business user. For example, a column in an employee table might be called emp_id. This column can be renamed to the more business focused name payroll_number. Calculated columns are also renamed with aliases (see Chapter Eight).

Most table aliases are used to reduce the length of table names to reduce Statement complexity. The only non-cosmetic use of aliases is for self joins, where a table is joined to itself (see chapter four). An alias is used to declare two instances of the same table. Aliases are created using the AS keyword and then the alias name. The alias name must always be enclosed in double quotes if it contains a space. If there is no space in the alias name, it can be left as a free standing string.

For example the following 'Full name' alias includes a space thus double quotes are used:

SELECT first_name||' '|| last_name AS "Full name" FROM
employees;

The following 'Fullname' alias does not include a space thus it is not quoted.

SELECT first_name||' '|| last_name AS Fullname FROM
employees;

Conclusion

The key constructs of SQL were covered. A firm understanding of these building blocks is critical to understanding the language. Some SQL statements with also introduced, do not worry about the syntax at this time as their meaning will become apparent in later chapters. Please do spend some time to understand NULLs as they are the source of confusion even to experienced programmers.

Chapter Three

Overview

This chapter introduces the SELECT statement. The statement is used to retrieve data from tables. In this chapter the statement is used to retrieve data from a single table. The Oracle and SQL server implementations are demonstrated.

Retrieving Data from Single Tables

The SQL SELECT statement is used to retrieve data from one or more tables in a database. It is the most frequently used SQL statement. The statement is generally used to produce business reports. The retrieved data can be optionally transformed or formatted using functions and operators, or filtered and sorted according to stated business requirements.

In its simplest form, the mandatory clauses are the SELECT and FROM clause. The SELECT clause lists the columns to be retrieved and the FROM clause specifies the source table(s) from which the stated columns originate. Once a table has been introduced in the FROM clause, any column from that table can be included in the SELECT list of columns. The order of the columns is syntactically unimportant; however, business rules should dictate the column order.

The generic syntax of the simple SELECT statement with its two mandatory SELECT and FROM clauses is as follows:

```
SELECT column1, column2
FROM Table_Name;
Note that column1, column2 are columns from Table_Name.
```

There must always be spaces between the words, and SQL keywords are not case sensitive. The column names are used as the heading for each column in the result and must be separated by commas. In the business environment these column names will appear as fields in reports thus the business relevance of the name is important. If the name is not business focused aliases should be used to rename them.

SQL server examples use the AdventureWorks2012 database while the Oracle examples use the Oracle 11g HR database. In the T-SQL (SQL server) examples, it is mandatory to prefix the table names with the schema names while in oracle the schema name can be ignored because you will connect to the HR schema. Thus the HR schema is implicitly stated.

To display the BusinessEntityID, FirstName and LastNames columns from the AdventureWorks2012 Person.Person table the following command is issued.

```
USE AdventureWorks2012;
GO
SELECT BusinessEntityID,FirstName,LastName
FROM Person.Person;
Subset of Output
```

BusinessEntityID	FirstName	LastName
1	Ken	Sánchez
2	Terri	Duffy
3	Roberto	Tamburello

Table 2.1

The USE AdventureWorks command specifies that the AdventureWorks2012 database should be used for the subsequent query.

The displayed output is only a subset of all the rows returned. The query returns the values contained in the three listed columns for each row in the Person.Person table. The statement uses the SELECT keyword to list the required columns, and the FROM keyword specifies the originating Person.Person table. Each column name is separated by a comma.

The Oracle syntax is exactly the same. To return all the rows and columns of a table an asterisk (*) is used to replace the column list in the SELECT clause. For example to return all rows and columns from the HumanResources.Department table the following statement is used.

```
USE AdventureWorks2012;
GO
SELECT * FROM HumanResources.Department;
Subset of output
```

DepartmentID	Name	GroupName	ModifiedDate
1	Engineering	Research and Development	2002-06-01 00:00:00.000
2	Tool Design	Research and Development	2002-06-01 00:00:00.000

Table 2.2

The output shows a subset of all the 16 rows returned from the query. The sterisk (*)wildcard character after the SELECT keyword indicates that all columns from every row should be retrieved.

The following Oracle example returns the employee_id, first_name and last_name columns of all employee rows in the employees table.

SELECT employee_id,First_name,Last_name

FROM

employees;

Subset of output

EMPLOYEE_ID	FIRST_NAME	LAST_NAME
100	Steven	King
101	Neena	Kochhar
102	Lex	De Haan

Table 2.3

Sorting Qery Results

Query results usally display data in the order in which they are stored in the database tables.

In the business environment, a requirement might arise to sort the query results in date, numerical or alphabetical order. This might be in decending or ascending order. For example, there might be a requirement to list employee details, starting from the youngest to the oldest. This is achived in SQL by using the optional ORDER BY clause. This clause is applied after the mandatory SELECT and FROM clauses. The keywords *desc* or *asc* are used to direct the sort order. Desc indicates descending order with the geatest values displayed first, while asc indicates ascending order, with the least values displayed first. The sorting syntax is the same in T-SQL and Oracle SQL.

The general syntax for sorting a select query is as follows:

SELECT column1, column2
FROM Table_Name
ORDER BY column1 desc/asc

The ORDER BY clause specifies the column used for the sorting. The column can be any column that exists in the table specified in the FROM clause even if it is absent from the SELECT column list. It is important to note that sorting does not limit the number of retrieved rows; it only displays the rows in the stated order. Thus a sorted query and an unsorted query will always return the same number of rows. ORDER BY only specifies the order in which they are displayed.

Sorting Based on Dates

In SQL, recent dates are considered 'greater than' past dates—thus today is considered greater than yesterday.

If a query is executed to display employee details without a sorting order, the output will be retuned in the order in which the rows are stored. For example, the following query displays employee details without a sort order:

USE AdventureWorks2012;

GO

SELECT BusinessEntityID, LoginID, JobTitle, BirthDate

FROM humanResources.Employee;

Subset of Output

BusinessEntityID	LoginID	JobTitle	BirthDate
1	adventure-works\ ken0	Chief Executive Officer	1963-03-02
2	adventure-works\ terri0	Vice President of Engineering	1965-09-01
3	adventure-works\ roberto0	Engineering Manager	1968-12-13

Table 2.4

Notice that the details are displayed according to the BusinessEntityID number. This is because the rows are stored in that order. The statement is now amended to sorts employee details based on dates of birth in decending order, starting with the youngest to the oldest.

USE AdventureWorks2012;

GO

SELECT BusinessEntityID, LoginID, JobTitle, BirthDate

FROM humanResources.Employee

ORDER BY BirthDate DESC

Subset of output

BusinessEntityID	LoginID	JobTitle	BirthDate
115	adventure-works\ angela0	Production Technician—WC50	1985-07-01
69	adventure-works\ steve0	Production Technician—WC60	1985-05-07
133	adventure-works\ michael1	Production Technician—WC40	1985-02-04

Table 2.5

Notice that the results have been sorted based on the BirthDate column values. The youngest employee, born on 1985-07-01 is displayed first, and then the older employees are sequentially displayed. It is also possible to sort with more than one column.

Sorting Characters

With characters the later characters are greater than the earlier characters thus z is greater than a. The following Oracle SELECT statement sorts employee first_names details in a acsending alphabetical order.

SELECT employee_id, First_name, Last_name

FROM employees

ORDER BY First_name ASC;

Subset of Output

EMPLOYEE_ID	FIRST_NAME	LAST_NAME
121	Adam	Fripp
196	Alana	Walsh
147	Alberto	Errazuriz

Table 2.6

The employee details have been sorted starting with the least character A and progresses right to Z.

Sorting Numbers

Query results can also be sorted based on numbers. For example the following oracle query sorts employee names based on their salary in decending order:

```
SELECT first_name, last_name, salary
FROM employees
ORDER by salary DESC;
Output (subset of rows)
```

FIRST_NAME	LAST_NAME	SALARY
Steven	King	24000
Neena	Kochhar	17000
Lex	De Haan	17000
John	Russell	14000

Table 2.7

The employees have been sorted starting with the highest salary to the lowest.

Filtering Data with Comparison Operators

In most business scenarios, only a subset of the table data will be required. Thus the table data will be filtered to retrieve only data that meets a certain condition. This is achieved in SQL by adding a WHERE clause to the statement. A condition is specified within the

WHERE clause. The condition evaluates expressions that use table columns as operands. The condition uses comparison operators (=, <>, BETWEEN, IN, LIKE, NULL) and logical operators (AND, OR, NOT) to evaluate the column values. The condition always evaluates to TRUE, FALSE or UNKNOWN. If a row column value within the condition evaluates to TRUE, the row is returned. If it evaluates to FALSE or UNKNOWN the row is ignored. Note that the values TRUE and FALSE are not displayed in your query results. Only the rows that evaluate to TRUE are displayed.

The Oracle and T-SQL syntax is the same.

The general syntax is:

```
SELECT column1, column2
FROM Table_Name
WHERE column1 = expression
ORDER BY column1 desc/asc
```

The column in the WHERE clause can be any column from the table specified in the FROM clause. The columns and expressions in the WHERE clause must have the same data types. The ORDER BY clause is optional. For example, the following T-SQL statement retrieves all available shifts in the shifts table of the AdventureWorks2012 database.

```
USE AdventureWorks2012;
GO
SELECT *
```

FROM HumanResources.Shift;

Output

ShiftID	Name	StartTime	EndTime	ModifiedDate
1	Day	07:00:00.0000000	15:00:00.0000000	2002-06-01 00:00:00.000
2	Evening	15:00:00.0000000	23:00:00.0000000	2002-06-01 00:00:00.000
3	Night	23:00:00.0000000	07:00:00.0000000	2002-06-01 00:00:00.000

Table 2.8

The three available shifts are listed. If only the evening shift was required, the following query would be used:

```
USE AdventureWorks2012;
GO
SELECT *
FROM HumanResources.Shift
WHERE Name ='Evening';
```

Output

ShiftID	Name	StartTime	EndTime	ModifiedDate
2	Evening	15:00:00.0000000	23:00:00.0000000	2002-06-01 00:00:00.000

Table 2.9

The query now includes a WHERE clause that specifies a condition on the Name column of the shift table. The condition uses the equal (=) comparison operator to compare all the values in the Name column of the shift table to a string literal called 'Evening'. Only the second row of the table has a Name column value of Evening. Thus only row 2 is returned. Notice that the string literal is enclosed between single quotes. The string search is case sensitive. All the other comparison operators can be used in this way. For example the less than (<) comparison operator can be used to return the details of employees whose BusinessEntityID is less than three.

```
USE AdventureWorks2012;
GO
SELECT BusinessEntityID, LoginID, JobTitle
FROM HumanResources.Employee
WHERE BusinessEntityID <3;
Output
```

BusinessEntityID	LoginID	JobTitle
1	adventure-works\ken0	Chief Executive Officer
2	bdventure-works\terri0	Vice President of Engineering

Table 2.10

The query returns the BusinessEntityID, loginid, and jobtitle of the two employees rows whose BusinessEntityID column value is less than 3. All the other employee rows are ignored. Notice that the number literal 3 is not enclosed with quotes.

Filtering Data with the BETWEEN and IN Operators

The BETWEEN operator is used to return rows whose column values exist within a specified range in the WHERE clause. The upper and lower values within the range are also included.

The next query will display all employees whose BusinessEntityID number is between 100 and 102 inclusive.

```
USE AdventureWorks2012;
GO
SELECT BusinessEntityID, JobTitle, VacationHours
FROM HumanResources.Employee
WHERE BusinessEntityID BETWEEN 100 AND 102;
Output
```

BusinessEntityID	JobTitle	VacationHours
100	Production Technician—WC50	7
101	Production Technician—WC50	3
102	Production Supervisor—WC10	66

Table 2.11

The query retuns only the rows where the BusinessEntityID column values are within the specified value range of 100 to 102 inclusive.

The IN operator limits your results to a set of listed values. It differs from the equality operator in that while the equality operator limits the results to a single value, the list operator specifies a list of comma-seperated values. The same rules about literals apply. Strings are surrounded by single quotes while numbers are free standing.

The following example demonstrates the functionality of the IN operator. Here a listing of all contacts whose first name is in the following set (e.g., 'Gustavo', 'Humberto', 'Pilar') are retrieved.

```
USE AdventureWorks2012;
GO
SELECT BusinessEntityID, FirstName, LastName
FROM Person.Person
```

WHERE FirstName IN ('Gustavo','Humberto','Pilar')

ORDER BY FirstName asc;

Output

BusinessEntityID	FirstName	LastName
291	Gustavo	Achong
601	Gustavo	Camargo
297	Humberto	Acevedo
299	Pilar	Ackerman
121	Pilar	Ackerman

Table 2.12

In this query only the rows whose FirstName column values are in the set of names specified by the IN operator are returned.

Filtering for Null Values

The IS Null operator is used in conditions to test column values for nulls. Other comparison operators cannot be used to evaluate null values. Note that nulls are not empty spaces (") that can be evaluated with other comparison operators. The following example returns all rows that have null values in the midle name column of Person.person table in the adventrueworks2012 database.

USE AdventureWorks2012;

GO

SELECT BusinessEntityID, FirstName, LastName,

   MiddleName

FROM Person.Person

WHERE MiddleName IS NULL;

Subset of Output

BusinessEntityID	FirstName	LastName	MiddleName
295	Kim	Abercrombie	NULL
2170	Kim	Abercrombie	NULL
2357	Sam	Abolrous	NULL

Table 2.13

The results lists all contacts with a null middlename. Note that the equality operator will not work in this instance. If we executed the following statement switching IS NULL with = null, no results will be returned.

```
USE AdventureWorks2012;
GO
SELECT BusinessEntityID, FirstName, LastName, MiddleName
FROM Person.Person
WHERE MiddleName = NULL;
```

The above query returns no results because the equality operator cannot evaluate null values. The NOT NULL operator is the opposite of IS NULL.

Filtering with Logical Operators

Logical operators are used to connect two expressions in the WHERE clause. They include AND, OR, and NOT. They are used when a query result needs to satisfy more than one condition. The AND operator indicates that the expressions on both sides of the operator must be

TRUE for the condition to be TRUE. The OR operator indicates that one or both expressions must be true to return TRUE. The NOT operator negates its operands.

The syntax is: Operand Logical Operator Operand.

For example, to return the details of a person whose firstname is Michael and lastname is Raheem, the following query is used.

```
USE AdventureWorks2012;
GO
SELECT BusinessEntityID, FirstName, LastName, MiddleName
FROM Person.Person
WHERE FirstName = 'Michael'
AND LastName ='Raheem';
Output
```

BusinessEntityID	FirstName	LastName	MiddleName
10	Michael	Raheem	NULL

Table 2.14

The query uses the AND operator in the WHERE clause to evaluate two expressions (FirstName = 'Michael' and LastName ='Raheem'). The single row returned satisfied both expressions because for that row, the firstname column value is Michael and lastname column value is Raheem.

The OR operator is used when only one or both expressions have to be true to return a result. For example, the following statement returns details of any person whose firstname is Marjorie or whose lastname is Abel.

```
USE AdventureWorks2012;
GO
SELECT BusinessEntityID, FirstName, LastName, MiddleName
FROM Person.Person
WHERE FirstName = 'Marjorie'
OR LastName ='Abel';
Output
```

BusinessEntityID	FirstName	LastName	MiddleName
293	Catherine	Abel	R.
1293	Marjorie	Lee	M.

Table 2.15

Two rows are returned. Note that a row is returned if either or both expressions are true. For example, the first row is returned because the value of the lastname column is Abel, which returns a TRUE value for the second expression. The fact that the firstname Catherine returns a FALSE result in the other expression is ignored.

The NOT operator negates an expression. If an expression evauates to TRUE, the NOT operator inverts the result to FALSE. The following Oracle HR example demonstrates this. The first query returns all the rows from the regions table.

```
SELECT *
FROM regions;
Output
```

REGION_ID	REGION_NAME
1	Europe
2	Americas
3	Asia
4	Middle East and Africa

Table 2.16

Now a query is written to return only regions whose name is not equal to Europe or Asia.

```
SELECT *
FROM regions
WHERE NOT Region_Name IN ('Europe','Asia');
Output
```

REGION_ID	REGION_NAME
2	Americas
4	Middle East and Africa

Table 2.17

The NOT operator negates the Region_Name IN ('Europe','Asia') expression thus only the rows with region_name values excluded from this expression are returned.

The Order of Logical Operator Execution

By default, SQL is executed sequentially from left to right. In situations where multiple logical operators are needed, this might lead to ambiguities and wrong results. To resolve this issue, paranthesis are included to force the order of execution. For example, during data name cleansing operations, there might be a requirement to identify an employee whose last name is known but whose middlename or title are null. The following statement is used for an employee whose lastname is Zwilling.

```
USE AdventureWorks2012;
GO
SELECT BusinessEntityID, Title, FirstName, LastName,
    MiddleName
FROM Person.Person
WHERE MiddleName IS NULL OR Title IS NULL AND
    LastName ='Zwilling';
Output subset
```

BusinessEntityID	Title	FirstName	LastName	MiddleName
3	NULL	Roberto	Tamburello	NULL
4	NULL	Rob	Walters	NULL
10	NULL	Michael	Raheem	NULL

Table 2.18

This query returns incorrect results because there are several rows where the lastname is not Zwilling. This is because the OR expression (MiddleName IS NULL OR Title IS NULL) is executed independently, returning incorrect rows. This issue is resolved by using parentheses to force the results of the OR operation to be connected (AND) with the results of the last expression (LastName ='Zwilling'). The following statement is used.

```
USE AdventureWorks2012;
GO
```

SELECT BusinessEntityID, Title, FirstName, LastName,
    MiddleName
FROM Person.Person
WHERE (MiddleName IS NULL OR Title IS NULL) AND
    LastName ='Zwilling';
Output

BusinessEntityID	Title	FirstName	LastName	MiddleName
64	NULL	Michael	Zwilling	J

Table 2.19

This is the correct output because this is the only row where the person's lastname is Zwilling and his title is null.

Filtering with T-SQL Pattern Matching Operators

It is sometimes necessary to search for an unknown pattern of words. All the previous operators used the exact string or number being searched. For example, if you need to list all the persons whose first name begins with A, you will need to use the LIKE operator. The LIKE operator uses wildcards to define your search patterns.

Wildcards are special reserved symbols used to replace unknown characters within your search patterns. They serve as placeholders within the pattern and can be single or a string of characters. The three main types of wildcards are % (percentage), [] (brackets), and _ (underscore). By default characters specified in T-SQL wildcards are not case sensitive. Oracle wildcards are case sensitive.

The % wildcard is used to match any number of characters, including spaces, between, after, or before a specified search string. To list all contacts whose lastname begins with an A, the following code is used:

```
USE AdventureWorks2012;
GO
SELECT LastName, FirstName, MiddleName
FROM Person.Person
WHERE LastName LIKE 'A%';
```

Subset of Output

LastName	FirstName	MiddleName
Abbas	Syed	E
Abel	Catherine	R.
Abercrombie	Kim	NULL

Table 2.20

The result lists all the names that start with A followed by any number of characters after the A. The % wildcard is used to indicate that any number of characters can be added to the initial A. Note that the wildcard could be placed anywhere in the search string. For example, to list the contacts whose lastname ends with a c, the following code is used:

```
USE AdventureWorks2012;
GO
SELECT LastName, FirstName, MiddleName
FROM Person.Person
WHERE LastName LIKE '%c';
```

Output

LastName	FirstName	MiddleName
Kotc	Pamala	M.
Tomic	Dragan	NULL
Tomic	Dragan	K

Table 2.21

The % wildcard is used before the search string indicates that any number of characters can be substituted in its place. The statement lists persons whose lastname ends with a c.

Integers are implicitly converted to strings when used in wildcards.

The _ (underscore) wildcard is used to replace a single character in the search parttern. It can also be used anywhere in the search pattern with the LIKE operator. For example, if you need to identify persons whose lastname ends with '_bel', the following statement is used:

```
USE AdventureWorks2012;
GO
SELECT LastName, FirstName, MiddleName
FROM Person.Person
WHERE LastName LIKE '_bel';
Output
```

LastName	FirstName	MiddleName
Abel	Catherine	R.

Table 2.22

The results show a person whose last name ends with 'bel' (Abel). The _ has been replaced by A and concatenated with bel. Note that this wildcard can be used anywhere in the search string.

The Brackets [] Wildcard

The brackets wildcard is used to specify a list of characters, any one of which can match a character in the specified position in the search pattern. This means if the bracket in the LIKE operator contains [rq], the r or q will be used as the replacement character.

This wildcard is best used with the % wildcard. Suppose we need a list of all contacts whose last name begins with r or q? The following code will be used:

```
USE AdventureWorks2012;
GO
SELECT LastName, FirstName, MiddleName
FROM Person.Person
WHERE LastName LIKE '[rq]%'
Subset of Output
```

LastName	FirstName	MiddleName
Quintana	Mary Lou	M.
Quintana	Monica	L.
Raheem	Bethany	L
Raheem	Devon	NULL

Table 2.23

The result lists only the contacts whose lastname begin with either q or r. This brackets ([]) operator is only available on the SQL server.

Filtering with Oracle Pattern Matching Operators

Oracle conditions use the same T-SQL pattern matching operators, with the exception of the brackets. The main difference in Oracle is that the patterns to be matched are case sensitive. For example, the following statement tries to return all employee names that start with (lowercase) a.

```
SELECT first_name, Last_name
FROM employees
WHERE first_name LIKE 'a%';
```

No rows are returned when the statement is executed. This is because there are no first_names that begin with a lowercase a. If the statement is altered to search for first_names that begin with an uppercase A, some rows are returned as follows:

```
SELECT first_name, Last_name
FROM employees
WHERE first_name LIKE 'A%';
Subset of Output
```

FIRST_NAME	LAST_NAME
Amit	Banda
Alexis	Bull
Anthony	Cabrio

Table 2.24

The results now show the employees whose first_names begin with A.

Filtering Data with Expressions Using Functions and Operators (What-IF Analysis)

Fuctions and operators can be embedded within the WHERE clause of a statement to filter data. They are generally used for what-if analysis and data conversions. A simple example of a business what-if analysis secnario where an operator is used is to find out which employees will earn 20000 or more if all salaries are increased by 3000. To do this analysis, the following statement is executed:

```
SELECT first_name, last_name, salary AS Current_salary,
    salary+3000 AS New_salary
FROM employees
WHERE (salary+3000) >= 20000;
Output
```

FIRST_NAME	LAST_NAME	CURRENT_SALARY	NEW_SALARY
Steven	King	24000	27000
Neena	Kochhar	17000	20000
Lex	De Haan	17000	20000

Table 2.25

The output shows that only three employees will earn 20000 or more if salaries were increased by 3000. This filtering is achieved by using the plus operator to add 3000 to the current salary of each employee. The result of this addition is then checked against 20000. If the salaries are greater than or equal to 20000, they are returned. There is more on calculated fields in chapter eight.

Filtering Data with Expressions Using Functions and Operators (Data Conversion)

Sometimes the data in tables might not be stored in a suitable format for a particular type of business analysis. For example, there might be a requirement to find out which employees where hired on the first day of any month in the oracle database. The following statement is is used:

```
SELECT first_name, last_name, salary AS Current_salary,
    hire_date
FROM employees
WHERE TO_CHAR(HIRE_DATE,'DD') = 1;
Output
```

FIRST_NAME	LAST_NAME	CURRENT_SALARY	HIRE_DATE
Payam	Kaufling	7900	05/01/2003
John	Russell	14000	10/01/2004
Allan	McEwen	9000	08/01/2004
Samuel	McCain	3200	07/01/2006

Table 2.26

The output shows that four employees were hired on the first of any month. This is achieved by embedding the TO_CHAR function that converts/extracts the day number of each hire_date. The date data type has been transformed to the number 1. All qulifying rows whose hire_date day is 1 are returned. More on functions in chapter eight. The SQL server functions are also used in the same manner. For example, the following statement returns all employees who were hired on the first day of any month:

```
USE AdventureWorks2012;

GO

SELECT BusinessEntityID, JobTitle, HireDate

FROM HumanResources.Employee

WHERE DATEPART(DAY,HireDate) = 1;

Output (subset of rows)
```

63	Production Technician—WC60	2004-03-01
185	Production Technician—WC20	2003-04-01
197	Production Technician—WC40	2003-02-01
211	Quality Assurance Manager	2003-04-01

Table 2.27

The T-SQL DATEPART function was used on the hiredate column to extract the hiredate number of each employee. These number was then compared to 1 and the matching rows were returned.

Returning the TOP n Rows with T-SQL

If the rows of a table are stored sequentially, it can be useful to be able to retrieve only a given number of them without using a filtering condition. For example, the rows of the employee table in the SQL server database are stored sequentially according to their BusinessEntityIDs from 1 through 290. To retrieve the first five rows, the TOP function is used in the SELECT clause as follows.

```
USE AdventureWorks2012;

GO

SELECT TOP(5) BusinessEntityID,OrganizationLevel,JobTitle
```

FROM HumanResources.Employee;

Output

BusinessEntityID	OrganizationLevel	JobTitle
1	0	Chief Executive Officer
2	1	Vice President of Engineering
3	2	Engineering Manager
4	3	Senior Tool Designer
5	3	Design Engineer

Table 2.28

The statement retrieves the first five rows of the table.

Returning the TOP n Rows with Oracle Inline View

The TOP function is not available in Oracle, but an inline view or WITH clause can be used to return the top n rows. Inline views are subqueries placed in the FROM clause of a SELECT statement. The subquery returns a pseudo-column called *rownum*. This invisible column is always present when a SELECT query returns data from an Oracle database. The pseudo-column returns number of the row as it was retrieved from the database. The pseudo-column must be explicitly called in the SELECT column list for it to become visible. For example, the following query shows the row numbers of each row returned by a query on the employees table:

```
SELECT first_name, last_name, salary, rownum FROM
    employees
WHERE employee_id <103;
Output
```

FIRST_NAME	LAST_NAME	SALARY	ROWNUM
Steven	King	24000	1
Neena	Kochhar	17000	2
Lex	De Haan	17000	3

Table 2.29

Notice that the rownum column returns the number of each row according to how they were retrieved from the table, from the first row to the third row.

To return the top 3 rows from the employees table the following code is used.

```
SELECT *
FROM (SELECT * FROM employees) employees2
WHERE rownum <= 3;
```
Output

EMPLOYEE_ ID	FIRST_ NAME	LAST_ NAME	E-MAIL	PHONE_NUMBER
100	Steven	King	SKING	515.123.4567
101	Neena	Kochhar	NKOCHHAR	515.123.4568
102	Lex	De Haan	LDEHAAN	515.123.4569

Table 2.30

The subquery uses the rownum pseudo-column to limit the number of rows returned to only the first three rows. Note that the pseudo-column acts like a calculated field and cannot be referenced directly in the WHERE clause. Thus a VIEW, WITH clause or Inline subquery must be used to realise the column before it can be used in the WHERE clause of an oracle SELECT query. There is more on subqueries in chapter five.

Returning Distinct Rows

Table data might become corrupted with duplicate rows. Duplicate rows are rows that have exactly the same value for each column. These duplicate rows cause queries to return inaccurate results. For example the results of calculations might be exaggerated. The DISTINCT keyword is used in SELECT queries to return only a single instance of a duplicate row ignoring the others. For example, the following oracle statement creates a table and inserts duplicate rows (table creation is treated in chapter eleven):

```
CREATE TABLE new_regions1
(region_id NUMBER,
region_name VARCHAR2(25));
INSERT INTO new_regions1 (region_id,region_name) VALUES
     (1,'AUSTRALIA');
INSERT INTO new_regions1 (region_id,region_name) VALUES
     (1,'AUSTRALIA');
INSERT INTO new_regions1 (region_id,region_name) VALUES
     (5,'ASIA');
INSERT INTO new_regions1 (region_id,region_name) VALUES
     (5,'ASIA');
```

The table has been created and two duplicate rows have been inserted as shown below:

```
SELECT * FROM new_regions1;
Output
```

REGION_ID	REGION_NAME
1	AUSTRALIA
1	AUSTRALIA
5	ASIA
5	ASIA

Table 2.31

The output shows a table with two duplicate rows. To return only a single instance of each duplicate the following statement is issued:

SELECT DISTINCT * FROM new_regions1;

Output

REGION_ID	REGION_NAME
1	AUSTRALIA
5	ASIA

Table 2.32

The DISTINCT keyword has been used to return only a single instance of each duplicate row.

Conclusion

The chapter demonstrated how to return and filter data from a single table. Most of the SQL SELECT constructs are similar in Oracle and SQL server. The few deviations where also presented. Table creation and data insertion statements were also included to illustrate the management of duplicate rows. These statements are covered in chapters seven and eleven.

Chapter Four

Overview

This chapter extends the use of the SELECT statement to return data from more than one table using joins. The different types of joins are covered.

Retrieving Data from More than One Table

As discussed in the opening chapters, due to E-R modelling and normalisation related data in OLTP databases are stored in different related tables. This reduces data redundancy, optimises storage, and improves data maintenance operations. However, this arrangement poses a problem because in the real world the data in all these tables is required to seamlessly answer business questions with reports. It will not do to simply return data from each individual table and try to stitch the results together. This problem is resolved using SQL joins. Joins are used to consistently retrieve data from more than one table and present the results as though all the data originated from a single table. Joins in Oracle and T-SQL are equivalent.

Joining More than One Table

Joins are conditions placed in the WHERE or FROM clause of a SELECT query. Joins consistently retrieve data from one (Self join) or more tables based on the logical relationship between the tables. They utilise all the operators used for single table queries. They can also be used in WHERE clause of other DML queries such as UPDATE DELETE and INSERT. This chapter is focused on joins in SELECT statements.

For example, the HumanResources.Employee and Person.Person tables in the AdventureWorks2012 SQL server database store different bits of information about employees. The HumanResources.Employee table stores information about the employees BusinessEntityID, HireDate, LoginID, JobTitle, etc. while the Person.Person table stores the employees personal information such as their BusinessEntityID, first names, last names, etc. These two tables have a logical relationship that is established and maintained by the common BusinessEntityID column. This common column ensures that when data is stored or retrieved for a particular BusinessEntityID value in either of these two tables, the data refers to the same employee.

When there is a business requirement to return data from these two tables, the required columns from both tables are specified in the SELECT list of the query. The two tables are declared in the FROM clause. Then the two tables are joined by their common column in the condition of a WHERE clause. For each join condition satisfied (when the values of the common columns specified in the condition are related), a new output row is created by retrieving the values of the columns from both tables specified in the SELECT list. The result of a join query can be loosely regarded as a table created from different table columns, with the join condition acting as the primary key logically linking the tables together. The simplest generic syntax for joining tables in SELECT statements is as follows:

```
SELECT table1.col1, table2.col1,table1.col3,table2.col2
FROM table1,table2
WHERE Condition(table1.col1 is_related_to table2.col1)
```

Once a table has been declared in the FROM clause of the statement, all of its columns become available for usage anywhere else in the statement. Qualifying the column name with the table name is unnecessary if the table columns have different names. The WHERE condition uses comparison operators to compare values from the joined tables columns. As a rule, when retrieving data from more than one table, always include at least one column from each table in the join condition.

Joins and Constraints

There is no explicit relationship between joins in SELECT queries and constraints but constraints ensure the correctness and consistency of join results. Primary and foreign key constraints ensure the logical relationship between the tables is maintained. These logically related columns must have the same data type and must have the same business meaning. Note that the column names might be different in each table.

Types of Joins

Joins are classed based on types of relationships they test in the WHERE clause condition. The conditions use all SQL operators to test the relationships between common columns. The most important joins include inner joins (equi-joins), outer joins (left outer joins and right outer joins), self joins, and cross joins

Inner joins use comparisons operators (=, <>,) to match values between logically related columns from two or more tables. The most common type of an inner join is the equi-join. This join uses the equality comparison operator. Whenever the values of the joining columns of a row are equal the rows from both tables are returned as the result of the query. These joins can be introduced in the FROM or WHERE clause of a query.

T—SQL Equip-Join in the WHERE Clause

Inner joins can be included with other filters in the WHERE clause of a SELECT query. This join type is supported by most DBMSs. It is the older join type and is easier to understand than the joins in the FROM clause.

For example, the Employee FirstName and LastName are stored in the Person.Person table while the NationalIDNumber and job_title is stored in the HumanResources.Employee table. Both tables also have a common BusinessEntityID column that represents the basis of their logical relationship. AN equi-join is used to retrieve all this information from both tables based on this column. The following two statements return a subset of data from each table. A final query uses a equi-join to combine the results from each individual query.

```
USE AdventureWorks2012;
GO
SELECT BusinessEntityID,jobtitle,NationalIDNumber
FROM HumanResources.Employee;
```

Output: Subset of rows and columns from the HumanResources.
Employee table

BusinessEntityID	jobtitle	NationalIDNumber
1	Chief Executive Officer	295847284
2	Vice President of Engineering	245797967
3	Engineering Manager	509647174

Table 4.1

```
USE AdventureWorks2012;
GO
SELECT BusinessEntityID,FirstName,LastName
FROM Person.Person
```

Output: Subset or rows and columns from the person.person table.

BusinessEntityID	FirstName	LastName
1	Ken	Sánchez
2	Terri	Duffy
3	Roberto	Tamburello

Table 4.2

An equi—join on the common BusinessEntityID can now be used
to return data from all these columns from both tables as follows:

```
USE AdventureWorks2012;
GO
SELECT Employee.BusinessEntityID,FirstName,LastName,Nat
    ionalIDNumber,jobtitle,NationalIDNumber
FROM HumanResources.Employee, Person.Person
```

WHERE Employee.BusinessEntityID = Person.

BusinessEntityID;

Output (subset of returned rows)

Business EntityID	First Name	Last Name	National IDNumber	jobtitle	National IDNumber
1	Ken	Sánchez	295847284	Chief Executive Officer	295847284
2	Terri	Duffy	245797967	Vice President of Engineering	245797967
3	Roberto	Tamburello	509647174	Engineering Manager	509647174

Table 4.3

The output shows the rows from the two tables returned as though the query was applied to a single table. This result is obtained because of the join applied in the WHERE clause as a condition (WHERE Employee.BusinessEntityID = Person.BusinessEntityID ;). Whenever the BusinessEntityID value from both tables match the condition is satisfied and the rows from both tables are returned. For example, when the BusinessEntityID from both tables is 1, the HumanResources. Employee table returns the specified columns of row 1, which are NationalIDNumber =295847284, jobtitle = Chief Executive Officer and NationalIDNumber =295847284. The Person.Person table also returns its row 1 column values, which are FirstName = Ken and LastName= Sánchez. This happens every time matches are found until the result is complete. This same procedure is executed for all join types when the stated conditions are satisfied.

Qualifiying Column Names

When the multiple tables used have the same column name, you must use the qualified name of the common column name in the query. The qualified name is the table name followed by a period followed by the column name. This specifies which table the column is coming from. In the previous example, the BusinessEntityID column name is common for both tables, thus in the SELECT and WHERE clause the qualified names are used (Employee.BusinessEntityID and Person.BusinessEntityID).

Table Name Aliases

Table aliases are used to simplify coding. Due to the fact that some queries have to use multiple qualified column names for multiple common columns, the code might become messy and difficult to read. Table aliases are strings or a character used to abbreviate table names. This makes it easier to reference the table anywhere in the query without having to spell out the full table name. For example the previous query could be rewritten with table aliases as follows:

```
USE AdventureWorks2012;
GO
SELECT e.BusinessEntityID,p.FirstName,p.LastName,e.
    NationalIDNumber,e.jobtitle,e.NationalIDNumber
FROM HumanResources.Employee e, Person.Person p
WHERE e.BusinessEntityID = p.BusinessEntityID;
```

This query returns the same results but is more readable because the table names have been abbreviated to e for HumanResources.Employee and p for Person.Person in the FROM clause. These abbreviated names are then used to qualify the column names (e.BusinessEntityID and p.BusinessEntityID).

T-SQL Inner Joins in the FROM Clause

The recomended join method in modern databases is to introduce the join in the FROM clause. These joins have a performance advantage when there are other constraints apart from the join itself in the WHERE clause. Joins in the FROM clause are slightly more complicated and are also applied in the same fasion in Oracle and SQL server. Using the previous examples, the join between the HumanResources.Employee and Person.Person tables are included in the FROM clause. The key words JOIN and ON will be added to the FROM clause, and the WHERE clause is removed if no further filtering is required. Note that the keywords JOIN and INNER JOIN mean exactly the same thing and can be used interchangeably.

For example, the following code was used in the previous examples:

```
USE AdventureWorks2012;
GO
SELECT Employee.BusinessEntityID,FirstName,LastName,Nat
    ionalIDNumber,jobtitle,NationalIDNumber
FROM HumanResources.Employee, Person.Person
WHERE
Employee.BusinessEntityID = Person.BusinessEntityID;
```

It is modified to:

```
USE AdventureWorks2012;
GO
SELECT Employee.BusinessEntityID, FirstName, LastName,
    NationalIDNumber, jobtitle, NationalIDNumber
FROM HumanResources.Employee JOIN Person.Person ON
(Employee.BusinessEntityID = Person.BusinessEntityID);
```

Both methods retrieve the same information from the database.

If further filtering is required, the WHERE clause is introduced after the FROM cluase. For example, if only the employee having a BusinessEntityID equal to 1 is required, the previous statement is modified to include a WHERE clause as follows:

```
USE AdventureWorks2012;
GO
SELECT Employee.BusinessEntityID, FirstName, LastName,
    NationalIDNumber,
jobtitle, NationalIDNumber
FROM HumanResources.Employee JOIN Person.Person ON
(Employee.BusinessEntityID = Person.BusinessEntityID)
WHERE
Employee.BusinessEntityID = 1;
Output
```

Business EntityID	First Name	Last Name	National IDNumber	jobtitle	National IDNumber
1	Ken	Sánchez	295847284	Chief Executive Officer	295847284

Table 4.4

Only one row is retrieved. This is because there is only a single employee whose BusinessEntityID =1. This extra filtering has been achieved by including the WHERE clause after the join.

Oracle Inner Joins

Oracle treats inner joins in exactly the same way as SQL server. For example, in the Oracle HR database the employees table stores the Salary, First_Name and Job_Id of each employee while the jobs table stores the Job_ID and Job_Name. The job_id is the common column that forms the logical relationship between both tables. Sample rows from both tables are first returned to show the logical relationship between them. The first query returns employee rows:

SELECT First_Name,Salary,job_id
FROM Employees;
Output(subset of rows and columns)

FIRST_NAME	SALARY	JOB_ID
Steven	24000	AD_PRES
Neena	17000	AD_VP
Lex	17000	AD_VP

Table 4.5

Now job rows are returned as follows:

SELECT job_id, job_title

FROM jobs;

Output(subset of rows and columns)

JOB_ID	JOB_TITLE
AD_PRES	President
AD_VP	Administration Vice President
AD_ASST	Administration Assistant

Table 4.6

To retrieve the Salary, Frist_Name and Job_Name of each employee, the two tables will have to be joined as follows:

SELECT First_Name,Salary,Job_Title

FROM Employees, Jobs

WHERE Employees.Job_ID = Jobs.Job_Id

ORDER BY employee_id;

Output(subset of rows)

FIRST_NAME	SALARY	JOB_TITLE
Steven	24000	President
Neena	17000	Administration Vice President
Lex	17000	Administration Vice President

Table 4.7

The rows from the employees and jobs table have been returned and merged in a single output. This happens because the two tables have been joined by their common job_id column. Whenever there is a match between the column values, rows from both tables are returned.

For example, employee 100 has a Job_Id of AD_PRES in the employees table. This value is also present in the Job_Id column of the jobs table. The Job_Name for this row is president. Thus, president is retrieved for employee 100 called Steven.

Outer Joins

Outer joins extend the functionality of inner joins. Inner joins only retrieve rows where there is a matching value found in both join columns. Outer joins return all rows from the outer joined table and only the rows where a match is found in the other table.

Outer joins are generally used in the business environment to test whether a certain event has occurred on an entity. Typically a row is stored for each occurrence of the events in a monitoring table. For example most companies have different payroll cycles for different employees. After each cycle the payment details are stored in a payroll history table. Now if at some point in the month a report is required to list all employees payment status (both paid and unpaid) an outer join will be required.

There are three types of outer joins. They are LEFT, RIGHT, and FULL outer joins.

T-SQL LEFT and RIGHT OUTER JOIN

Outer joins can only be declared in the FROM clause. The LEFT keyword indicates that the table preceding LEFT OUTER JOIN is the outer joined table. This is the table where all row values are retuned even if no match is found in the column of the other table. The order of the columns in the ON join condition is irrelevant. For example, in the production planning process, finished products are inspected and reviewed. These reviews are stored in the Production.ProductReview table. The finished products are stored in the Production.Product table. Thus, to find out which of a set of products have been reviewed as well as those that have not been reviewed, the Production.Product table is LEFT outer joined to the Production.ProductReview table. The tables are logically related by their common productID column.

The following statement returns the set of products to be checked for reviews from the Production.Product table:

```
USE
AdventureWorks2012;
SELECT ProductID, Name FROM Production.Product
WHERE ProductID IN (798, 937, 1,321);
Output
```

ProductID	Name
1	Adjustable Race
321	Chainring Nut
798	Road-550-W Yellow, 40
937	HL Mountain Pedal

Table 4.8

The following statement returns a listing of all the reviewed products from the set of productids:

USE

AdventureWorks2012;

GO

SELECT ProductID, ReviewerName, ReviewDate, Rating

FROM Production.ProductReview

WHERE ProductID IN (798, 937, 1,321);

Output (only a subset of columns shown)

ProductID	ReviewerName	ReviewDate	Rating
937	David	2007-12-15 00:00:00.000	4
937	Jill	2007-12-17 00:00:00.000	2
798	Laura Norman	2007-12-17 00:00:00.000	5

Table 4.9

Notice that product 937 has been reviewed twice while product 1 and 321 have not been reviewed. To list which of the selected products have and have not been reviewed in a single report, the following statement is issued:

USE AdventureWorks2012;

GO

SELECT p.ProductID, Name, ReviewerName, ReviewDate, Rating

FROM Production.Product p LEFT OUTER JOIN Production.

ProductReview r

ON r.ProductID = p.ProductID

WHERE p.ProductID IN (798,937,1,321);

Output

Product ID	Name	Reviewer Name	ReviewDate	Rating
1	Adjustable Race	NULL	NULL	NULL
321	Chainring Nut	NULL	NULL	NULL
798	Road-550-W Yellow, 40	Laura Norman	2007-12-17 00:00:00.000	5
937	HL Mountain Pedal	David	2007-12-15 00:00:00.000	4
937	HL Mountain Pedal	Jill	2007-12-17 00:00:00.000	2

Table 4.10

The output includes all the rows from the Production.Product table (product id 798, 937, 1,321). This is because this table is declared to the left of the LEFT OUTER JOIN keywords. The Production.ProductReview table returns only the rows where a match is found between the two productid columns values. Nulls are returned when matches are not found. For example, in the first row of the output productid 1 and Name Adjustable Race are returned from the Production.Product table but the ReviewerName, ReviewDate and Rating return nulls from the Production.ProductReview table because productid 1 is not in the table. When a match is found, as in the case of productid 798, all the row values are returned from both tables. It is important to note that when nulls are returned from the table on the other side of an outer join, it generally means that the row was not returned at all rather than that the rows contained null values.

T-SQL RIGHT OUTER JOIN and the Influence of the WHERE Clause

The RIGHT OUTER JOIN is the polar opposite of the LEFT OUTER JOIN. In this join, the table on the right side is outer joined to the table on the left side of the JOIN declaration. The syntax is exactly the same as the LEFT OUTER join. For example, if the join from the previous example is switched from left to right all the qualified rows from the Production.ProductReview table will be returned while only the matching rows from the Production.Product table will be returned, as shown below:

```
USE AdventureWorks2012;
GO
SELECT p.ProductID,Name,ReviewerName,ReviewDate,Rating
FROM Production.Product p RIGHT OUTER JOIN Production.
    ProductReview r
ON p.ProductID = r.ProductID
WHERE p.ProductID IN (798,937,1,321);
Output
```

Product ID	Name	Reviewer Name	ReviewDate	Rating
937	HL Mountain Pedal	David	2007-12-15 00:00:00.000	4
937	HL Mountain Pedal	Jill	2007-12-17 00:00:00.000	2
798	Road-550-W Yellow, 40	Laura Norman	2007-12-17 00:00:00.000	5

Table 4.11

The output returns all the rows within the specified set of productids (973 and 798) from the Production.ProductReview table and only the matching rows from the Production.Product table. Note that all the productid values in the Production.ProductReview table also exist in the Production.Product thus the output looks like an inner join.

Oracle OUTER JOINS

The Oracle OUTER JOIN syntax is equivalent to the SQL server version. For example, in the Oracle HR database the list of employees who have and have not changed departments can be obtained with the following OUTER JOIN statement. The employees table is LEFT OUTER joined with the Job_History table, therefore all employee rows will be returned regardless of whether they have changed jobs or not.

```
SELECT First_Name,Last_Name,Start_Date,End_Date
FROM Employees LEFT OUTER JOIN Job_History ON
(Employees.Employee_Id = Job_History.Employee_Id)
ORDER BY Employees.Employee_Id;
Output (subset of rows returned)
```

FIRST_NAME	LAST_NAME	START_DATE	END_DATE
Steven	King	—	—
Neena	Kochhar	09/21/1997	10/27/2001
Neena	Kochhar	10/28/2001	03/15/2005
Lex	De Haan	01/13/2001	07/24/2006
Alexander	Hunold	—	—

Table 4.12

The result lists all the employee names including those who have never changed departments. For example Steven King has not changed jobs thus the start_date and end_date return NULLs while a stat_date and end_date are returned for Lex De Haan who has changed jobs. The employee table is LEFT OUTER JOIN to the Job_History table on their common Employee_Id column. Thus all employees from the employee table are retrieved while only matching rows are retrieved from the Job_History table. The FULL OUTER JOIN retrieves all rows from both tables.

SELF JOINS

Some business questions can only be resolved by using self joins. SELF JOINS are used to join a table to its self. In this situation, the same table name will be required twice in the join condition, causing syntactic errors. This situation is resolved by using aliases to distinguish the separate instances of the same table.

An example in the Oracle HR database is the employees table. This table stores the employee details such as names and e-mail addresses. The Manager_ID of each employee is also stored in the same row as the employee name in this same table. A sample of rows to show the data structure can be seen with the following statement:

```
SELECT employee_id, first_name, last_name, manager_id
FROM employees;
Output (subset of returned rows)
```

EMPLOYEE_ID	FIRST_NAME	LAST_NAME	MANAGER_ID
100	Steven	King	—
101	Neena	Kochhar	100
102	Lex	De Haan	100
103	Alexander	Hunold	102
104	Bruce	Ernst	103

Table 4.13

The output shows that each employee's manager is stored in the same row as the employee. Notice that employee 100 has a null value for manager_id

To retrieve the name of each employee and his or her manager name, two instances of the employees table are needed. The first instance retrieves the employee name while the second retrieves the employee's manager name. The following statement is used:

```
SELECT e.employee_id,e.first_name, e.last_name, e1.last_
    name AS "Manager Name"
FROM employees e, employees e1
WHERE e.manager_id = e1.employee_id
ORDER BY e.employee_id;
Output (subset of rows)
```

EMPLOYEE_ID	FIRST_NAME	LAST_NAME	Manager Name
101	Neena	Kochhar	King
102	Lex	De Haan	King
103	Alexander	Hunold	De Haan
104	Bruce	Ernst	Hunold

Table 4.14

This query uses aliases to references the same employee table twice (employees e, employees e1). The database treats the aliased table as two separate tables. All the employee_ids, first_name and last_name of each employee and their manager name are retrieved. The tables are inner joined on the employee_Id and manager_Id columns. Note that logically the manager_Id is effectively the employee_Id of each manager. For example when the manager_ id in table e is 100 and the employee_id of table e1 is 100 first_name and Last_Name values of table e (Neena Kouchar) is returned and the last name of table e1 King is returned. Note that employee Steven King is not included in the result set. This is because in the employee table, the manager_Id value is NULL for the Steven King row. Self joins work in the same fashion in SQL server and Oracle. SELF JOINS can also be defined in the FROM clause as an INNER JOIN.

Joining More than Two Tables

Business requirements might necessitate the joining of more than two tables. This can be achieved by using joins in the WHERE or FROM clause of a statement. When the number of tables to be joined exceeds two, the tables must be joined in pairs. The result from each pair is then joined to obtain the final result. When the WHERE clause is used to create multiple pairs of joins, logical operators (AND, OR) are used to string them together, and additional filters can be included. When the FROM clause is used for multiple join pairs, the JOIN and ON pair are used to state the tables and column pairs. The WHERE clause is needed to add further filters to the JOIN pairs when the FROM clause is used. For example, four tables are needed to retrieve complete employee details from the adventureworks2012 database; the following statement is used to join the four required tables. An extra filter is included to restrict the number of employees:

```
USE AdventureWorks2012;
GO
SELECT h.BusinessEntityID,h.JobTitle,h.HireDate,n.
    FirstName,p.Rate,a.AddressLine1
FROM HumanResources.Employee h,HumanResources.
    EmployeePayHistory p, Person.Address a,
Person.Person n,Person.BusinessEntityAddress e
WHERE h.BusinessEntityID = p.BusinessEntityID
AND a.AddressID = e.AddressID
AND e.BusinessEntityID = h.BusinessEntityID
AND n.BusinessEntityID = h.BusinessEntityID
AND h.BusinessEntityID < 3;
Output
```

Business EntityID	Job Title	Hire Date	First Name	Rate	Address Line1
1	Chief Executive Officer	2003-02-15	Ken	125.50	4350 Minute Dr.
2	Vice President of Engineering	2002-03-03	Terri	63.4615	7559 Worth Ct.

Table 4.15

The output is a result of four WHERE join pairs and a filter to restrict the returned result to the two employees whose businessentityid is less than three. The same results can be obtained using FROM clause join pairs as follows:

```
USE AdventureWorks2012;
GO
SELECT h.BusinessEntityID,h.JobTitle,h.HireDate,n.
    FirstName,p.Rate,a.AddressLine1
FROM HumanResources.Employee h JOIN HumanResources.
    EmployeePayHistory p ON h.BusinessEntityID =
    p.BusinessEntityID
JOIN Person.BusinessEntityAddress e ON e.BusinessEntityID
    = h.BusinessEntityID
JOIN Person.Address a ON a.AddressID = e.AddressID
JOIN Person.Person n ON n.BusinessEntityID =
    h.BusinessEntityID
WHERE h.BusinessEntityID < 3;
Output
```

Business EntityID	Job Title	Hire Date	First Name	Rate	Address Line1
1	Chief Executive Officer	2003-02-15	Ken	125.50	4350 Minute Dr.
2	Vice President of Engineering	2002-03-03	Terri	63.4615	7559 Worth Ct.

Table 4.16

The same 2 row are returned using the JOIN and ON pairs on table pairs. The trick to using the FROM clause to join multiple tables is to declare a new table with every JOIN step and join it to a table declared in the previous step. Note that some tables might have to be joined more than once. Both statements are equivalent and personal programming style should dictate which one to use. However FROM joins are generally marginally faster than WHERE joins.

Cross Joins

Cross joins (not available in Oracle) are used to retrieve every row combination from the joined tables. They effectively deliver a Cartesian product of the two tables. If a both tables have five rows, the cross join will retrieve 25 (5 * 5) rows. The same output can be achieved by simply selecting columns from two tables and omitting a join in the WHERE or FROM clause. The following T-SQL example CROSS joins the shift table to itself. The shift table has the following rows:

SELECT *

FROM HumanResources.Shift

Output

Shift ID	Name	StartTime	EndTime	ModifiedDate
1	Day Period	07:00:00. 0000000	15:00:00. 0000000	2002-06-01 00:00:00.000
2	Evening	15:00:00. 0000000	23:00:00. 0000000	2002-06-01 00:00:00.000
3	Night	23:00:00. 0000000	07:00:00. 0000000	2002-06-01 00:00:00.000

Table 4.17

The Output shows three rows. If this table is now joined to itself with a CROSS join a Cartesian product of nine rows are returned as follows:

USE AdventureWorks2012;

GO

SELECT *

FROM HumanResources.Shift CROSS JOIN

    HumanResources.Shift s1;

Output

Shift ID	Name	StartTime	EndTime	ModifiedDate
1	Day Period	07:00:00.0000000	15:00:00.0000000	2002-06-01 00:00:00.000
2	Evening	15:00:00.0000000	23:00:00.0000000	2002-06-01 00:00:00.000
3	Night	23:00:00.0000000	07:00:00.0000000	2002-06-01 00:00:00.000
1	Day Period	07:00:00.0000000	15:00:00.0000000	2002-06-01 00:00:00.000
2	Evening	15:00:00.0000000	23:00:00.0000000	2002-06-01 00:00:00.000
3	Night	23:00:00.0000000	07:00:00.0000000	2002-06-01 00:00:00.000
1	Day Period	07:00:00.0000000	15:00:00.0000000	2002-06-01 00:00:00.000
2	Evening	15:00:00.0000000	23:00:00.0000000	2002-06-01 00:00:00.000
3	Night	23:00:00.0000000	07:00:00.0000000	2002-06-01 00:00:00.000

Shift ID	Name	StartTime	EndTime	ModifiedDate
1	Day Period	07:00:00.0000000	15:00:00.0000000	2002-06-01 00:00:00.000
1	Day Period	07:00:00.0000000	15:00:00.0000000	2002-06-01 00:00:00.000
1	Day Period	07:00:00.0000000	15:00:00.0000000	2002-06-01 00:00:00.000
2	Evening	15:00:00.0000000	23:00:00.0000000	2002-06-01 00:00:00.000
2	Evening	15:00:00.0000000	23:00:00.0000000	2002-06-01 00:00:00.000
2	Evening	15:00:00.0000000	23:00:00.0000000	2002-06-01 00:00:00.000
3	Night	23:00:00.0000000	07:00:00.0000000	2002-06-01 00:00:00.000
3	Night	23:00:00.0000000	07:00:00.0000000	2002-06-01 00:00:00.000
3	Night	23:00:00.0000000	07:00:00.0000000	2002-06-01 00:00:00.000

Table 4.18

Note that the same result can be obtained by simply not joining the tables as follows

```
USE AdventureWorks2012;
GO
SELECT *
FROM HumanResources.Shift, HumanResources.Shift s1;
```

Conclusion

This chapter covered the different join types. A Join is the best method used to retrieve data from more than one table. My preference is to use the WHERE inner join over the FROM inner join because its meaning is simpler to understand by a new user. Outer joins are very useful but costly. Tables should be redesigned to avoid outer joins.

Chapter Five

Overview

In this chapter the different types of subqueries are covered. They can be used to retrieve data from more than one table. They can also be used to replace joins.

Subqueries

Subqueries are queries that retrieve data from one or more tables and views. Subquery implementation is equivalent between Oracle and SQL server. Subqueries can be used to return data from more than one table and seamlessly present the results, like a query based on a single table. They can be used within the SELECT, WHERE, HAVING, and FROM clauses.

Subqueries are SELECT statements that are nested inside another SELECT statement. They are sometimes referred to as inner SELECT statements, while the main query housing the subquery is called the query or outer SELECT statement. The subquery must be enclosed in brackets. Some subqueries return results independently without referencing the outer query while others, called correlated subqueries, must reference the outer query.

They can be used with both single row and multiple row comparison operators. When a subquery is used with a single row comparison operator (=, >, <>) it must return only a single or zero column value, while when used with a multiple row comparison operator (IN, ANY, ALL, EXIST) it can return zero, one, or more values.

Subqueries in the SELECT Clause as a Calculated Column

A subquery can be included as a column in the column list of a SELECT statement. This type of subquery is a scalar because it only uses single row operators to return a single value.

They are used to answering multipart business questions with one query. Without subqueries, these multipart business questions might require several independent queries. It becomes problematic to stitch these individual query results to get the correct coherent answers to the question. For example, using the Oracle HR database, departments and employees information is stored in two separate tables. To derive what department name where Employee_Id 100 (Steven King) works, two queries are required. The first query retrieves the department_ID from the employee table while the second retrieves the department_name from the department table as follows:

First query:

```
SELECT Employee_Id,First_Name,Last_name,Department_Id
FROM Employees
WHERE Employee_Id = 100;
Output
```

EMPLOYEE_ID	FIRST_NAME	LAST_NAME	DEPARTMENT_ID
100	Steven	King	90

Table 5.1

The results show that employee_id 100 is in department_id 90.

Second query to return the department name:

SELECT Department_Name
FROM Departments
WHERE Department_Id = 90;
Output

DEPARTMENT_NAME
Executive

Table 5.2

The result shows that department 90 is the executive department. Thus, employee 100 works for the executive department. It now becomes difficult to consistently stitch the individual results together.

These two queries can be combined in a single query by including the subquery as a column in the SELECT list of the first query as follows (this subquery is a calculated column that is treated in more detail in chapter eight).

SELECT Employee_Id,First_Name,Last_name, Department_Id,
(SELECT Department_Name
FROM Departments
WHERE Department_Id = 90)As "Department_Name"
FROM Employees
WHERE Employee_Id = 100;
Output

EMPLOYEE _ID	FIRST _NAME	LAST _NAME	DEPARTMENT _ID	Department _Name
100	Steven	King	90	Executive

Table 5.2

The results show that employee_id 100 is in the executive department. Most subqueries can be replaced by joins to achieve the same results.

Subqueries in the WHERE Clause as Part of a Condition Expression

Subqueries can be used as part of the condition expression in the WHERE clause of an outer query. In this situation, the subquery is used to retrieve the rows to be compared with the rows of the outer query. The following T-SQL example uses the multiple row IN comparison operator to return the firstname and lastname of persons who work in department 16:

```
USE AdventureWorks2012;
GO
SELECT FirstName, LastName
FROM Person.Person
WHERE BusinessEntityID
IN (SELECT BusinessEntityID from HumanResources.
    EmployeeDepartmentHistory
WHERE DepartmentID = 16);
Output
```

FirstName	LastName
Ken	Sánchez
Laura	Norman

Table 5.3

The results show that Ken Sánchez and Laura Norman are the only two people who work in department 16. The subquery retrieves the set of department 16 BusinessEntityIDs from the HumanResources. EmployeeDepartmentHistory table.Then the outer query retrieves the firstnames and lastnames of persons whose BusinessEntityIDs are present in the list returned by the subquery. If the equals to (=) single row comparison operator was used, the query would have failed because the subquery returned more than one row. For example, if the IN is replace with =:

```
USE AdventureWorks2012;
GO
SELECT FirstName, LastName
FROM Person.Person
WHERE BusinessEntityID
= (SELECT BusinessEntityID from HumanResources.
    EmployeeDepartmentHistory
WHERE DepartmentID = 16 and EndDate IS NULL);
Output
```

Msg 512, Level 16, State 1, Line 1

Subquery returned more than 1 value. This is not permitted when the subquery follows =, !=, <, <=, >, or >=, or when the subquery is used as an expression.

Subqueries Using ANY and ALL Multiple Row Comparison Operators

The ANY operator in the WHERE clause indicates that the outer query will return all rows that match with any value in the set of values returned by the subquery. The ALL operator in the WHERE clause indicates that the outer query will return all rows that match with ALL values in the set of values returned by the subquery.

For example, If a subquery returns a set of (1,2,3), then the condition WHERE >ANY (1,2,3) will indicate return all rows greater than >1,or>2, or>3 (i.e., greater than the lowest value in the set). The condition WHERE >ALL (1,2,3) will indicate return all rows greater than all the values returned by the subquery (i.e., greater than the highest value in the set). For example, to display all employees whose salary is greater than or equal to the maximum salary of either department 80 or 90 of the Oracle HR database, the following query is used:

```
SELECT First_Name,Salary,Department_Id
FROM Employees
WHERE Salary >= ANY (SELECT MAX(Salary) AS "Dept_Sal"
FROM Employees
WHERE Department_Id IN (90,80)
GROUP BY Department_Id);
Output
```

FIRST_NAME	SALARY	DEPARTMENT_ID
Steven	24000	90
Neena	17000	90
Lex	17000	90
John	14000	80

Table 5.4

The output displays four employees whose salaries are greater than or equal to any of the maximum salaries returned by the subquery. The maximum salaries of departments 80 and 90 returned by the subquery can be displayed by running the subquery as follows:

SELECT MAX(Salary) AS "Dept_Sal"

FROM Employees

WHERE Department_Id IN (90,80)

GROUP BY Department_Id;

Output

Dept_Sal
24000
14000

Table 5.5

The maximum salaries in each department are 24000 and 14000, so the outer query that uses the ANY operator returned the four employees whose salary is greater than or equal to any of those figures. If the ANY is replaced by ALL, the database returns only the employees whose salary is greater than or equal to all the values returned by the nested subquery.

In the following example, the previous query is used. The only difference is that the ANY is replaced with ALL:

```
SELECT First_Name,Salary,Department_Id
FROM Employees
WHERE Salary >= ALL (SELECT MAX(Salary) AS "Dept_Sal"
FROM Employees
WHERE Department_Id IN (90,80)
GROUP BY Department_Id);
Output
```

FIRST_NAME	SALARY	DEPARTMENT_ID
Steven	24000	90

Table 5.6

The subquery is executed first and returns a list of salaries between 24000 and 14000. The outer query takes this list and determines which employees have a salary greater than or equal to both values in this list. The only employee who meets this criterion is Steven, with a salary of 24000. Thus only Steven is displayed.

Subqueries in the FROM Clause

Subqueries can also be used in the FROM clause. When defined in the FROM clause, they act like a named table and are called inline views. All the columns defined in the subquery become available to the outer query. This type of subquery in Oracle is used to replicate the functionality of T-SQL common table expressions (CTE). The main rule is to name the subquery with an alias and use the alias name to reference the subquery column names in the outer query. For example, the following T-SQL statement returns employee details obtained from a subquery:

```
USE AdventureWorks2012;
GO
SELECT Employee_details.BusinessEntityID,Employee_
    details.JobTitle,Employee_details.Rate,Employee_details.
    AddressLine1
FROM
(SELECT h.BusinessEntityID,h.JobTitle,n.FirstName,p.Rate,a.
    AddressLine1
FROM HumanResources.Employee h,HumanResources.
    EmployeePayHistory p,Person.Address a,Person.Person
    n,Person.BusinessEntityAddress e
WHERE h.BusinessEntityID = p.BusinessEntityID
AND a.AddressID = e.AddressID
AND e.BusinessEntityID = h.BusinessEntityID
AND n.BusinessEntityID = h.BusinessEntityID
AND h.BusinessEntityID <4 )AS Employee_details ;
Output
```

Business EntityID	Job Title	FirstName	Rate	AddressLine1
1	Chief Executive Officer	Ken	125.50	4350 Minute Dr.
2	Vice President of Engineering	Terri	63.4615	7559 Worth Ct.
3	Engineering Manager	Roberto	43.2692	2137 Birchwood Dr

Table 5.7

Three employee details are returned by the query. The outer query uses the Employee_details alias to reference the subquery columns. If the data returned by the subquery becomes a frequent business requirement, it should be converted into a view.

Correlated Subqueries with EXISTS Operator

Subqueries that are synchronised with the outer query are called correlated subqueries. Correlated subqueries are re-evaluated for every row returned by the parent query. The queries are synchronised by referencing columns from the outer query within the inner query. They increase the efficiency, flexibility, and functionality of subqueries. The IN operator can be replaced by the EXISTS operator in a correlated subquery to return the same results in a more efficient manner. This is because the EXISTS operator only tests for existence and does not return any rows. It only returns a TRUE or FALSE value to the condition thus less network traffic is incurred. For example, the following correlated query is used to return the names of employees who work in department 16:

```
USE AdventureWorks2012;
GO
SELECT FirstName, LastName
FROM Person.Person P
WHERE EXISTS (SELECT * from HumanResources.
    EmployeeDepartmentHistory H
WHERE DepartmentID = 16
AND P.BusinessEntityID = H.BusinessEntityID);
Output
```

FirstName	LastName
Ken	Sánchez
Laura	Norman

Table 5.8

The output is the same as when the IN operator is used, but during performance tuning the EXISTS operator is preferred. All these subquery operators are equivalent in T-SQL and Oracle SQL.

Conclusion

The different types of subqueries were covered. They are useful but should be used with caution as they might have a negative impact on performance. Joins are generally processed more efficiently and should be used when possible. The EXISTS operator should take precedence over the IN operator because it is more efficient.

Chapter Six

Overview

The use of set operators in SQL is covered. The deviations in Oracle and SQL server are also highlighted.

Set Operators

SQL set operators use mathematical set theory rules to manipulate data. Set operators are used to process the results of two or more equivalent queries. They are generally used to simplify queries that might otherwise be difficult or impossible to create using joins. There are three types of SQL set operators: UNION (UNION ALL), INTERSECT, and MINUS (EXCEPT).

The UNION operator is used to combine the results of two or more queries into one. Set operators are also used in ETL (Extract Transform Load) applications to capture data changes in tables using the MINUS (EXCEPT) operators. In these situations, an old image of the table is compared with the changed version of the table so that only the changed rows are retrieved and loaded to target tables. The INTERSECT operator is used to find common rows returned by queries. The UNION and INTERSECT operators are used in a similar manner in both SQL server and Oracle. The MINUS operator is used in Oracle to return the row difference between the results of two queries while SQL server uses the EXCEPT operator to achieve the same goal. The combined queries are only equivalent if the number of columns in the select list of both queries is the same and the data types of each corresponding column are the same. An individual set operator can only process two queries at a time, but they can be layered to process more than two queries.

UNION Operator

The UNION operator is used to combine data from two equivalent queries. It can be used as a simple UNION or as UNION ALL. The simple UNION returns only one occurrence of duplicate rows returned by the queries while the UNION ALL returns all rows including duplicates. The UNION operator is used in the business environment to work around certain database design or business process Loopholes.

For example, a company may store their normal business regions in one table and store their favourite business regions in another, so to get a report that shows both business regions (normal and favourite), the UNION operator is required. The following Oracle example demonstrates the usage. The normal regions table in the Oracle HR schema contains the following data.

SELECT * FROM regions;
Output

REGION_ID	REGION_NAME
1	Europe
2	Americas
3	Asia
4	Middle East and Africa

Table 6.1

A new favourite_regions table is now created. Four rows are then inserted as follows:

```
CREATE TABLE favourite_regions
( region_id NUMBER,
region_name VARCHAR2(25));
INSERT INTO favourite_regions (region_id,region_name)
    VALUES (1,'Europe');
INSERT INTO favourite_regions (region_id,region_name)
    VALUES (2,'Atlantis');
INSERT INTO favourite_regions (region_id,region_name)
    VALUES (3,'Pandora');
INSERT INTO favourite_regions (region_id,region_name)
    VALUES (4,'The Borge');
```

The next table displays the rows of the new_regions table:

```
SELECT * FROM favourite_regions;
```

Output

REGION_ID	REGION_NAME
1	Europe
2	Atlantis
3	Pandora
4	The Borge

Table 6.2

Now, to see all the regions from both tables in one result set, the UNION operator combines two queries that retrieve data from the two tables as follows. The ORDER BY clause can be used to order the result set after the second query.

SELECT region_id,region_name FROM regions

UNION

SELECT region_id,region_name FROM favourite_regions

ORDER BY region_id;

Output

REGION_ID	REGION_NAME
1	Europe
2	Americas
2	Atlantis
3	Asia
3	Pandora
4	Middle East and Africa
4	The Borge

Table 6.3

The result shows that all the rows from both tables are returned. Notice that region_id value 1 and region_name value Europe are present in both tables but the UNION operator returns only one occurrence.

To return all rows including the duplicates the following UNION ALL statement is executed.

SELECT region_id,region_name FROM REGIONS

UNION ALL

SELECT region_id,region_name FROM favourite_regions

ORDER BY region_id;

Output

REGION_ID	REGION_NAME
1	Europe
1	Europe
2	Americas
2	Atlantis
3	Pandora
3	Asia
4	The Borge
4	Middle East and Africa

Table 6.4

The resulting output shows all eight rows including the two instances of the region_id value 1 and region_name value Europe. The UNION operator is the same in SQL server.

INTERSECT Operator

The INTERSECT operator is used to return rows that are common to two or more query results. The same rules apply. The number of columns and their data types must be the same in each query. Using the tables of the previous example, the INTERSECT operator will be used to discover which region is both a normal and favourite region. The results of queries on the regions and favourite_regions tables are INTERSECTED. The following query is used:

```
SELECT region_id,region_name FROM regions
INTERSECT
SELECT region_id,region_name FROM favourite_regions
ORDER BY region_id;
```

The output is:

REGION_ID	REGION_NAME
1	Europe

Table 6.5

The output is so because region_id value 1 and region_name value Europe is common in both query results.

MINUS and EXCEPT Operators

The MINUS and EXCEPT operators are used by Oracle and SQL server respectively to process set difference operations. The operator looks for differences between rows returned by a specified query and a comparison query. The unique rows found in the specified query are returned.

Oracle MINUS Operator

The Oracle MINUS operator will only return unique rows that are present in the first query but absent in the second query. For example, the MINUS operator can be used to identify the difference between the regions and favourite_regions tables from the previous examples as follows:

```
SELECT region_id,region_name FROM regions
MINUS
SELECT region_id,region_name FROM favourite_regions;
```

The output is:

REGION_ID	REGION_NAME
2	Americas
3	Asia
4	Middle East and Africa

Table 6.6

This output shows the unique rows present in the regions table but absent in the favourite_regions table.

SQL Server EXCEPT Operator

The EXCEPT operator returns the unique rows present in the first query but absent in the second query. Their application for reporting and ETL applications is the same as in Oracle. For example, the shift table in the AdventureWorks2012 database contains the following rows:

SELECT * FROM HumanResources.Shift;
Output

ShiftID	Name	StartTime	EndTime	ModifiedDate
1	Day	07:00:00. 0000000	15:00:00. 0000000	2002-06-01 00:00:00.000
2	Evening	15:00:00. 0000000	23:00:00. 0000000	2002-06-01 00:00:00.000
3	Night	23:00:00. 0000000	07:00:00. 0000000	2002-06-01 00:00:00.000

Table 6.7

An identical table called shift_target is then created, and one row is inserted as follows:

```
USE AdventureWorks2012;
GO
CREATE TABLE HumanResources.Shift_target(
ShiftID int,
Name nvarchar(50),
StartTime time(7),
EndTime time(7),
ModifiedDate datetime);
GO
INSERT INTO HumanResources.Shift_target (ShiftID,Name,St
    artTime,EndTime,ModifiedDate)
VALUES (4,'Extra_hours','12:00:00','23:30:00',GETDATE());
GO
```

The created shift_target table contains the following row:

```
SELECT * FROM HumanResources.Shift_target;
```

ShiftID	Name	StartTime	EndTime	ModifiedDate
4	Extra_ hours	12:00:00. 0000000	23:30:00. 0000000	2012-05-31 12:48:30.477

Table 6.8

The EXCEPT operator can now be used to identify the unique rows present in the shift table but absent in the shift_target table as follows:

```
USE AdventureWorks2012;
GO
SELECT * FROM HumanResources.Shift
```

EXCEPT

SELECT * FROM HumanResources.Shift_target;

The output is as follows:

ShiftID	Name	StartTime	EndTime	ModifiedDate
1	Day	07:00:00. 0000000	15:00:00. 0000000	2002-06-01 00:00:00.000
2	Evening	15:00:00. 0000000	23:00:00. 0000000	2002-06-01 00:00:00.000
3	Night	23:00:00. 0000000	07:00:00. 0000000	2002-06-01 00:00:00.000

Table 6.9

The output shows all the rows of the shift table. This result can be used as a report or as an incremental INSERT during ETL processing.

SET Operator Precedence

It is always prudent to force the execution order when multiple set operators are used together. This guarantees the truthfulness of the results. The order is forced using parentheses to enclose query pairs. For example:

USE AdventureWorks2012;

GO

(SELECT * FROM HumanResources.Shift

EXCEPT

SELECT * FROM HumanResources.Shift_target)

INTERSECT

SELECT * FROM HumanResources.Shift;

The first query pair will be returned first. Then the rows returned will be intersected with the rows returned by final query.

Conclusion

The Oracle and SQL server set operators were covered in this chapter. The application of set constructs for data warehousing will be covered in chapter seven.

Chapter Seven

Overview

This chapter covers statements that create and modify table data. The effects of constraints on these statements are also covered. The application of these statements in data warehousing environments is also demonstrated.

Inserting and Updating Data

Databases tables are empty at the point of creation. In some cases these tables are populated by scripts bundled with the installation. For example, the Oracle sample HR database used for these examples was populated on creation.

The INSERT statement is used to insert new rows into database tables. The UPDATE statement is used to change the values of the inserted rows. The inserted and updated rows have to be committed in order for the table changes to be made permanent. If the database operation mode is not automatic commit, then an explicit commit command is required to save the table changes. The default operating mode of Oracle and SQL server is to auto-commit these statements, thus an explicit commit is not required to save these changes to the database. The query editor will automatically indicate the number of rows affected by these statements. Just like SELECT, both statements are data manipulation language statements (DML). Their usage is also similar in Oracle and SQL server.

Inserting a Single Full Row of Data

Generally, a single INSERT statement is used to populate a single table with one or more rows. The data type of each value must also match the data type of the destination column. A full (all columns are populated) or partial (some columns are ignored) row can be inserted into a table. The usage of the INSERT statement is totally dependent upon the structure and constraints on the database table. For example, you cannot insert a partial row into a table where there is a NOT NULL constraint imposed on each column. The simplest single row INSERT statement syntax is as follows:

```
INSERT INTO table_name (col1,col2,col3)
VALUES(val1,val2,val3)
```

Col1, col2 and col3 are the destination table columns, while VALUES (val1,val2,val3) are the values being inserted into the columns. The data type of values must match column data types or can be implicitly converted by the database. For example, to insert a new country in the Oracle countries table, the following statement is used:

```
INSERT INTO COUNTRIES
    (COUNTRY_ID,COUNTRY_NAME,REGION_ID)
VALUES ('CM','Cameroon',4);
```

The insert succeeded. The new row can be seen by running the following query:

```
SELECT * FROM countries WHERE country_id ='CM';
Output
```

COUNTRY_ID	COUNTRY_NAME	REGION_ID
CM	Cameroon	4

Table 7.1

This statement inserted a full row of values in the countries table.

Inserting a Single Partial Row of Data

The previous example provided a value for each column. This is not mandatory; values must only be provided for columns that do not have explicit or implicit not null constraints. For example, to insert a partial row into the countries table, the following code is used:

```
INSERT INTO COUNTRIES (COUNTRY_ID,COUNTRY_NAME)
VALUES ('PK','Pakistan');
```

A new partial row is inserted that omits the region_id column. A null is implicitly inserted for this column as shown.

```
SELECT * FROM countries WHERE country_id ='PK';
Output
```

COUNTRY_ID	COUNTRY_NAME	REGION_ID
PK	Pakistan	—

Table 7.2

The output show the inserted partial row with a null value inserted for the omitted region_id column.

INSERTS and Table Constraints

Generally, any INSERT statement that violates a database constraint will fail. For example, if an attempt is made to insert a duplicate value into the country_id column of the countries table, the insert fails as follows:

```
INSERT INTO COUNTRIES
    (COUNTRY_ID,COUNTRY_NAME,REGION_ID)
VALUES ('UK','United Kingdom',1);
Output
ORA-00001: unique constraint (HR.COUNTRY_C_ID_PK) violated
```

The insert fails because UK already exists as a value in the country_ id primary key.

Another aspect to consider is automatic value generation. Sometimes the primary key of a table is automatically generated. In this instance, the INSERT will fail if you provide a value for this column. In SQL server these types of columns are called identity columns. Oracle does not use identity columns. For example, the following statement attempts to insert a new row into the HumanResources.Department table:

```
USE AdventureWorks2012;
GO
INSERT INTO HumanResources.Department (DepartmentID,N
    ame,GroupName,ModifiedDate)
VALUES (17,N'Analyst','Research and
    Development',GETDATE());
```

Output

Msg 544, Level 16, State 1, Line 1 Cannot insert explicit value for identity column in table 'Department' when IDENTITY_ INSERT is set to OFF.

This code fails because a value has been provided for the primary key (DepartmentID) which is an auto-generating identity column. To get around this, the column value is excluded from the INSERT values. The column name is also excluded so that the number of columns and values are identical. The following code should be used:

```
USE AdventureWorks2012;
GO
INSERT INTO HumanResources.Department
    (Name,GroupName,ModifiedDate)
VALUES (N'Analyst','Research and Development',GETDATE());
```

The new row is successfully inserted. A value is automatically generated for the DepartmentID column as shown.

```
SELECT * FROM HumanResources.Department
WHERE Name = 'Analyst';
```
Output

DepartmentID	Name	GroupName	ModifiedDate
17	Analyst	Research and Development	2012-07-05 20:26:43.720

Table 7.3

This table cannot support partial INSERTS because each column has the NOT NULL constraint enabled. Also notice the optional N prefixing the Analyst VALUE. This denotes that the subsequent string is in Unicode that extends beyond Western European languages into Chinese.

Inserting Multiple Rows of Data

There are two main scenarios that present an opportunity to INSERT multiple rows of data into a table. The first case is when the data already resides in other tables in your database. The second case is when the data values reside in a text file or are simply known. The first case uses a SELECT subquery as a data source retrieving data from other tables and inserting to the destination table. The second case is manual, where the values will have to be entered into a single INSERT statement. Multiple rows can inserted into duplicate tables using the SELECT * statement. In the next section a single statement issued to create and populate a duplicate of an existing table with multiple rows.

Creating Duplicate Tables

SELECT * statements can be used to create table copies. All the rows of the original table are INSERTED into the new table. The two tables will be structurally the same but most constraints are not inherited by the new table. For example, to create a copy of the Oracle HR employees table, the following syntax is used:

```
CREATE TABLE employee1 AS SELECT * FROM employees;
Output
Table created
```

A new identical table called employee1 is created. This table is also populated with all the rows from the source employees table.

In T-SQL, to create a copy of the HumanResources.Department table, the following syntax is used:

```
USE AdventureWorks2012;
GO
SELECT * INTO HumanResources.Department2
FROM HumanResources.Department;
Output
(17 row(s) affected)
```

A new identical table called HumanResources.Department2 is created. All the rows from the HumanResources.Department have also been copied into the new table. Since there are fewer constraints in these duplicate tables, they are ideal for the remaining examples of this chapter.

INSERTING Multiple Rows Using INSERT SELECT

The INSERT SELECT statement is used to insert multiple rows into a destination table. The rows are retrieved from a source table with a SELECT subquery within the INSERT outer query. All applicable SELECT clauses can be used in the SELECT subquery. The INSERT query inserts the retrieved rows into a destination table. The INSERT INTO SELECT statement can be used in both Oracle and SQL server. For example, if all the rows of the new oracle employee1 table are deleted, the INSERT INTO SELECT statement can be used to repopulate it as follows:

DELETE FROM employee1;

Output

107 row(s) deleted.

The DELETE statement empties the table as shown below.

SELECT * FROM employee1;

Output

No data found

To repopulate the table with the first four rows from the employees table the following INSERT INTO SELECT statement is executed:

INSERT INTO employee1

SELECT * FROM employees WHERE employee_id <104;Output

4 row(s) inserted.

This repopulates the employee1 table with four the rows from the employees table as shown.

SELECT * FROM employee1;

Output: Only a subset of columns shown

EMPLOYEE_ ID	FIRST_ NAME	LAST _NAME	E-MAIL	PHONE_ NUMBER
100	Steven	King	SKING	515.123.4567
101	Neena	Kochhar	NKOCHHAR	515.123.4568
102	Lex	De Haan	LDEHAAN	515.123.4569
103	Alexander	Hunold	AHUNOLD	590.423.4567

Table 7.4

Note that the statement works as intended because both tables have exactly the same structure, so the value to column order is maintained and the correct data types are used. It is always better programming practice to list the destination columns in an insert statement.

T-SQL also uses the same syntax. The following statement deletes all the rows of the created departments2 table:

DELETE FROM HumanResources.Department2;

Output

(17 row(s) affected)

The following statement confirms that the table is in fact empty:

SELECT * FROM HumanResources.Department2;

Output

No rows returned. The INSERT INTO SELECT statement is now going to be used to retrieve three rows from the departments table and insert them into the departments2 table as follows:

USE AdventureWorks2012;

GO

SET IDENTITY_INSERT HumanResources.Department2

    ON;--Turn OFF Identity property

GO

INSERT INTO HumanResources.Department2 (DepartmentID,

    Name,GroupName,ModifiedDate)

SELECT DepartmentID,Name,GroupName,ModifiedDate

FROM HumanResources.Department

WHERE DepartmentID < 4;

The Identity property is turned off so that it becomes possible to insert non automatic values into the DepartmentID column. The following statement retrieves the three inserted rows:

SELECT * FROM HumanResources.Department2;
Output

DepartmentID	Name	GroupName	ModifiedDate
1	Engineering	Research and Development	2002-06-01 00:00:00.000
2	Tool Design	Research and Development	2002-06-01 00:00:00.000
3	Sales	Sales and Marketing	2002-06-01 00:00:00.000

Table 7.5

Manually Inserting Non-Database Multiple Rows

It is sometimes necessary to insert new rows that do not originate from database objects. In this case the column values will be manually edited into your INSERT ALL statement. This method can also be used to insert rows into different tables. With Oracle, this group INSERT ALL uses a subquery with the dummy DUAL table. The DUAL table is a table created during the installation of oracle. It consists of a single row. It is generally used to complete the syntax of SQL statements which do not need a source table.

For example:

```
INSERT ALL
INTO departments (DEPARTMENT_ID, DEPARTMENT_
    NAME, MANAGER_ID, LOCATION_ID ) VALUES
    (290,'Security',100,1300)
INTO departments (DEPARTMENT_ID, DEPARTMENT_
    NAME, MANAGER_ID, LOCATION_ID )
    VALUES(300,'Analysis',107,1400)
INTO employee1 (EMPLOYEE_ID,LAST_NAME,EMAIL,HIRE_
    DATE,JOB_ID) VALUES(EMPLOYEES_
    SEQ.NEXTVAL,'Doe','jdoe@hotmail.
    com','04/01/2012','IT_PROG')
SELECT * FROM DUAL;
```

The code uses the INSERT ALL statement to insert two rows into the departments table and one row into the employee1 table. The string ('04/01/2012') is implicitly converted by the database into a date data type in the employees1 table. The inserted employee1 row is displayed as follows:

```
SELECT * FROM employee1 WHERE last_name = 'Doe';
Output
```

EMPLOYEE _ID	FIRST _NAME	LAST _NAME	E-MAIL	PHONE _NUMBER	HIRE _DATE
220	—	Doe	jdoe@ hotmail.com	—	04/01/2012

Table 7.6

A single partial row is inserted into the employee1 table. The primary key value 220 is generated by a sequence (more on sequences later in this chapter). Notice that nulls are inserted for first_name and phone_number because values were not specified for them. Next is the result of the INSERT into the departments table.

```
SELECT * FROM departments WHERE department_id
    in(290,300);
Output
```

DEPARTMENT_ID	DEPARTMENT_NAME	MANAGER_ID	LOCATION_ID
290	Security	100	1300
300	Analysis	107	1400

Table 7.7

Two full rows have been inserted into the departments table.

Multiple manual inserts in T-SQL use a very simple syntax. The number of rows affected by the INSERT statement can also be captured and returned to a client application with the @@ROWCOUNT global variable. The following example illustrates this:

```
USE AdventureWorks2012;
GO
INSERT INTO HumanResources.Department
    (Name,GroupName,ModifiedDate)
VALUES ('Reporting','Analytics',GETDATE()),
('Security','Assurance',GETDATE()),
('Gastro','Food',GETDATE())
```

GO

Output

SELECT * FROM HumanResources.Department

WHERE name IN('Reporting','Security','Gastro');

DepartmentID	Name	GroupName	ModifiedDate
18	Reporting	Analytics	2012-07-09 10:12:29.607
19	Security	Assurance	2012-07-09 10:12:29.607
20	Gastro	Food	2012-07-09 10:12:29.607

Table 7.8

This statement INSERTS three sets of values into the HumanResources.Department table. The INSERT INTO and VALUES keywords are only stated once. The three sets of values are separated by commas. Notice that the departmentID column is omitted by the INSERT statement; its values are generated by the IDENTITY property.

Transforming Data during INSERTS

Data is sometimes stored in undesirable formats. It is generally more efficient to correct these data anomalies within the database tables than during reporting where functions are embedded in SELECT statements. During data migration or data cleansing activities, functions are embedded within INSERT statements so that the data in tables are in the right format for reporting.

Using the previous example, the data in the table is deleted and the following statement is used to repopulate it with three rows:

```
USE AdventureWorks2012;
GO
SET IDENTITY_INSERT HumanResources.Department2
    ON;--SWITCH OFF IDENTITY CONSTRAINT
GO
INSERT INTO HumanResources.Department2 (DepartmentID,
    Name,GroupName,ModifiedDate)
SELECT (DepartmentID + 1),UPPER(Name),UPPER(GroupNam
    e),GETDATE()
FROM HumanResources.Department
WHERE DepartmentID < 4;
```

Here is the output

```
SELECT * FROM HumanResources.Department2;
```

DepartmentID	Name	GroupName	ModifiedDate
2	ENGINEERING	RESEARCH AND DEVELOPMENT	2012-07-06 18:30:55.617
3	TOOL DESIGN	RESEARCH AND DEVELOPMENT	2012-07-06 18:30:55.617
4	SALES	SALES AND MARKETING	2012-07-06 18:30:55.617

Table 7.9

The output shows that the name and groupname columns values have been transformed from lowercase to uppercase with the UPPER function during the INSERT. The departmentIDs have also been incremented by 1.The data is now in the required format, so transformations will not be required during reporting.

INSERT and SEQUENCES

Oracle and SQL server 2012 uses SEQUENCES to generate automatic primary keys. As opposed to SQL server IDENTITY columns, SEQUENCES are not tied to any table column. Sequences are not constraints on tables so their order can be violated without raising an error. They are used as a black box to generate an arithmetic progression of numbers for any column. Sequences are covered in more detail in chapter twelve.

For example:

The department table in our Oracle HR schema has a primary key department_id. This column needs to be incremented by 10 for each new row. The current maximum value is 270.There is a sequence called DEPARTMENTS_SEQ that can be used for this purpose. Thus to INSERT a new row into this column, the following statement is used:

```
INSERT INTO departments (DEPARTMENT_ID,
    DEPARTMENT_NAME, MANAGER_ID, LOCATION_ID )
VALUES (DEPARTMENTS_SEQ.
    NEXTVAL,'Analysis',107,1400);
```

To see the inserted row, the following statement is issued:

SELECT * FROM departments WHERE department_name = 'Analysis';

Output

DEPARTMENT _ID	DEPARTMENT _NAME	MANAGER _ID	LOCATION _ID
280	Analysis	107	1400

Table 7.10

The DEPARTMENTS_SEQ.NEXTVAL function is included in the values list and generates the next available department_id primary key (280) for the newly inserted analysis department.

In SQL server 2012 there is the option of using either sequences or the identity property to generate automatic primary key values. Unlike identity column values, sequence values can be changed. If sequences are used the NEXT VALUE FOR function is used in the INSERT values list. For example, all the data in the departments2 table is deleted and a sequence is used to generate new primary key values for two new rows as follows (the sequence is called HumanResources.Test_seq and increments by 1):

Delete all rows with the following query

DELETE FROM HumanResources.Department2;

A sequence is now created as follows: (see chapter twelve for sequence creation).

CREATE SEQUENCE HumanResources.Test_seq START WITH
    1 INCREMENT BY 2 MINVALUE 1
MAXVALUE 10000 CYCLE;

The table is now populated using a sequence.

USE AdventureWorks2012;
GO
INSERT INTO HumanResources.Department2 (DepartmentID,
    Name,GroupName,ModifiedDate)
VALUES (NEXT VALUE FOR HumanResources.
    Test_seq,'PRESS','PR',GETDATE()),
(NEXT VALUE FOR HumanResources.Test_seq,'DEFENCE','SE
    CURITY',GETDATE());

Two rows are inserted and can be seen below.

SELECT * FROM HumanResources.Department2

DepartmentID	Name	GroupName	ModifiedDate
1	PRESS	PR	2012-07-06 20:00:13.127
2	DEFENCE	SECURITY	2012-07-06 20:00:13.127

Table 7.11

The two new departmentID values have been generated by the
sequence.

Data Warehousing Incremental INSERTS USING the EXCEPT (MINUS for ORACLE) Operator

Set difference operators are particularly important in ETL applications where data is routinely being migrated from one database table in a source environment to a copy of same table in a target environment. The goal is to minimise the amount of data being moved from the source table to the target table. Set difference operators are used to identify only the new or updated rows for the migration. This process is known as incremental loading. The common rows are thus ignored, improving performance and avoiding duplications. In the following example, a copy of the HumanResources.Shift table is created to act as a target table. Then one row of the original HumanResources.Shift table is updated and another row inserted. The original HumanResources. Shift table will act as the source table. The following statement creates a full copy of the original HumanResources.Shift table with all its rows:

```
USE AdventureWorks2012;
GO
SELECT * INTO HumanResources.Shift_dw
FROM HumanResources.Shift;
```

The HumanResources.Shift_dw table is created with all the rows from the HumanResources.Shift table as shown.

```
SELECT * FROM HumanResources.Shift_dw;
Output
```

ShiftID	Name	StartTime	EndTime	ModifiedDate
1	Day	07:00:00.0000000	15:00:00.0000000	2002-06-01 00:00:00.000
2	Evening	15:00:00.0000000	23:00:00.0000000	2002-06-01 00:00:00.000
3	Night	23:00:00.0000000	07:00:00.0000000	2002-06-01 00:00:00.000

Table 7.12

The table is an exact replica of the HumanResources.Shift table. The HumanResources.Shift table rows are now updated and inserted as follows:

```
UPDATE HumanResources.Shift
SET Name = 'Night_period'
WHERE ShiftID = 3;
```

The previous statement changed the name of shiftid 3 from Night to Night_period. A new row is now inserted as follows:

```
INSERT INTO HumanResources.Shift (Name,StartTime,EndTi
    me,ModifiedDate)
VALUES ('Extra_hours','12:00:00','23:30:00',GETDATE());
```

A new shift row is inserted where the name is Extra_hours. The identity property is implicitly used to generate the new shiftid. The updated HumanResources.Shift now looks like this:

```
SELECT * FROM HumanResources.Shift;
Output
```

ShiftID	Name	StartTime	EndTime	ModifiedDate
1	Day	07:00:00. 0000000	15:00:00. 0000000	2002-06-01 00:00:00.000
2	Evening	15:00:00. 0000000	23:00:00. 0000000	2002-06-01 00:00:00.000
3	Night_ period	23:00:00. 0000000	07:00:00. 0000000	2002-06-01 00:00:00.000
4	Extra_ hours	12:00:00. 0000000	23:30:00. 0000000	2012-07-15 17:47:04.840

Table 7.11

The third and fourth rows are the only rows where changes have occurred; they are the only rows eligible to be inserted into the HumanResources.Shift_dw target table. The following statement does an incremental INSERT from the HumanResources.Shift table source to the HumanResources.Shift_dw table target (the EXCEPT operator is used):

```
INSERT INTO HumanResources.Shift_dw (Name,StartTime,En
    dTime,ModifiedDate)
SELECT Name,StartTime,EndTime,ModifiedDate FROM
    HumanResources.Shift
EXCEPT
SELECT Name,StartTime,EndTime,ModifiedDate FROM
    HumanResources.Shift_dw;
Output
(2 row(s) affected)
```

Only the qualifying rows three and four have been inserted into the target HumanResources.Shift_dw as shown below: The identical rows have been ignored by the EXCEPT operator.

SELECT * FROM HumanResources.Shift_dw;

Output

ShiftID	Name	StartTime	EndTime	ModifiedDate
1	Day	07:00:00. 0000000	15:00:00. 0000000	2002-06-01 00:00:00.000
2	Evening	15:00:00. 0000000	23:00:00. 0000000	2002-06-01 00:00:00.000
3	Night	23:00:00. 0000000	07:00:00. 0000000	2002-06-01 00:00:00.000
4	Night_ period	23:00:00. 0000000	07:00:00. 0000000	2002-06-01 00:00:00.000
5	Extra_ hours	12:00:00. 0000000	23:30:00. 0000000	2012-07-15 17:47:04.840

Table 7.12

UPDATING Tables

The UPDATE statement is used to modify existing data in database tables or views. UPDATE statements can modify one or more columns of one or more rows based on the validity of a given condition. All rows of a table can also be updated if the UPDATE statement is issued without a condition. The new values that replace the previous values can be constants or data retried from other tables using a SELECT subquery. The success of UPDATE statements are also subject to database constraints. UPDATES will always fail if they violate database constraints. The Oracle and SQL server UPDATE statement syntax are generally equivalent.

Updating Tables with Constant Values

The simple general syntax to update all rows without a condition is:

```
UPDATE table_name
SET col1 = val1, col2 = val2;
```

Col1 and col2 are the column names of the table, val1 and val2 are new values used to update the current values of col1 and col2 for each row.

The simple general syntax to update specific rows based on the validity of a condition is:

```
UPDATE table_name
SET col1 = val1, col2 = val2
WHERE condition = TRUE
```

Col1 and col2 are the column names of the table, val1 and val2 are new values used to update the current values of col1 and col2 for each row where the condition is true.

The Oracle examples will use a copy of the regions table. A copy of the table is first created thus:

```
CREATE TABLE regions1 AS SELECT * FROM regions;
Table created:
The current data in the tables is:
SELECT * FROM regions1;
Output
```

REGION_ID	REGION_NAME
1	Europe
2	Americas
3	Asia
4	Middle East and Africa

Table 7.13

Updating Specific Rows Based on the Validity of a Condition

Most business operations will only require updates on a subset of rows that satisfy a condition. The condition is specified in the WHERE clause of the UPDATE statement. For example, to UPDATE a specific region_name, the following UPDATE statement is used with a condition that specifies the rows to be updated:

```
UPDATE regions1
SET region_name = 'Asia Minor'
WHERE region_id = 3;
Output
SELECT * FROM regions1;
```

REGION_ID	REGION_NAME
1	Europe
2	Americas
3	Asia Minor
4	Middle East and Africa

Table 7.14

Only one row has been updated. The value of region_name of row three has been updated from Asia to Asia Minor. This is because only row three satisfies the condition of the UPDATE statement.

Updating All Rows

Now to UPDATE all rows of the table the following UPDATE statement is issued without a WHERE clause condition.

UPDATE regions1

SET region_name = 'UNKNOWN'

Output

SELECT * FROM regions1;

REGION_ID	REGION_NAME
1	UNKNOWN
2	UNKNOWN
3	UNKNOWN
4	UNKNOWN

Table 7.15

In this example, all the rows have been updated because no condition was specified. The region_name column value of each row has been updated to the constant value UNKNOWN. The syntax for T-SQL is exactly the same. The next section examines some advanced T-SQL update options.

T-SQL Update OUTPUT Clause

The T-SQL optional OUTPUT clause can be used to return information about changed row values. This clause can be executed after INSERT, UPDATE, and DELETE statements. When any of these statements change a row's value, the initial and current values are stored in internal tables called deleted and inserted. When invoked, the OUTPUT clause automatically queries the SQL server deleted and inserted tables to return the changes. This can be used to keep an audit of table changes over time. In data warehousing applications, they can be used with triggers to manage slowly changing dimensions. For example, the shift table has the following rows:

```
SELECT * FROM HumanResources.shift;
```

ShiftID	Name	StartTime	EndTime	ModifiedDate
1	Day	07:00:00.0000000	15:00:00.0000000	2002-06-01 00:00:00.000
2	Evening	15:00:00.0000000	23:00:00.0000000	2002-06-01 00:00:00.000
3	Night	23:00:00.0000000	07:00:00.0000000	2002-06-01 00:00:00.000

Table 7.16

The following statement updates the first row and uses the OUTPUT clause to show the changed values from the name column.

```
UPDATE TOP(1) HumanResources.shift
SET NAME ='Day Period'
```

OUTPUT Deleted.name AS Initial_name, Inserted.name AS
    Updated_name;
Output

Initial_name	Updated_name
Day	Day Period

Table 7.17

The UPDATE statement uses the TOP function to identify only the first row for the update. The UPDATE changes the name column value from Day to Day Period. The OUTPUT clause is used to implicitly query the deleted and inserted tables and returns the initial and current values of the name column for that row.

UPDATES Using SELECT Subqueries

All the previous UPDATE statements used constant values or expressions to replace the current value. This is static and forces the programmer to hardcode values in their programs. This is sometimes undesirable when designing reusable ETL applications. In the ideal ETL world, it is better to store the new values in a table and then use an UPDATE SELECT statement to update the current values with the values from the table. For example, a new person.TopPerson table is created and populated with the first three rows of the person.person table. The data in the first_name column has been corrupted with the UPPER function and a concatenation operator. The data in the firstname column is correct and will be used as a control column for comparisons:

The following statement creates the person.TopPerson table populated with the top 3 rows from the Person.Person table.

```
USE AdventureWorks2012;
GO
SELECT TOP (3) BusinessEntityID,UPPER('@
    ve'+FirstName+'lg')AS First_name,Firstname
INTO Person.TopPerson
FROM Person.Person;
```

The first_name column demonstrates how functions and operators can be embedded in queries to transform data.

Below is a listing of the created table with muddled names.

```
SELECT * FROM Person.TopPerson;
Output.
```

BusinessEntityID	First_name	Firstname
285	@VESYEDLG	Syed
293	@VECATHERINELG	Catherine
295	@VEKIMLG	Kim

Table 7.18

The created table is now UPDATED with the correct names from the Person.Person table using a subquery.

```
UPDATE Person.TopPerson
SET First_Name =
(SELECT Firstname FROM Person.Person
```

WHERE Person.BusinessEntityID = TopPerson.

BusinessEntityID);

The updated Person.TopPerson table is now displayed as follows.

SELECT * FROM Person.TopPerson;

Output

BusinessEntityID	First_name	Firstname
285	Syed	Syed
293	Catherine	Catherine
295	Kim	Kim

Table 7.19

The UPDATE SELECT statement is used to correct the muddled first_names in the Person.TopPerson Table. Notice that the new correct values are retrieved from the Person.Person table.

UPDATES and Table Constraints

As previously stated, updates will always fail if they violate any database constraint.

For example, in the Oracle HR database, there is a constraint that stipulates that the employee last_name should never be null. If we try to set any last_name to null, an error will be raised as follows:

UPDATE employees

SET last_name = NULL

WHERE employee_id = 100;

When we try to run this update, the following error is raised:

ORA-01407: cannot update ("HR"."EMPLOYEES"."LAST_
NAME") to NULL

With SQL server, if we try to update any BusinessEntityID with a number that already exists, the primary key constraint will be violated and the update will fail and return an error. For example:

```
USE AdventureWorks2012;
UPDATE Person.person
SET BusinessEntityID = 1
WHERE BusinessEntityID =10;
```

The following error is returned when the statement is executed:

Msg 2627, Level 14, State 1, Line 1

Violation of PRIMARY KEY constraint 'PK_Person_ BusinessEntityID'. Cannot insert duplicate key in object 'Person. Person'. The duplicate key value is (1).

The statement has been terminated.

MERGE Statements for Data Validation and Verification

The MERGE statement is very useful and can be used in data verification, correction and validation activities where a master data table (an authority table that is accepted to contain the most valid and correct data) is used to correct, standardise and cleanse a subtable.

The merge statement can be used to combine multiple DML statements. The statement retrieves data from one or more tables and uses decision logic to determine how to apply the retrieved rows in a destination table. The MERGE statement can be used to combine SELECT, INSERT, and DELETE statements. The MERGE statement compares source and destination table values in a condition and performs one action if the values match and another if the values do not match. The next example demonstrates how to use the MERGE statement in Oracle. A new table is first created and loaded with four rows:

```
CREATE TABLE new_regions
(region_id NUMBER, region_name VARCHAR2(25));
INSERT INTO new_regions (region_id,region_name) VALUES
    (1,'AUSTRALIA');
INSERT INTO new_regions (region_id,region_name) VALUES
    (2,'AMERICAS');
INSERT INTO new_regions (region_id,region_name) VALUES
    (5,'ASIA');
INSERT INTO new_regions (region_id,region_name) VALUES
    (7,'ARABIA');
```

The following table shows the rows of the new table.

```
SELECT * FROM new_regions;
```

REGION_ID	REGION_NAME
1	AUSTRALIA
2	AMERICAS
5	ASIA
7	ARABIA

Table 7.20

This new_regions table can now be merged with data from the regions table. The rows of the regions table are shown below:

SELECT * FROM regions;

REGION_ID	REGION_NAME
1	Europe
2	Americas
3	Asia
4	Middle East and Africa

Table 7.21

The MERGE statement can now be used synchronise the new_regions table with data from the regions table. The regions table is acting like the master data table which corrects the new_regions table.

```
MERGE INTO new_regions n
USING (SELECT region_id, region_name
FROM regions ) r
ON(r.region_id = n.region_id)
WHEN MATCHED THEN UPDATE SET n.region_name =
    r.region_name
```

WHEN NOT MATCHED THEN INSERT (n.region_id,n.

region_name)

VALUES (r.region_id,r.region_name);

The result of the MERGE is shown below:

SELECT * FROM new_regions ORDER BY region_id ;

REGION_ID	REGION_NAME
1	Europe
2	Americas
3	Asia
4	Middle East and Africa
5	ASIA
7	ARABIA

Table 7.22

As an example, the MERGE statement UPDATES the new_regions table with data from the regions table whenever the region_ids of the two tables match. When the region_id value 1 is matched in both tables the region_ name is updated from AUSTRALIA to Europe. When the region_ids do not match, new rows are INSERTED into the new_region table from the regions table. For example, when region_ids 3 and 4 are not matched, regions_id 3 and 4 details (Asia, Middle East and Africa) are inserted into the table.

The T-SQL version of the MERGE statement works in a similar way. A new table called Person.AddressTypeS is created and synchronised with the Person.AddressType table: The new table is created with the following statement:

```
USE AdventureWorks2012;
GO
CREATE TABLE Person.AddressTypeS(
AddressTypeID int,
NameName nvarchar(50),
ModifiedDate datetime);
INSERT INTO Person.AddressTypeS (AddressTypeID,NameNa
    me,ModifiedDate)
VALUES (1,'Procurement',GETDATE()),
(11,'Banking',GETDATE()),
(2,'Payment',GETDATE());
```

A new table called Person.AddressTyeS is created and three rows are inserted into it. The contents of the table is shown below.

SELECT * FROM Person.AddressTypeS;

AddressTypeID	NameName	ModifiedDate
1	Procurement	2012-05-27 00:47:45.130
11	Banking	2012-05-27 00:47:45.130
2	Payment	2012-05-27 00:47:45.130

Table 7.24

This table data can now be synchronised with the Person. AddressType table. The contents of the table is shown next:

SELECT * FROM Person.AddressType ;

AddressType ID	Name	Rowguide	ModifiedDate
1	Billing	B84F78B1-4EFE-4A0E-8CB7-70E9F112F886	2002-06-01 00:00:00.000
2	Home	41BC2FF6-F0FC-475F-8EB9-CEC0805AA0F2	2002-06-01 00:00:00.000
3	Main Office	8EEEC28C-07A2-4FB9-AD0A-42D4A0BBC575	2002-06-01 00:00:00.000
4	Primary	24CB3088-4345-47C4-86C5-17B535133D1E	2002-06-01 00:00:00.000
5	Shipping	B29DA3F8-19A3-47DA-9DAA-15C84F4A83A5	2002-06-01 00:00:00.000
6	Archive	A67F238A-5BA2-444B-966C-0467ED9C427F	2002-06-01 00:00:00.000

Table 7.25

```
USE AdventureWorks2012
MERGE Person.AddressTypeS AS n
USING (SELECT AddressTypeID, Name,ModifiedDate FROM
    Person.AddressType) AS a
ON (n.AddressTypeID = a.AddressTypeID)
WHEN MATCHED THEN
UPDATE SET n.NameName = a.Name
WHEN NOT MATCHED THEN
INSERT (AddressTypeID, NameName, ModifiedDate)
VALUES (a.AddressTypeID, a.Name, a.ModifiedDate);
```

The MERGE statement UPDATES and INSERTS data into the new Person.AddressTypeS with data from Person.AddressType table.

The table is updated whenever the addressTypeID of both tables match. For example, when AddressTypeID value 1 is matched, the NameName field is updated from procurement to billing. When the values do not match, rows are inserted into the table. For example, addressTypeIDs 3, 4, 5 and 6 are inserted into the table.

AddressTypeID	NameName	ModifiedDate
1	Billing	2012-05-27 00:47:45.130
2	Home	2012-05-27 00:47:45.130
3	Main Office	2002-06-01 00:00:00.000
4	Primary	2002-06-01 00:00:00.000
5	Shipping	2002-06-01 00:00:00.000
6	Archive	2002-06-01 00:00:00.000
11	Banking	2012-05-27 00:47:45.130

Table 7.25

Using INSERT and SELECT CASE to Transform Data

The SELECT CASE expression can be used to INSERT rows into database tables. These INSERTS can be part of a business intelligence drive in an organisation. The rationale is that the data should be stored in the best format, avoiding the requirement to decode values during data retrieval with inefficient SELECT statements. This also ensures that there is only one version of truth available to reporting tools, as some reporting tools might not have the SELECT CASE functionality. The syntax is the same as used in SELECT statements, the main difference being rather than simply returning the transformed values, the values are derived and saved in the database. The next example creates a new_regions2 tables and uses the SELECT CASE to populate the currency column with decoded region_id values from the regions table:

The table is created as follows:

CREATE TABLE new_regions2
(Region_id NUMBER,
Region_name VARCHAR2(25),
Currency VARCHAR2(25));

The table is created and can now be populated with the following values from the regions table.

SELECT * FROM regions;

REGION_ID	REGION_NAME
1	Europe
2	Americas
3	Asia
4	Middle East and Africa

Table 7.26

The normal INSERT SELECT statement is used but a CASE expression is used to define the values of the currency column as follows:

INSERT INTO new_regions2(Region_id,Region_name,Currency)
SELECT region_id, region_name,CASE region_id

WHEN 1 THEN 'Euros'

WHEN 2 THEN 'US Dollars'

WHEN 3 THEN 'Yen'

ELSE 'Franc CFA' END AS Currency

FROM regions;

The currency column has now been populated with the real currency values as follows:

SELECT * FROM new_regions2;

Output

REGION_ID	REGION_NAME	CURRENCY
1	Europe	Euros
2	Americas	US Dollars
3	Asia	Yen
4	Middle East and Africa	Franc CFA

Table 7.27

The currencies are now stored in the database and can be retrieved without using CASE statements in SELECT statements. Please refer to chapter eight for details about the SELECT CASE statement.

Conclusion

The UPDATE and INSERT statements were covered in this chapter. The application of these statements in data warehousing environments was also covered. DDL statements for creating tables where also introduced. These DDL object creation statements are covered in more detail in chapter eleven.

Chapter Eight

Overview

This chapter covers functions calculated columns and operators. These are potentially the most challenging constructs in declarative SQL. However each of the functions is explicitly presented to capture their intended use and business applicability. The deviations in Oracle and SQL server are also covered.

Calculated or Virtual Columns and Functions

The list of columns specified in SELECT statements usually includes only physical columns from tables or views. Sometimes the data in these columns might not be in the required format. For example, in the SQL server AdventureWorks2012 database, in the Person.person table a person's full name is split up into the first name and last name columns. This is correct from a table design perspective (third NF) but is inappropriate when you need to display all the names as a single string for mailing purposes. This situation is resolved by including a calculated or virtual column in the column list of the SELECT statement. This virtual column will use operators or functions to format the data and deliver the required results. These virtual columns do not exist in the database table, they disappear once the statement terminates. They can be optionally named using an alias. Aliases are assigned using the AS keyword. If the alias name does not include a space or special character, it can be declared without double quotes. If it includes a special character or space, it must be declared with double quotes. For example:

Alias names with no space character:

SELECT salary+100 AS salary_increase from employee;
Alias names with spaces :
SELECT salary+100 AS "salary increase" from employee;

T-SQL Calculated Columns

The syntax for creating T-SQL calculated columns is similar to the Oracle syntax; the difference is in the choice of operator and functions used. The first example uses the concatenation operator (+).

The first and last name of a person whose BusinessEntityID is 100 in the SQL server AdventureWorks2012 database Person.Person table is listed as follows:

USE AdventureWorks2012
GO
SELECT FirstName,LastName
FROM Person.Person
WHERE BusinessEntityID = 100;
Which outputs:

FirstName	LastName
Lolan	Song

Table 8.1

The output shows both names in different columns. To get the full contact name from the two columns the concatenation operator is used.

```
SELECT FirstName + LastName As Fullname
FROM Person.Person
WHERE BusinessEntityID = 100;
```
Which outputs

Fullname
LolanSong

Table 8.2

Notice that the firstname and lastname have been concatenated into one virtual column called fullname. The AS keyword is used to name the virtual column with an alias called fullname. The alias name is not surrounded by double quotes because it does not contain a space.

Notice that the full name is strung together as one word (LolanSong). To separate the words you must include an empty string literal between the two columns in the SELECT statement. To do this, use single quotes and an empty space between the column names. The statement changes to:

```
SELECT FirstName +' '+LastName As Fullname
FROM Person.Person
WHERE BusinessEntityID = 100;
```
Outputing

Fullname
Lolan Song

Table 8.3

The results now shows the names separated by two spaces.

Another important use of virtual columns is for mathematical calculations. A typical situation is when you have separate columns for quantity sold and unit price in a sales table. To display the total revenue for orders with more than forty items, you will need to multiply the quantity sold by the unit price in a virtual column. The statement for this is:

```
USE AdventureWorks2012
GO
SELECT SalesOrderID,OrderQty,UnitPrice,OrderQty*UnitPrice
    AS "Total Revenue"
FROM Sales.SalesOrderDetail
WHERE OrderQty >40;
Output:
```

SalesOrderID	OrderQty	UnitPrice	Total Revenue
50270	44	17.0955	752.202
67266	41	31.4955	1291.3155

Table 8.4

The results shows the unit price and quantity as well as the virtual column Total Revenue, which is the product of quantity and unit price. Note that all basic mathematical operators can be used in this context and the alias name Total Revenue is surrounded by double quotes because of the space between the words.

Oracle Virtual Columns

Oracle virtual columns are used in the same manner as their SQL server counterpats. However they use different operators and functions. For example a double pipe symbol (||) is used to concatenate the first and last name of an employee 100 in the Oracle HR employee table.

The following code is used:

```
SELECT first_name||' '||last_name AS Fullname FROM
    employees
WHERE employee_id = 100;
Output
```

FULLNAME
Steven King

Table 8.5

The first double pipe is used to concatenate the first_name with the space, and the second double pipe is used to conatenate the space and the last name, resulting in the aliased fullname column.

Special Virtual Columns Using the SELECT CASE Expression

Virtual columns can also be created using the CASE expression. The CASE expression is defined as one of the columns in the SELECT list. It could be used to add more intelligence into a report by qualifying rows based on the validity of a condition. For example, it could be used to qualify all employees earning more than 1700 as high earners while those earning less are qualified as low earners. However, the case expression is usually used in reports to transform coded values to more business-oriented words. For example, the currency of a country could be stored using the code UKS. This code can be transformed to the more understandable currency name called pound sterling in reports. The case expression adds decision logic to SQL. It evaluates a list of conditions and returns one of multiple alternative results. The CASE expression is equivalent in Oracle and SQL server.

There are two variations of the CASE expression—the simple and searched CASE expressions.

Oracle Simple CASE Expression

The simple CASE expression is based on equality. It checks if the values returned from a stated column are equal to a set of stated values or expressions. Each time a match is found, the THEN clause is used to output a preset value or expression. The simple CASE expression has the following syntax:

```
SELECT col1, col2, CASE col3
WHEN vale1 THEN preset_value1
WHEN valu2 THEN preset_value2
ELSE default_value END
FROM table_name
END;
```

All the columns must originate from the table specified in the FROM clause. This expression compares col3 values to each of the values (value1 and value2) specified in each WHEN clause. For each row, if a match is found, the THEN clause outputs the preset_value and ignores the other WHEN clauses. If no match is found, the ELSE clause is executed and outputs the stated default_value. Note that the ELSE clause is optional. If the ELSE clause is omitted, NULLs will be returned if no matches are found. The simple case expression allows for only an equality check in the WHEN clause.

In the following example, a virtual currency column is created to display the currency of each region. The following is the current contents of the regions table:

SELECT * FROM regions;

REGION_ID	REGION_NAME
1	Europe
2	Americas
3	Asia
4	Middle East and Africa

Table 8.6

Each region is displayed without a currency. The CASE statement is now used to return virtual column currency for each region based on their region_ids:

SELECT region_id, region_name,CASE region_id
WHEN 1 THEN 'Euros'
WHEN 2 THEN 'US Dollars'

WHEN 3 THEN 'Yen'

ELSE 'Franc CFA' END AS Currency

FROM regions;

Output

REGION_ID	REGION_NAME	CURRENCY
1	Europe	Euros
2	Americas	US Dollars
3	Asia	Yen
4	Middle East and Africa	Franc CFA

Table 8.7

The calculated currency column displays the simple SELECT CASE results. The Region_Id column displays the original Region_Ids. The currency column transforms the Region_Id to the values stated in the THEN clause of the CASE statement. For example, when the region_id is equal to 1 in the first WHEN clause, the 1 is returned as Euros by the THEN clause. The fourth row currency value Franc CFA is returned by the ELSE clause because there was no WHEN test for region_id equals 4 thus the stated default currency is displayed.

Search Case Expression

The search CASE expression is based on the validity of a condition rather than on equality. The searched CASE expression evaluates the condition and returns the preset value in the THEN clause if the condition evaluates to TRUE for any row.

If no condition is found to be true, the optional value in the ELSE clause is returned. The searched CASE expression has the following syntax:

```
SELECT col1, col2, CASE col3
WHEN condition_1_is_true THEN preset_value1
WHEN condition_2_is_true THEN preset_value2
ELSE defult_value END
FROM table_name
END;
```

For example, the following statement returns the salaries of five employees:

```
SELECT employee_id, First_Name,Last_Name,Salary
FROM employees
WHERE employee_id <105;
```

EMPLOYEE_ID	FIRST_NAME	LAST_NAME	SALARY
100	Steven	King	24000
101	Neena	Kochhar	17000
102	Lex	De Haan	17000
103	Alexander	Hunold	9000
104	Bruce	Ernst	6000

Table 8.8

The search case statement is then used to return predefined salary qualifications for each salary range as follows.

```
SELECT First_Name,Last_Name,Salary,
CASE WHEN Salary < 7000 THEN 'LOW SALARY'
WHEN Salary BETWEEN 7000 AND 10000 THEN 'MEDIUM
    SALARY'
WHEN Salary BETWEEN 10000 AND 20000 THEN 'HIGH SALARY'
ELSE 'SUPER SCALE'
END AS "SALARY RANGE"
FROM Employees
WHERE employee_id <105;
```

Output

FIRST_NAME	LAST_NAME	SALARY	SALARY RANGE
Steven	King	24000	SUPER SCALE
Neena	Kochhar	17000	HIGH SALARY
Lex	De Haan	17000	HIGH SALARY
Alexander	Hunold	9000	MEDIUM SALARY
Bruce	Ernst	6000	LOW SALARY

Table 8.9

The CASE statement returns LOW SALARY when the salary is below 7000, as in the case of Bruce Ernst, who earns 6000. It displays MEDIUM SALARY when the salary is between 7000 and 10000 as in the case of Alexander Hunold, who earns 9000. It displays HIGH SALARY when the salary is between 10000 and 20000, as in the case of Neena, who earns 17000. It displays SUPER SCALE when the salary is not within any of the declared ranges, as in the case of Steven King, who earns 24000.

BUILT IN Functions

BUILT IN functions are relational objects that are created and are available for use once a DBMS is installed. They are used to facilitate and accomplish complex data manipulation operations on table data. Some fuction operations include counting, summing, formating, averaging, and ranking table data. Fuctions are used in SQL statements by stating their names and specifying zero or more operands. They always return a result. The operands or arguments of a function are usually database table columns, literals, or a combination of both. In the business environment, developers can also build user-defined functions using programmable T-SQL or PL/SQL to solve certain business-related issues. An example of a user-defined function could be a payroll function used to process employee salaries. These functions are covered in part two of this book. Functions can be used in SELECT, DELETE, INSERT, and UPDATE statements.

The general syntax of a function is: Function_name (operand1, operand2 . . .);

Functions expect a specific data type for its operands. If data with the wrong data type is entered as an operand, the fuction tries to implicitly convert it to the expected data type, and if it fails, the query will also fail. For example, numbers stored as characters will be implicitly converted to numbers by the numeric function before being used. However, a date cannot be implicitly converted into a number, so the query fails. The three general types of functions are scalar, aggregate, and analytic.

Scalar functions manipulate single rows in tables, returning a value for eash row. Aggregate functions manipulate groups of rows and return a single result for the group. Analytic functions manipulate several rows or groups to return several results for each group.

One of the greatest difference between DBMSs is in their implementation of functions. The differences in function implementation between Microsoft SQL server and Oracle are covered in this chapter. Since there are hundreds of fuctions, only the top four functions of each type are covered.

The three general types of functions have a subset of function groups, which include arithmetic functions, date and time functions, aggregate functions, conversion functions, system functions, character functions, analytic functions, and miscellaneous functions. Calculated columns will be used in the examples to demonstrate how to use these functions in different SELECT statements. Different functions will be applied to the same data to illuminate their operational differences.

Aggregate Functions

Aggregate functions return a single row based on calculations across several rows. They are very useful in summarising data for reporting and analysis. They can appear in SELECT statements as well as the ORDER BY and HAVING clauses. Most aggregate functions ignore nulls and can be used with the DISTINCT keyword to ignore duplicate values. The exception to this is the COUNT * function. Aggregate functions are the same in Oracle and SQL server.

AVG(n)

The AVG(n) function calculates the arithmetic average of the data values contained within a column. It returns a numeric data type value. The column must contain numeric values or any non-numeric data type that can be implicitly converted to a numeric data type. An example is the calculation of the average unit price from the AdventureWorks2012 Sales.SalesOrderDetail:

```
USE AdventureWorks2012
GO
SELECT AVG(UnitPrice)AS "Average Unit Price",
AVG (DISTINCT(UnitPrice)) AS "Individual Average Unit Price"
FROM Sales.SalesOrderDetail;
Outputs
```

Average Unit Price	Individual Average Unit Price
465.0934	408.7945

Table 8.10

The first AVG(UnitPrice) returns 465.0934, which is the average unit price including duplicate unit prices, while the second AVG (DISTINCT(UnitPrice)) returns 408.7945, which is the average unit price and includes only unique prices in the average calculation.

MAX(n)

The MAX(n) function derives the maximum data value of the column. The column can contain numeric, string, or date data type values. The returned value always has the same data type as its arguments. An example is demonstrated by calculating the maximum unit price and the most recent date modification from the Sales. SalesOrderDetail table:

```
USE AdventureWorks2012
GO
SELECT MAX(UnitPrice)AS "Most expensive product",
Max(ModifiedDate) AS "Most resent modification"
FROM sales.SalesOrderDetail;
Outputs
```

Most expensive product	Most resent modification
3578.27	2008-07-31 00:00:00.000

Table 8.11

The first MAX(UnitPrice)returns 3578.27, which is the most expensive product, and the second Max(ModifiedDate) returns 2008-07-31 00:00:00.000, which is the most recent modification date. Note that in most databases, today's date is greater than yesterday's date. The functions return the type of its operands that are numeric and date data types respectively.

MIN(N)

The MIN(n) function derives the minimum data value of the column. It is the polar opposite of the MAX(n) function. The column can contain numeric, string, or date data type values. The returned value always has the same data type as its arguments.

An example is demonstrated by calculating the minimum unit price and the earliest date modification from the Sales. SalesOrderDetail table:

```
USE AdventureWorks2012;
GO
SELECT MIN(UnitPrice)AS "Cheapest product",
MIN(ModifiedDate) AS "Earliest modification"
FROM sales.SalesOrderDetail;
Output
```

Cheapest product	Earliest modification
1.3282	2005-07-01 00:00:00.000

Table 8.12

The first MIN(UnitPrice) returns 1.3282, which is the cheapest product, and the second MIN(ModifiedDate) returns 2005-07-01 00:00:00.000, which is the date of the earliest modification.

COUNT(n), COUNT (*)

COUNT(n) returns the number non NULL data values in a column including duplicates. If the DISTINCT key word is specified, both NULLS and duplicates are ignored.

COUNT (*) calculates the number of all rows, including duplicates and nulls returned by a query. It is the only function that cannot be applied to a column. Count always returns a numeric data type.

An example is demonstrated by counting all the MiddleNames in the person.person table. Notice that the same column (MiddleName) is being used to demonstrate how this function manipulates the same set of values differently with different options.

USE AdventureWorks2012

SELECT COUNT(*)AS "Every Row in the table",

Count(MiddleName)AS "All stored middle names",

Count (DISTINCT(MiddleName)) AS "Individual Middle Names"

FROM Person.Person;

Output

Every Row in the table	All stored middle names	Individual Middle Names
19972	11473	70

Table 8.13

The first COUNT(*) returns the value 19972, which is the total number of rows returned by the query including NULLs and duplicates. The second COUNT (MiddleName) returns 11473, which is the total number of middle names excluding NULLs but including duplicates. The third COUNT (DISTINCT(MiddleName) returns 70, which is the number of unique MiddleNames excluding NULLs and duplicates.

SUM(n)

The SUM(n) function calculates the mathematical addition of all data values in a column. The column must contain numeric values or any non-numeric data type that can be implicitly converted to a numeric data type. It always returns a numeric data type.

```
USE AdventureWorks2012
GO
SELECT SUM(UnitPrice)AS "Total Unit Price",
SUM(DISTINCT(UnitPrice)) AS "Sum Of Individual Unit Price"
FROM sales.SalesOrderDetail;
Output
```

Total Unit Price	Sum Of Individual Unit Price
56423747.6147	117324.0357

Table 8.14

The first SUM(UnitPrice) returns 56423747.6147, which is the sum of all unit prices including duplicates. The second SUM(DISTINCT(UnitPrice)) returns 117324.0357, which is the sum of all unit prices, excluding duplicates.

Aggregate Functions and Grouping

Once an aggregate function is applied to a column in the select list of a SELECT statement any other column in the select list must also have an aggregate function applied to it or it must be included in a GROUP BY clause. For example, the following statement, which determines the maximum VacationHours, fails:

```
USE AdventureWorks2012
GO
SELECT MAX(VacationHours)AS "Longest Holiday", Gender
FROM HumanResources.Employee;
Output
Msg 8120, Level 16, State 1, Line 1
```

Column 'HumanResources.Employee.Gender' is invalid in the select list because it is not contained in either an aggregate function or the GROUP BY clause.

The error message is self-explanatory. The error can be corrected by either including the gender column in a GROUP BY clause or applying an aggregate function to it. The business requirement will generally direct this decision. The statement can be corrected by grouping genders as follows.

```
SELECT MAX(VacationHours)AS "Longest Holiday", Gender
FROM HumanResources.Employee
GROUP BY Gender;
Outputing
```

Longest Holiday	Gender
99	F
99	M

Table 8.15

A single row is returned for each group, one row each for M and F.

Arithmetic Functions

These scalar functions (which operate on individual rows) perform mathematical manipulations on numeric operands and return numeric values. They accept numeric input operands and return numeric values. They are used the same way in Oracle and SQL server. The main difference is in the spelling of some of the functions. Virtual fields will be used in the examples to demonstrate how to use these functions in different configurations. They include:

(ABS(n),

This function returns the absolute value of the operand n. The absolute value is always a positive number thus negative numbers are converted to positive numbers. For example:

```
USE AdventureWorks2012
GO
SELECT UnitPrice, (UnitPrice - 1000) As "negative number",
ABS(UnitPrice - 1000) AS "Absolute Numbers"
FROM sales.SalesOrderDetail
WHERE SalesOrderDetailID = 15
Output
```

UnitPrice	negative number	Absolute Numbers
809.76	-190.24	190.24

Table 8.16

In the first column, unitprice is 809.76. The negative number (UnitPrice - 1000) calculates 809.76-1000, which evaluates to—190.24. The ABS function then converts this value to 190.24 in the third column.

(CEILING(n) for SQL server), FLOOR(n), (CEIL(n) for Oracle)

The CEILING(n) function returns the smallest integer value greater or equal to the specified operand n. The FLOOR(n) function is the polar opposite of the CEILING(n) function. It returns largest integer equal to or less than *n*. They manipulate numeric data type operands or any non-numeric data type that can be implicitly converted to a numeric data type by the database. It always returns numeric data types. Oracle version is called CEIL(n). An SQL server example is:

```
SELECT UnitPrice, FLOOR(UnitPrice ) As "Floor Numbers",
CEILING(UnitPrice) AS "Ceiling Numbers"
FROM sales.SalesOrderDetail
WHERE
SalesOrderDetailID = 15;
Output
```

UnitPrice	Floor Numbers	Ceiling Numbers
809.76	809.00	810.00

Table 8.17

In the first column, unitprice is 809.76. The FLOOR(UnitPrice) returns 809.00, which is the largest integer less than 809.76. The CEILING(UnitPrice) returns 810.00, which is the smallest integer greater than 809.76.

SQRT(n)

The SQRT(n) function returns the square root of *n*. It manipulates numeric data type operands or any non-numeric data type that can be implicitly converted to a numeric data type by the database. It always returns numeric data types. An SQL server example is:

```
SELECT SQRT(9) AS "Square root";
```

Outputs

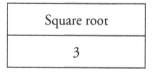

Square root
3

Table 8.18

Oracle needs the DUAL table to execute the same function when applied on a free standing literal. The statement is:

SELECT SQRT(9) AS "Square root" FROM DUAL;
Output

Square root
3

Table 8.19

Character Functions

Character functions are used to manipulate data and return characters or numeric values. They are scalar functions. Note that the words character and string are used interchangeably. They include:

UPPER(x), LOWER(x)

The UPPER function transforms all lowercase characters in a string to uppercase. The LOWER function transforms uppercase strings to lowercase. They always return stings. An example is can be demonstrated by transforming the FirstName of person 250 in the Person.Person table to uppercase and lowercase characters.

```
USE AdventureWorks2012
GO
SELECT Firstname, UPPER(FirstName) AS
    "UPPER_FIRST_NAME",
LOWER(FirstName) AS "LOWER_FIRST_NAME"
From Person.Person
WHERE BusinessEntityID =250;
```

Output:

Firstname	UPPER_FIRST_ NAME	LOWER_FIRST_ NAME
Sheela	SHEELA	sheela

Table 8.20

The FirstName column is displayed without the transformation. The second virtual column "UPPER_FIRST_NAME" is used to display the uppercase transformed name. The final virtual column LOWER_FIRST_NAME shows the FirstName transformed to lowercase.

RTRIM(x) LTRIM(x) T-SQL

These functions are not equivalent between Oracle and SQL server. In SQL server the functions remove leading and trailing spaces. LTRIM removes leading spaces from the left while RTRIM removes trailing spaces from the right. They always return strings. The following example demonstrates the use of these functions in SQL server. The functions are used to trim character constants in SQL server.

```
SELECT ('Remove From Left') AS "Leading spaces Present",
    LTRIM('Remove From Left') AS "Leading spaces removed",
```

('Remove From Right ')+'Right spaces present' AS "With

Trailing Saces",

RTRIM('Remove From Right ')+'Spaces removed' AS "Without

Trailing Saces";

Leading spaces Present	Leading spaces removed	With Trailing Spaces	Without Trailing Spaces
Remove From Left	Remove From Left	Remove From Right Right spaces present	Remove From Right Spaces removed

Table 8.21

The first column displays a string with leading spaces. The second column uses the LTRIM function to remove these spaces from the string. The third column displays a variable with trailing spaces. The forth column uses the RTRIM function to remove these trailing spaces.

LTRIM(string,'variable'), RTRIM(string,'variable') for Oracle

With Oracle these functions remove all the characters from string defined by a variable from the left or right end of a string. LTRIM removes from the left and RTRIM removes from the right. This can be demonstrated in the following example, which trims employee Steven's name:

```
SELECT First_Name,
LTRIM(First_Name,'St')AS "St Removed",
RTRIM (First_Name,'en') AS "en Removed"
FROM employees
WHERE Employee_ID = 100;
Output:
```

FIRST_NAME	St Removed	en Removed
Steven	even	Stev

Table 8.22

Steven is displayed in the first column First_Name without the trim function. The second column uses LTRIM to remove *St* from the FirstName to display *even*. The final column uses the RTRIM function to remove *en* from the FirstName to display *Stev*. Note that these functions are case sensitive.

(LENGTH(n for oracle)) (LEN(n) for SQL Server)

The LENGTH(n) function is used in Oracle to calculate the length of an input string n. This length includes leading and trailing blanks.

The LEN(n) Function is used in SQL server to calculate the length of an input string n. This length excludes trailing blanks.

This function is one of the few character functions that return numbers. The input is always a string. An SQL Server example is:

```
USE AdventureWorks2012
GO
SELECT LEN('Length including Leading Blanks') AS "Length1",
LEN('Length excluding Leading Blanks ') AS "Length2";
Output
```

Length1	Lenth2
37	31

Table 8.23

Both strings have thirty seven characters. There are thirty-one alphanumeric characters and six blank spaces. The LEN() function in the first column counts all the characters including leading blank spaces, thus displaying thirty seven. The LEN() function in the second column counts only the alphanumeric characters ignoring the trailing spaces, thus displaying thirty one.

An Oracle example is:

SELECT
LENGTH('Length including Leading Blanks') AS "Length1",
LENGTH('Length excluding Leading Blanks ') AS "Lenth2"
FROM DUAL;
Output

Length1	Lenth2
41	41

Table 8.24

In Oracle, both columns count and display forty-one. This is because the LENGTH() function in Oracle includes trailing and leading blanks in calculations.

SUBSTR (x, y, substring_length) Oracle; (SUBSTRING (x, y, substring_length) for SQL server)

This function is equivalent in Oracle and SQL server. It returns a portion of string x, beginning at position y, for substring_length number of characters. Where x is a string and y and substring_length are numbers.

In Oracle, to determine the position, if position x is negative, then the string characters are counted from the end to the beginning (right to left). If the position is positive, then the string is counted from the beginning to end (left to right). Once the position is established, the substring_length is always counted left to right.

An SQL server example is:

USE AdventureWorks2012

GO

SELECT FirstName, SUBSTRING(FirstName,1,3) AS
    "Short_name",

SUBSTRING(FirstName,3,4) AS "Short_name2"

FROM Person.Person

WHERE BusinessEntityID =20;

Output

FirstName	Short_name	Short_name2
Wanida	Wan	nida

Table 8.25

The first column displays Wanida, which is the name of person 20. The second column displays Wan. This is because the SUBSTRING fuction started extracting at position 1 and extracts 3 characters (w, a, and n). The third column displays nida. Similarly, the function started extracting at position 3 (n) and extracts 4 characters (nida).

An Oracle example is:

```
SELECT First_Name, SUBSTR(First_Name,1,3) AS
    "Short_name",
SUBSTR(First_Name,-3,3) AS "Short_name2"
FROM employees
WHERE Employee_ID = 100;
Output
```

FIRST_NAME	Short_name	Short_name2
Steven	Ste	ven

Table 8.26

The first column displays Steven, which is the First_name to be substringed. The second column displays Ste. This is because the SUBSTR fuction started extracting at position 1 and extracts 3 characters (s, t, and e). The third column displays *ven*. This is because the function started extracting at position—3 (v: from the right) and extracts 3 characters (v, e, and n).

RPAD(x,y,z), LPAD(x,y,z), Oracle Only

These functions are used only with Oracle databases. The same result can be achived in SQL server by nesting several string functions. Data in databases is somtimes stored with leading or trailing spaces. This becomes problematic for report formating and ETL (Extraction, Transformation, and Load) applications. The RPAD(x,y,z) and LPAD(x,y,z) are used to fill these black spaces in x, to a length of y with a string z that you specify.

LPAD() fills leading blanks while RPAD() fills trailing spaces. For example:

```
SELECT
RPAD('My name is Victor ',25,'@') AS "Right_Padded",
LPAD('My name is Victor',25,'E') AS "Left_Padded"
FROM DUAL;
```
Outputs

Right_Padded	Left_Padded
My name is Victor	EEE My name is Victor

Table 8.27

The SELECT statement uses the dummy DUAL table to ensure correct SQL syntax. The first column uses the RPAD() function to replace the trailing spaces in the constant ('My name is Victor ') with @ while the second column uses the LPAD() function to replace the leading spaces in the constant string ('My name is Victor') with E.

Data Conversion Functions with Implicit and Explicit Data Conversion

It is sometimes necessary to combine different types of data to improve information retrieved from databases. For example, there could be a requirement to retrieve an employee's name and salary in the same column. This presents a problem because it is impossible to combine a string with a number. The salary will have to be converted into a string by a conversion function before they can be combined. Conversion functions are used to convert from one data type to another and are usually used with format models. They are scalar functions. Databases usually automatically convert data from one data type to another when possible. This is called implicit conversions. However, to be sure about outputs, different data types must be explicitly converted to the target data type. The format models are there to tell the database how to interpret and convert different data types. Some of the functions are identical in Oracle and SQL server. The syntax is usually as follows:

Conversion_Function(<Data>, '<format>'); or Conversion_
   Function(<Data> AS Data_Type[style]);
Format and style are declared using several variations of dd/
   mm/yyyy (day/year/month)
T-SQL Data Conversion Functions

The functions include:

CAST(x AS data type [(length)], CONVERT

The CAST function is used by SQL server to convert from one data type to another. This function converts x to a compatible data type specified by the data type operand. The length operand is optional. It returns the specified data type. The CAST function is equivalent in Oracle and SQL server.

The following example shows how the CAST function is used:

USE AdventureWorks2012
GO
SELECT SalesOrderID,'Total sales is' +' '+CAST(LineTotal AS
   NCHAR) AS "Total Sales",
ModifiedDate

FROM Sales.SalesOrderDetail

WHERE SalesOrderDetailID = 15

AND ModifiedDate = CAST('2005-07-01 00:00:00.000' AS

DATETIME);

Outputs

SalesOrderID	Total Sales	ModifiedDate
43661	Total sales is 809.760000	2005-07-01 00:00:00.000

Table 8.28

In this example, the LineTotal is a number data type so it cannot be appended to the string 'Total sales is' using the + operator. So the CAST function is used to convert it into a string(CAST(LineTotal AS NCHAR)) before the + operator can be used.

In the WHERE clause, the date literal string '2005-07-01 00:00:00.000' is converted to a date before it can be compared to the ModifiedDate field. Note that the date is in the expected yyyy/mm/dd (or mm/yyyy/dd) format and would have been implicitly converted. This is because the database language setting is us_english. However if the date string is changed to '01-07-2005 00:00:00.000' (i.e., (dd/mm/yyyy)) then no results will be returned because the database does not understand the (dd/mm/yyyy) date format. The CONVERT function will be needed to resolve this issue.

CONVERT (data_type [(length)], x [, style])

The CONVERT function is similar to the CAST function but has more advanced options. For example, the style option can be used. These styles tell the database how to interpret a string.

Styles are declared by their relative number. For example, to tell the database that a date string should be interpreted as mm/dd/yyyy (month/day/year), the number 101 is used. For dd/mm/yyyy (day/month/year), number 103 is used in the CONVERT function. Using the prevous example, the CONVERT function can be used to convert the '01-07-2005 00:00:00.000'(dd/mm/yyyy) date as follows:

```
USE AdventureWorks2012
GO
SELECT SalesOrderID,'Total sales is' +' '+CAST(LineTotal AS
    NCHAR) AS "Total Sales",
ModifiedDate
FROM Sales.SalesOrderDetail
WHERE SalesOrderDetailID = 15
AND ModifiedDate = CONVERT(DATETIME,'01-07-2005
    00:00:00.000',103)
Output
```

SalesOrderID	Total Sales	ModifiedDate
43661	Total sales is 809.760000	2005-07-01 00:00:00.000

Table 8.29

Oracle Data Conversion Functions

The following conversion functions are used only in Oracle. The output of some of these functions is dependent on the database territory settings.

TO_DATE(CHAR, fmt)

This function converts a string into a date. The optional fmt operand specifies how the string should be interpreted and converted into a date. They are defined using date masks such as (DD-MM-YY), which tells the database how to interpret the string (day-month-year). The models should be treated with care because using an inappropriate model will lead to incorrect results. For example, the following string '02/01/2012' can be interpreted and converted in two ways, depending on the format model:

('02/01/2012' 'DD-MM-YYYY') This string will be interpreted
     as (02-JANUARY-2012) while
('02/01/2012', 'MM-DD-YYYY') This string will be interpreted
     as (01-FEBRUARY-2012)

An example is of implicit date conversion is:

SELECT

first_name,last_name,hire_date

FROM Employees

WHERE hire_date = '01/13/2001';

Output

FIRST_NAME	LAST_NAME	HIRE_DATE
Lex	De Haan	01/13/2001

Table 8.30

The character string literal '01/13/2001' is implicitly converted into the date 01/13/2001. This automatic conversion is correct because the database territory and language setting is American thus dates are implicitly interpreted as MONTH-DAY-YEAR. If the settings had been United Kingdom dates will be implicitly interpreted as DAY-MONTH-YEAR, thus the query will fail because 13 is not a valid month. This date is then compared with the Hire_Date. As a result, employee Lex is displayed. If the string was in a wrong format, the format model must be used to get the correct results. For example, if the same date was represented by the string '13-01-2001', then an implicit conversion would be impossible, as shown below:

```
SELECT
first_name,last_name,hire_date
FROM Employees
WHERE hire_date = '13-01-2001';
Output
ORA-01843: not a valid month
```

The only way to get the same correct result will be to explicitly convert the string using the format model as follows:

```
SELECT
first_name,last_name,hire_date
FROM Employees
WHERE hire_date = TO_DATE('13-01-2001','DD-MM-YYYY');
Outputs
```

FIRST_NAME	LAST_NAME	HIRE_DATE
Lex	De Haan	01/13/2001

Table 8.31

The same result is achieved using the format model. The 'DD-MM-YYYY' tells the database to interpret the string as DAY-MONTH-YEAR and the correct date is obtained.

TO_CHAR(Date,fmt)

This function converts dates to strings and is generally used to display the full names of dates. Individual parts of dates can also be retrieved using this function and parts of the format model. For example:

SELECT

FIRST_NAME,HIRE_DATE,

TO_CHAR(HIRE_DATE,'DD-MONTH-YYYY')AS full_date,

TO_CHAR(HIRE_DATE,'DD')AS day,

TO_CHAR(HIRE_DATE,'DAY')AS day_name,

TO_CHAR(HIRE_DATE,'MONTH')AS HIRE_MONTH,

TO_CHAR(HIRE_DATE,'YYYY')AS "HIRE_YEAR"

FROM Employees

WHERE EMPLOYEE_ID = 100;

Outputs

FIRST _NAME	HIRE _DATE	FULL _DATE	DAY	DAY _NAME	HIRE _MONTH	HIRE _YEAR
Steven	06/17/2003	17-JUNE -2003	17	TUESDAY	JUNE	2003

Table 8.32

In this example, the Hire_date (06/17/2003) is converted into a full date (17-JUNE—2003) in the virtual column called full_date. The individual parts of the date are then extracted by using the appropriate parts of the format model.

TO_CHAR(NUMBER, fmt), TO_NUMBER(CHAR,fmt)

The TO_CHAR function converts a number into a string. The TO_NUMBER function converts a string into a number. The optional fmt operand specifies the required format.

For example:

```
SELECT
First_Name ||' is Paid '|| TO_CHAR(Salary,'L99G999D99MI')
    AS "Formatted Salary",
First_Name ||' is Paid '|| TO_CHAR(Salary)AS "Unformatted
    Salary",
TO_NUMBER('0110') + Salary AS "New Salary"
FROM Employees
WHERE employee_id =100;
Outputs
```

Formatted Salary	Unformatted Salary	New Salary
Steven is Paid $24,000.00	Steven is Paid 24000	24110

Table 8.33

In the first column, formatted salary, the First_Name Field is concatenated with the formatted salary. The salary, which is a number data type, is first converted into a string. The format model ('L99G999D99MI') is used to format the salary into dollars. The second column is similar to the first but the format model is omitted.

The final column converts the string literal value '0110' into the number 110 and then adds this number to the salary (24000), which results in 24110.

Miscellaneous and Null Related Functions

These are general comparison functions and functions that facilitate the handling of null values. They are scalar functions. It is sometimes necessary to substitute a value for null columns values. This can help for reporting and data quality purposes. Differences between Oracle and SQL server are shown next. They include:

SQL server Null functions: COALESCE (Column, 'Replacement_ Value'), ISNULL (Column, 'Replacement _Value')

The COALESCE and ISNULL functions are used to replace null values in tables with a replacement value. The replacement value could be a column value or a constant. For example, in the Person.Person table, some of the column values for suffix, firstname, and title are null. The following example demonstrates how null values can be replaced with these functions. The first query shows the columns with null values:

```
USE AdventureWorks2012
GO
Select Title, Suffix, FirstName, MiddleName, LastName
FROM Person.Person
WHERE BusinessEntityID <4;
Output
```

Title	Suffix	FirstName	MiddleName	LastName
NULL	NULL	Ken	J	Sánchez
NULL	NULL	Terri	Lee	Duffy
NULL	NULL	Roberto	NULL	Tamburello

Table 8.34

It shows NULLs for Title and MiddleName. Now the NULL functions will be used to substitute these NULLs with alternative values.

```
USE AdventureWorks2012
GO
SELECT isnull(title,'Sir')AS New_title,
    LastName,isnull(Suffix,Lastname)AS New_suffix,
    FirstName, COALESCE(MiddleName,FirstName)AS
    New_middlename
FROM Person.Person
WHERE BusinessEntityID <4
Output
```

New_title	LastName	New_suffix	FirstName	New_middlename
Sir	Sánchez	Sánchez	Ken	J
Sir	Duffy	Duffy	Terri	Lee
Sir	Tamburello	Tamburello	Roberto	Roberto

Table 8.35

The ISNULL function replaces all the null values with the constant value *sir* in the New_title column. In the New_suffix column the ISNULL function replaces all the null suffixes with the lastnames. In the New_middlename column, the COALESCE function replaces the null middlename of the third row with the first name Roberto. The COALESCE function is also available in Oracle.

Oracle Null functions: NVL (Column, 'Replacement _Value'), NVL2 (Column,'Replacement _Value1', 'Replacement _Value2')

The NVL function replaces the null column value with the 'Replacement _Value' in Oracle.

With the NVL2 function, when the column is not null, then the function substitutes it with Replacement _Value1. When the column is null, the function returns Replacement _Value2.

For example, if we SELECT the first two rows from the employees table as follows:

```
SELECT Employee_id,First_name,Commission_pct,Manager_
    id FROM employees
WHERE Employee_id < 102 ;
Output
```

EMPLOYEE_ID	FIRST_NAME	COMMISSION_PCT	MANAGER_ID
100	Steven	—	—
101	Neena	—	100

Table 8.36

The Commission_pct column is NULL for both employees. Furthermore, the Manager_id is null for employee 100 but is present for employee 101.

The NVL function is then used to substitute the Commission_pct nulls with 2 and the NVL2 function is used to replace null Manager_id value with 150 and the non NULL Manager_id value with 200 as follows:

SELECT   Employee_id,First_name,NVL(Commission_pct,2)As New_comis,NVL2(Manager_id,150,200) AS New_manager FROM employees

WHERE Employee_id < 102 ;

Output

EMPLOYEE_ ID	FIRST_ NAME	NEW_ COMIS	NEW_ MANAGER
100	Steven	2	200
101	Neena	2	150

Table 8.37

The output shows that the null Commission_pct has been replaced by 2 using NVL. The null manager_id for employee 100 has been replaced by 200 and the manager_ id of employee 101 has been switched from 100 to 150. The NVL function is not available in SQL server 2012.

General comparison functions include:

GREATEST(),LEAST()

These are Oracle functions used to retrieve the greatest or smallest value from a list of values. They always return the data type of the input list. These functions are not available in SQL server. For example:

SELECT LEAST(5,-1,80)AS Lowest,GREATEST(5,-1,80) AS

Highest FROM DUAL ;

LOWEST	HIGHEST
-1	80

Table 8.38

The LEAST function is used to retrieve the lowest value, which is—1, while the greatest function is used to retrieve the highest number in the same list, which is 80.

Date and Time Functions

Date and time functions are least standardized functions between databases. These functions operate on date and time data types. Date functions usually return date string literals or numbers. These functions calculate the respective date or time portion of an expression or returns the number value between time intervals. When data is stored as a date data type, these functions can be used directly. When the date is stored as a number or string in the database, data conversion functions and format models should be used before the date time functions can be applied.

The date time functions for Oracle and SQL server are implemented differently but they generally return the same result.

Oracle date functions:

SYSDATE()

This function returns the current date of the database server. For example:

```
SELECT SYSDATE AS Today FROM DUAL;
```
Outputs:

TODAY
07/12/2012

Table 8.39

The current date is displayed.

```
ADD_MONTHS (date,Number_of _months),
    MONTHS_BETWEEN(date1,date2)
```

The ADD_MONTHS function is used to determine the resultant date when months are added to the specified date. The MONTHS_ BETWEEN() function returns the number of months between date1 and date2.

This example shows the date when employee 200 celebrated her two-year anniversary in her new job. The second column shows the number of months the employee has been with the company.

```
SELECT first_name, hire_date,ADD_MONTHS(hire_date,24)
    AS Two_Years,
CEIL(MONTHS_BETWEEN(sysdate,hire_date)) AS
    Number_Of_Months
FROM employees
WHERE employee_id = 200;
```

Output

FIRST_NAME	HIRE_DATE	TWO_YEARS	NUMBER_OF_ MONTHS
Jennifer	09/17/2003	09/17/2005	105

Table 8.40

In the third column, the ADD_MONTHS function is used to add 24 months to the hire date (09/17/2003), resulting in 09/17/2005. The fourth column uses the ADD_MONTHS function to calculate the number of months between the hire_date and today's date (06/03/2012 and 09/17/2003), which returns 105. The CEIL function is simply used to round the number of months value to the highest integer number.

LAST_DAY(date)

The LAST_DATE() function returns the last date of the month specified in the date operand.

For example, this function returns the last day of the current month:

SELECT SYSDATE AS Today, LAST_DAY(SYSDATE) AS
    Last_date_of_month FROM DUAL;

Output

TODAY	LAST_DATE_OF_MONTH
06/03/2012	06/30/2012

Table 8.41

This function returns 06/30/2012, the last date of June 2012.

SQL server date time functions:

SQL Server Date functions: GETDATE(), SYSDATETIME()

These functions derive the current database date and time. The SYSDATETIME()function returns a more precise time component. For example:

USE AdventureWorks2012
GO
SELECT SYSDATETIME()AS "NOW", GETDATE()AS "TODAY";
Output:

NOW	TODAY
2012-06-03 14:04:14.3389047	2012-06-03 14:04:14.350

Table 8.42

The current date and time of the database server is displayed.

DATEPART (datepart, date)

The DATEPART function returns an integer that represents the specified datepart of a specified date. It is equivalent to the EXTRACT function in Oracle. The datepart specifies the year, month, or day of a date. For example:

USE AdventureWorks2012
GO
SELECT GETDATE()AS Today, DATEPART(YEAR,GETDATE())
    AS This_year,

DATEPART(MONTH,GETDATE())AS This_month,

DATEPART(DAY,GETDATE()) AS This_day ;

Output

Today	This_year	This_month	This_day
2012-06-03 14:10:34.700	2012	6	3

Table 8.43

The function returns the year month and day of the current date.

DATENAME (datepart, date)

The DATENAME function returns a character string that represents the specified datepart of a specified date. The input operand is always a date and the datepart may include (DAY, MONTH, YEAR, QUARTER, WEEKDAY, SECOND, etc). For example:

USE AdventureWorks2012

GO

SELECT GETDATE()AS Today,

DATENAME(MONTH,GETDATE())AS Month_name,

DATENAME(WEEKDAY,GETDATE()) AS Day_name ;

Output

Today	Month_name	Day_name
2012-06-03 14:16:49.293	June	Sunday

Table 8.44

The names of today's month and year are returned.

*DATEDIFF (*datepart, startdate, enddate *)*

The DATEDIFF function returns an integer value for the difference between the startdate and enddate for a particular datepart. It is similar to the Oracle MONTHS_BETWEEN() function but has more flexibility because while Oracle can only handle the MONTH datepart, this function can handle DAY, MONTH, YEAR, QUARTER, WEEKDAY, SECOND, etc.

The next example demonstrates how this function is used to calculate the number of years, months, and days between an order Modifieddate and the current system date.

```
USE AdventureWorks2012
GO
SELECT GETDATE()AS Today, ModifiedDate,DATEDIFF(YEAR,
    ModifiedDate,GETDATE())AS "year_difference",
DATEDIFF(MONTH,ModifiedDate,GETDATE())AS
    "month_difference",
DATEDIFF(DAY,ModifiedDate,GETDATE()) AS "day_difference"
FROM Sales.SalesOrderDetail
Where SalesOrderID = 43660
Output
```

Today	ModifiedDate	year _difference	month _difference	day _difference
2012-06-03 15:41:36.470	2005-07-01 00:00:00.000	7	83	2529

Table 8.45

The year_difference column displays 7, which is the number of years between modifieddate and the current system date (2012-06-03 and 2005-07-01 00:00:00.000). The month_difference column displays 83, which is the number of months between modifieddate and the current system date. The day_difference column displays 2529, which is the number of days between modifieddate and the current system date

DATEADD (Datepart, Number, Date)

This function returns a specified date that is calculated by adding an interval number to a datepart. It is similar to the Oracle ADD_ MONTHS function but has more flexibility because while Oracle can only handle the MONTH datepart, this function can handle DAY, MONTH, YEAR, QUARTER, WEEKDAY, SECOND, etc.

The following example demonstrates how 2 is added to the DAY, MONTH and YEAR dateparts:

```
USE AdventureWorks2012
GO
SELECT GETDATE()AS Today,DATEADD(YEAR,2,GETDATE())
    AS two_years_time,
DATEADD(MONTH,2,GETDATE())AS two_months_time,
DATEADD(DAY,2,GETDATE()) AS Two_days_time
Output
```

Today	two_years_time	two_months_time	Two_days_time
2012-06-03 15:51:01.963	2014-06-03 15:51:01.963	2012-08-03 15:51:01.963	2012-06-05 15:51:01.963

Table 8.46

The Today column shows the current system date (2012-06-03 15:51:01.963). The other columns display the dates of each datepart plus 2.

Analytic Functions

Like aggregate functions, analytic functions compute sets of rows. But unlike aggregate functions, they return different results for each group. In fact, analytic functions can behave like aggregate functions if the optional partitioning clause is omitted. For example, the RANK () can behave like an aggregate function by ranking all employees based on their salaries. This same function can behave like an analytic function by ranking employees of each department based on their salaries. Thus, in the analytic application of the function, each department will have its own independent ranking. The Oracle and SQL server implementations of RANK () are exactly the same.

The RANK () as an analytic function: The general syntax of this function is

RANK ( ) OVER ([partition BY col1] ORDER BY col2 DESC/ASC)

The function classifies rows based on the values in the column specified in the ORDER BY clause—for example, salary. The ASC or DESC options determine the rank number. DESC implies that the highest value will be ranked as number 1. The function uses the PARTITION BY clause to generate different groups on which the function will be applied. For example, if the PARTITION BY department_id is used, each department value will become a group. RANK() always returns an integer. The rank of a row will be one plus the rank of the previous row. If two rows have the same value, they will be ranked equally and the next rank will be two plus the previous rank.

Oracle RANK() example:

```
SELECT employee_id, first_name, department_id, salary,
    RANK () OVER (PARTITION BY department_id ORDER BY
    salary DESC) AS Dept_ranks
FROM employees WHERE employee_id < 110
Output
```

EMPLOYEE _ID	FIRST _NAME	DEPARTMENT _ID	SALARY	DEPT _RANKS
103	Alexander	60	9000	1
104	Bruce	60	6000	2
105	David	60	4800	3
106	Valli	60	4800	3
107	Diana	60	4200	5
100	Steven	90	24000	1
102	Lex	90	17000	2
101	Neena	90	17000	2
108	Nancy	100	12008	1
109	Daniel	100	9000	2

Table 8.47

The employees returned of each department have been ranked based on their salary. Notice that each department is ranked individually. For example, employee 103 is ranked number 1 in department 60 because he has the highest salary in that department (9000), while employee 100 is ranked number 1 in department 90 because he has the highest salary in that department (24000). This individual ranking of departments is only possible because of the PARTITION BY department_id clause. Also notice that in cases where the employee salaries in a department are equal, both rows will have the same rank and the next rank is 2 plus the previous rank number. For example, in department 60, employee 105 and 106 have the same salary (4800) and are both ranked 3, and the next rank for employee 107 is 5. The DENSE_RANK() function can be used to override this behaviour and eliminate gaps in the ranks.

RANK () as an aggregate function:

If the PARTITION BY department_id clause is removed, the RANK function will act like an aggregate function. The RANK () will rank all the returned rows as a single group. Department differences will be ignored. For example:

SELECT employee_id, first_name, department_id, salary,
    RANK () OVER (ORDER BY salary DESC) AS Dept_ranks
    FROM employees WHERE employee_id < 110
Output

EMPLOYEE _ID	FIRST _NAME	DEPARTMENT _ID	SALARY	DEPT _RANKS
100	Steven	90	24000	1
101	Neena	90	17000	2
102	Lex	90	17000	2
108	Nancy	100	12008	4
103	Alexander	60	9000	5
109	Daniel	100	9000	5

104	Bruce	60	6000	7
105	David	60	4800	8
106	Valli	60	4800	8
107	Diana	60	4200	10

Table 8.48

The output shows all employees ranked as a group. The ranking of employees within individual departments is ignored.

System Functions

System functions provide extensive information about database objects and the database environment (metadata). Metadata is the data stored in system tables about database objects such as table names, user accounts, language settings, and so forth. They are very useful informational tools and are generally used to debug and tune database environment variables.

System functions in Oracle include:

SELECT SYS_CONTEXT

The SELECT SYS_CONTEXT function is used to return several parameters. It can be useful during debugging—for example, if dates are not being returned in the expected format, this function can be used to check the language and territory settings. Examples are:

SELECT SYS_CONTEXT ('USERENV', 'NLS_TERRITORY') AS
    Territory

FROM DUAL;

Output

TERRITORY
AMERICA

Table 8.49

The territory setting is returned as America.

The next function returns the database name

SELECT SYS_CONTEXT ('USERENV', 'DB_NAME')
FROM DUAL;

CURRENT_DB
XE

Table 8.50

The database name is returned as XE.

System functions in SQL server include:

SQL server has similar functions that return information about the server environment. They include HOST_ID (), DB_NAME(), HOST_NAME()and @@LANGUAGE.

The following query returns the values or all the mentioned functions:

USE AdventureWorks2012

GO

SELECT HOST_ID () AS Host_number,DB_NAME() AS

   Database_name,HOST_NAME ()Server_name,

@@LANGUAGE AS Language_setting;

Output

Host_number	Database_name	Server_name	Language_ setting
6084	AdventureWorks2012	USER-PC	us_english

Table 8.51

The functions return the stated session parameter values. To return all the language settings the sp_helplanguage function is used as follows:

sp_helplanguage us_english;

Output

langid	date format	date first	upgrade	name	aalias	months	short months	days	lcid	msglangid
0	mdy	7	0	us_english	EEnglish	January,February,March,April,May,June,July,August,September,October,November,December	Jan,Feb,Mar,Apr,May,Jun,Jul,Aug,Sep,Oct,Nov,Dec	Monday,Tuesday,Wednesday,Thursday,Friday,Saturday,Sunday	1033	1033

Table 8.52

Virtual Columns Used as Concrete Relational Objects (VIEWS, WITH, and CTEs)

It is sometimes necessary to use virtual columns like real columns. For example, there could be a requirement to return only the highest paid employees for each department. This request cannot be resolved by referencing the virtual column in the WHERE clause. It can be achieved either by adding a column to the table and inserting the calculated values or by using other relational objects such as views or common table expressions (CTE, SQL server only) to concretise the virtual column. Views and CTEs are covered in chapters twelve.

USING Views to References Virtual Columns

Views and subqueries can be used to concretise a virtual column so it can be used in the WHERE clause of a query. The following example shows how a view is used to return only the fourth highest paid employee in the Oracle employees table. Note that this example also applies to T-SQL. A view is first created, which includes the ranking virtual field called Dept_ranks.

```
DROP VIEW rank_salaries;
CREATE VIEW vw_rank_salaries AS
SELECT employee_id, first_name, department_id, salary,
    RANK () OVER ( ORDER BY salary DESC) AS Dept_ranks
FROM employees WHERE employee_id < 110;
```

Once the view is created a query can now be applied on the view that uses the Dept_ranks in the WHERE clause to return the employees of any rank. The following query returns the 4th ranked employee.

```
SELECT * FROM vw_rank_salaries
WHERE Dept_ranks = 4;
Output
```

EMPLOYEE _ID	FIRST _NAME	DEPARTMENT _ID	SALARY	DEPT _RANKS
108	Nancy	100	12008	4

Table 8.53

Using T-SQL CTEs to Reference Virtual Columns

The view example is also applicable to SQL server, but under certain circumstances it is better to use a CTE. CTEs are temporary views. They achieve the same result but are not permanent and cannot be referenced by queries outside the context of its creation. The following CTE can be used to return the highest paid employee from the SQL server AdventureWorks2012 database:

```
USE AdventureWorks2012
GO
WITH top_emp_sal_cte
AS
(SELECT DISTINCT(e.BusinessEntityID),e.JobTitle,h.Rate,d.
    DepartmentID,
DENSE_RANK() OVER ( ORDER BY h.Rate DESC)AS top_salaries
FROM HumanResources.Employee e,HumanResources.
    EmployeePayHistory h,HumanResources.
    EmployeeDepartmentHistory d
WHERE e.BusinessEntityID = d.BusinessEntityID
AND e.BusinessEntityID = h.BusinessEntityID)
SELECT * FROM top_emp_sal_cte
WHERE top_salaries = 1
ORDER BY DepartmentID DESC;
GO
```

Output

Business EntityID	JobTitle	Rate	DepartmentID	top_salaries
1	Chief Executive Officer	185.50	16	1

Table 8.54

The CTE creates a virtual column called top_salaries. This virtual column is used in the WHERE clause of a query within the CTE to retrieve only the highest paid employee. Note that queries that use CTE columns must be within the CTE.

Oracle CTEs Using Subqueries

The T-SQL CTE can be replicated in Oracle with subqueries defined in the FROM clause of the outer query (Inline View.) This statement is similar to T-SQL CTEs because the statement is temporary and cannot be referenced by other queries. For example, views were previously used to determine the fourth-highest paid employee in the Oracle employees table, and a subquery is now used to replicate the same results as follows:

```
SELECT *
FROM (SELECT employee_id, first_name, department_id,
    salary, RANK () OVER ( ORDER BY salary DESC) AS
    Dept_ranks
FROM employees WHERE employee_id < 110)Rank_numbers
WHERE Dept_ranks = 4;
Output
```

EMPLOYEE _ID	FIRST _NAME	DEPARTMENT _ID	SALARY	DEPT _RANKS
108	Nancy	100	12008	4

Table 8.55

The query uses a subquery in the FROM clause. The same results are obtained as when the view was used.

Conclusion

This chapter covered the use of functions and operators. Using them correctly profoundly extends the usefulness of SQL. The use of more advanced constructs such as SQL server CTEs and oracle WITH clause were also introduced. These advanced constructs are covered in chapter twelve.

Chapter Nine

Overview

This chapter covers the aggregation of data using some of the covered aggregate functions. Aggregated data generally forms the basis of advanced analytics.

Grouping Data

In the reporting world, facts such as revenue and cost are business measurements, while dimensions such as product and department are narrative business descriptions. It is sometimes necessary to return aggregated facts for management reporting. These fact measurements can be aggregated independently or based on descriptive dimensions. Aggregate functions are used to group a set of rows and return a single result. When an aggregate function is introduced in the select list, every other column in the list must also be aggregated or declared in the GROUP by clause. The functions are equivalent in Oracle and SQL server.

Independent Fact Aggregation

Independent fact aggregation simply aggregates a set of rows and returns a single value. For example, management may want to know the total number of products sold and the total revenue generated within a table for auditing purposes. This requirement can be satisfied with the following statement:

```
USE AdventureWorks2012;
GO
SELECT SUM(OrderQty) AS "Number Of Products",
SUM(LineTotal)AS "Revenue Of Product"
FROM Sales.SalesOrderDetail;
Output
```

Number Of Products	Revenue Of Product
274914	109846381.399888

Table 9.1

The query results in 274914 and 109846381.399888. These are aggregate totals of all rows returned by the query from the Sales.SalesOrderDetail table. It is obvious that these are pretty meaningless values because the numbers do not describe anything. Dimensions such as dates and orders will give more meaning to these numbers.

Fact Aggregation Based on Dimensions Using the GROUP BY Clause

In business intelligence reporting, these numerical values become more useful when they are described by dimensions such as the SalesOrderID. For example during profitability analysis it will be more useful to display these same totals for each SalesOrderID. To display the total OrderQty and LineTotal for each SalesOrderID, the GROUP BY clause must be used. To do this the following statement is used:

```
USE AdventureWorks2012;
GO
SELECT SalesOrderID,
```

SUM(OrderQty) AS "Number Of Products",

SUM(LineTotal)AS "Revenue Of Product"

FROM Sales.SalesOrderDetail

GROUP BY SalesOrderID;

Output (subset of rows)

SalesOrderID	Number Of Products	Revenue Of Product
43659	26	20565.620600
43660	2	1294.252900
43661	38	32726.478600
43662	54	28832.528900

Table 9.2

The result shows the OrderQty and LineTotal rolled into groups. Now a row is returned for each group (SalesOrderID). For example, SalesOrderID 43659 has a total OrderQty of 26 and Revenue Of Product of 20565.620600, while SalesOrderID of 43660 had a total OrderQty of 2 and Revenue Of Product of 1294.252900. These numbers represent a set of rows summed up for each group (SalesOrderID). For example, the set of rows that make up SalesOrderID 43660 can be shown as follows:

SELECT SalesOrderID,OrderQty, LineTotal

FROM Sales.SalesOrderDetail

WHERE SalesOrderID = 43660;

Output

SalesOrderID	OrderQty	LineTotal
43660	1	419.458900
43660	1	874.794000

Table 9.3

Output shows these rows, which are summed up for SalesOrderID 43660.

Understanding the Changing Input Calculation Context of Multiple Groups

Grouped calculation results are based on the input group values. These values are the input calculation context. For example, when the total revenue is summed based on a single group salesorderID number 43666, a single row is returned as follows:

```
SELECT SalesOrderID,SUM(LineTotal) AS total_revenue
FROM Sales.SalesOrderDetail
WHERE SalesOrderID = 43666
GROUP BY SalesOrderID;
Output
```

SalesOrderID	total_revenue
43666	5056.489600

Table 9.4

The single row is returned because the calculation is rolled up based on a single input value(43666) in the GROUP BY clause. If a second column is added to the GROUP BY clause, the calculation input contex is changed to include the new values from the new column. This will lead to the total value being divided to reflect the new calculation context. For example, if orderqty is added to the GROUP BY clause, the total_revenue will be split into two rows calculating the total_revenue of each quantity as follows:

```
SELECT SalesOrderID,OrderQty, SUM(LineTotal) AS
    total_revenue
FROM Sales.SalesOrderDetail
WHERE SalesOrderID = 43666
GROUP BY SalesOrderID, OrderQty;
Output
```

SalesOrderID	OrderQty	total_revenue
43666	1	4217.571800
43666	2	838.917800

Table 9.5

The total revenue is still the same but it has been split across two rows. This issue is important to consider when adding columns to the GROUP BY clause. As a rule, when an aggregate function is being used with the GROUP BY clause, all the columns in the SELECT list must be operands in an aggregate function or must be included in the GROUP BY clause. For example, if the CarrierTrackingNumber is included in the SELECT statement and is ommited from the GROUP BY clause, the query fails as follows:

```
USE AdventureWorks2012;
GO
SELECT SalesOrderID,CarrierTrackingNumber,
SUM(OrderQty) AS "Number Of Products",
SUM(LineTotal)AS "Revenue Of Product"
FROM Sales.SalesOrderDetail
GROUP BY SalesOrderID;
Output
Msg 8120, Level 16, State 1, Line 1
```

Column 'Sales.SalesOrderDetail.CarrierTrackingNumber' is invalid in the select list because it is not contained in either an aggregate function or the GROUP BY clause.

To correct this error, the CarrierTrackingNumber must be included in the GROUP BY clause as follows:

```
USE AdventureWorks2012;
GO
SELECT SalesOrderID,CarrierTrackingNumber,
SUM(OrderQty) AS "Number Of Products",
SUM(LineTotal)AS "Revenue Of Product"
FROM Sales.SalesOrderDetail
GROUP BY SalesOrderID,CarrierTrackingNumber;
Output(subset of rows)
```

74437	NULL	3	15.230000
47685	CC2F-4D47-8C	167	51197.988100
44962	NULL	1	3578.270000
73886	NULL	2	14.980000

Table 9.5

The query succeeds, displaying the required fields.

Filtering Groups with the HAVING Clause

It is sometimes necessary to filter the results of groups. This helps to limit the output results of a grouping SELECT statement. The keyword to use when filtering groups is HAVING.

An example is to identify the top orders in the Sales. SalesOrderDetailtable. The following STATEMENT is used to display only the orders where the total SUM of OrderQty is greater than 480.

```
GO
USE AdventureWorks2012;
GO
SELECT SalesOrderID,
MAX(OrderQty)AS "Maximum order",
MIN(OrderQty)AS "Minimum order",
sum(OrderQty)AS "Total order quantity"
FROM Sales.SalesOrderDetail
GROUP BY SalesOrderID
HAVING sum(OrderQty) > 450
ORDER BY SalesOrderID;
Output
```

SalesOrderID	Maximum order	Minimum order	Total order quantity
47355	28	1	475
47400	32	1	499
51131	25	1	483
51160	20	1	484
51721	24	1	484
51739	23	1	476
53465	21	1	460

Table 9.6

The result has been restricted to seven groups of salesOrderID HAVING the total number of OrderQty greater than 450.

Filtering Groups with the HAVING and WHERE Clause

It is sometimes necessary to filter some rows before the data is grouped. For example, if we wanted to see the highest number of orders where each transaction grossed more than 110 revenue, a WHERE clause will have to be used. The WHERE clause is added before the HAVING clause. The WHERE cluase will filter out all the rows where LineTotal is less than 110. After these rows have been filtered, the GROUP BY clause groups the results. Then the HAVING clause filters out the groups that have OrderQty of less than 450.

The statement for this is:

```
GO
USE AdventureWorks2012;
SELECT SalesOrderID,
MAX(OrderQty)AS "Maximum order",
MIN(OrderQty)AS "Minimum order",
sum(OrderQty)AS "Total order quantity"
FROM Sales.SalesOrderDetail
WHERE LineTotal > 110
GROUP BY SalesOrderID
HAVING sum(OrderQty) > 450;
Output
```

SalesOrderID	Maximum order	Minimum order	Total order quantity
47355	28	1	458

Table 9.7

The previous statement is used. The only addition to it is WHERE LineTotal > 110

The result displays only one SalesOrderID, which is 47355. The other 6 groups have been droped. This is because when rows where WHERE LineTotal is less than 110 are droped then the sum of their OrderQtys becomes less than 450.

Notice that the OrderQty of SalesOrderID 47355 is 458. This number is 17 less than 475 in the previous query. The folowing query shows the details of SalesOrderID 47355 where the lineTotal is less than 110, demonstrating why this number is less.

```
USE AdventureWorks;
SELECT SalesOrderID, OrderQty, LineTotal
FROM Sales.SalesOrderDetail
WHERE SalesOrderID = 47355 AND LineTotal < 110;
Output
```

SalesOrderID	OrderQty	LineTotal
47355	7	98.902300
47355	10	51.865000

Table 9.8

Notice that OrderQty 7 and 10 with LineTotals of 98.902300 and 51.865000 respectively are displayed. The line totals are less than 110, thus these two rows are eliminated from the previous grouping query. 10 + 7 = 17, resulting in the difference in the OrderQty between the two queries(The query which includes a WHERE clause and the query without it).

The WHERE clause is similar to the HAVING clause in that they are both used as filters in SELECT statements and both use the same operators. The difference is that the WHERE clause is used to filter individual rows while the HAVING clause is used to filter groups. The WHERE clause must be used before the GROUP BY clause.

Sumarizing Data at Different Aggregation Levels Using Oracle ROLLUP()

The ROLLUP() operator can be used to summarise hierachical data to different aggregation levels. For example, the total salary expenditure of a multinational company can be aggregated according to a geographical hierarchy such as regions and countries. The ROLLUP operator is used in the GROUP BY clause to generate subtotals for each country and region and finally a grand total of all rows. The oracle statement for this is as follows:

```
SELECT region_name,country_name, sum(salary) "AS Total
    Salary Cost"
FROM locations l,employees e,countries c,departments d,regions r
WHERE l.country_id = c.country_id
AND e.department_id = d.department_id
AND d.location_id = l.location_id
AND r.region_id = c.region_id
GROUP BY ROLLUP (region_name,country_name);
Output
```

REGION_NAME	COUNTRY_NAME	AS Total Salary Cost
Europe	Germany	10000
Europe	United Kingdom	311000
Europe	-	321000
Americas	Canada	19000
Americas	United States of America	344416
Americas	-	363416
-	-	684416

Table 9.9

The output shows salary subtotals for each country and region. For example, the subtotal for Germany is 10000 and the subtotal for Europe is 321000. The grand total for all regions is 684416. Note that this grand total only includes the sum of each region subtotal (Europe 321000 + Americas 363416).

Sumarizing Data at Different Aggregation Using T-SQL ROLLUP()

The T-SQL syntax for calculating aggregates at different levels is slightly different from Oracle. The ROLLUP operator is stated after the column list of the GROUP BY clause using a WITH clause. The following T-SQL example also calculates salary subtotals along a territory and state geographical hierarchy. The final row returns the grand total.

```
USE AdventureWorks2012;
GO
SELECT t.Name AS Territory_name,s.Name AS Province_
    Name, SUM(p.Rate) AS"AS Total Salary Cost"
```

FROM HumanResources.Employee h,HumanResources.

EmployeePayHistory p,Person.Address a,

Person.Person n,Person.BusinessEntityAddress e, Person.

StateProvince s,Sales.SalesTerritory t

WHERE h.BusinessEntityID = p.BusinessEntityID

AND a.AddressID = e.AddressID

AND e.BusinessEntityID = h.BusinessEntityID

AND n.BusinessEntityID = h.BusinessEntityID

AND s.StateProvinceID = a.StateProvinceID

AND t.TerritoryID =s.TerritoryID

GROUP BY t.Name,s.Name WITH ROLLUP;

Output (Subset of rows)

Territory_name	Province_Name	AS Total Salary Cost
Australia	Victoria	23.0769
Australia	NULL	23.0769
Canada	Alberta	23.0769
Canada	Ontario	23.0769
Canada	NULL	46.1538
Central	Michigan	23.0769
Central	Minnesota	85.2631
Central	NULL	108.34

Table 9.11

The output shows salary subtotals for each province and territory. For example, the subtotal for Michigan is 23.0769 while the subtotal for its parent state, Central, is 108.34. The final row shown below returns the grand total of 5611.7821 for all salaries.

Teritory_name	Province_Name	AS Total Salary Cost
NULL	NULL	5611.7821

Table 9.11

Conclusion

The concepts of grouping and filtering groups were covered. The tricky concept of filtering rows and filtering groups using the WHERE and HAVING clause is important in business environments and should be mastered.

Chapter Ten

Overview

This chapter covers how to handle the removal of rows from tables. Since data is an important corporate asset, this chapter includes precautions to follow when the DELETE statement is executed.

DELETING Data

The DELETE statement is used to delete table data in a database. The DELETE statement differs from all other DML statements (e.g., SELECT, INSERT, UPDATE) in that it always affects all the columns in a row. Other DML statements can be executed to affect all columns or only a few columns in a row. DELETE cannot be used to delete relational objects such as tables and views. (To delete relational objects the DROP statement is used.) DELETE can be used to delete specific rows that meet a stated condition, or to delete all rows in the table. DELETEs are also subjected to database constraints. DELETEs will always fail when they violate a constraint.

Since the default mode of most databases is to auto COMMIT, DELETE operations cannot be ROLLEDBACK. This means if all the records of a table are deleted, they are lost forever if backups are unavailable. A safe way to handle DELETEs is to switch off the database auto COMMIT mode and test the DELETE statements before committing the changes. When this happens you will have to explicitly tell the DBMS when to COMMIT changes to the database.

In this mode, DELETE statements can also be ROLLED back to restore the deleted rows.

Another method is to use a SELECT statement to review the rows that are going to be discarded by the DELETE. Always create duplicate tables for testing DELETE statements. By default, the query editor will return information about the number of rows affected by the DELETE statements. The following examples are based on the duplicate tables created in chapter seven.

DELETING All Rows

The simple DELETE statement syntax that deletes all table rows is as follows (Oracle and T-SQL use the same syntax):

```
DELETE FROM table_name;
```

The following code DELETES all the rows in the Oracle HR employees1 tables:

```
DELETE FROM employee1;
```

The editor returns the message "107 row(s) deleted". The table can now be repopulated thus:

```
INSERT INTO employee1 SELECT * FROM employees;
The editor returns the message "107 row(s) inserted."
DELETING Rows based on a condition.
```

In most instances, only a particular set of rows that satisfy a condition will need to be deleted. This limiting of qualifying rows can be achieved using a WHERE clause.

In the next example, all employees whose job_id is equal to 'AD_VP' are to be deleted. A SELECT query is first used to return and review all the rows that are going to be deleted. Then a DELETE statement is used to delete the qualifying rows. To retrieve all rows of employees whose job_id is equal to 'AD_VP', the following code is used:

```
SELECT * FROM employee1
WHERE
JOB_ID= 'AD_VP';
```

Output (only a subset of columns are shown)

EMPLOYEE _ID	FIRST _NAME	LAST _NAME	E-MAIL	PHONE _NUMBER
101	Neena	Kochhar	NKOCHHAR	515.123.4568
102	Lex	De Haan	LDEHAAN	515.123.4569

Table 10.1

The two qualifying employee rows are returned. To DELETE all the employees whose job_id is equal to 'AD_VP', the following code is used:

```
DELETE FROM employee1
WHERE
JOB_ID= 'AD_VP';
```

The 2 employee records have been deleted from the employee1 table and the editor returns the message: 2 row(s) deleted.

This can be verified by running the previous SELECT query:

```
SELECT * FROM employee1
WHERE
JOB_ID= 'AD_VP';
```

This query returns no data because all the employees whose job_id is equal to 'AD_VP' have been deleted. All the other employee rows are still in the employees1 table.

Oracle DELETE and Auto COMMIT

When a DELETE, UPDATE, or INSERT statement is issued, the final result of this statement depends on the database operation mode. If the database is using the default auto COMMIT mode, an implicit COMMIT is executed and the changes are written to the database. If the auto COMMIT mode is off, an explicit COMMIT is required to save these changes. Switching off the auto COMMIT helps you test your DELETE and UPDATE statements before saving the changes to the database with an explicit COMMIT statement.

Explicitly Committing Oracle DELETE Statements

With Oracle, if you are working with the DBMS SQL editor you can manually switch off the auto COMMIT mode by checking the auto COMMIT option box at the top left corner of the editor. If you are using SQL*Plus or any other client tool, the auto commit option can be switched off by issuing the following command:

SET AUTOCOMMIT OFF.

For example, in our previous example, if we switch off auto commit we can always ROLLBACK the DELETE statement if we are not happy with the results. The employees1 table is deleted and recreated so that the qualifying rows are present.

```
DROP TABLE employee1;
CREATE TABLE employee1 AS SELECT * FROM employees;
The table has been recreated.
DELETE FROM employee1
WHERE
JOB_ID= 'AD_VP';
Output
2 row(s) deleted.
```

The DELETE statement temporarily deletes the two rows where the JOB_ID= 'AD_VP' in the empolyee1 table. These rows have not been permanently deleted because a COMMIT has yet to be issued. If we now SELECT all rows where the employee JOB_ID= 'AD_VP', no rows are returned.

```
SELECT * FROM employee1
WHERE
JOB_ID= 'AD_VP'
Output
No data found
```

No rows returned because the rows have been temporarily deleted. If a ROLLBACK statement is now issued, all the temporarily deleted rows will be permanently restored to the table. For example the ROLLBACK command is issued as follows:

ROLLBACK;

The ROLLBACK command restores all the temporarily deleted rows to the employee1 table. Note that issuing a COMMIT at this stage would permanently delete these rows. If we now SELECT all rows where the employee JOB_ID= 'AD_VP', all the two restored rows are displayed.

```
SELECT * FROM employee1
WHERE
JOB_ID= 'AD_VP'
```
Output (only a subset of columns are shown)

EMPLOYEE _ID	FIRST _NAME	LAST _NAME	E-MAIL	PHONE _NUMBER
101	Neena	Kochhar	NKOCHHAR	515.123.4568
102	Lex	De Haan	LDEHAAN	515.123.4569

Table 10.2

The deleted rows have been restored to the table.

SQL Server DELETE and Auto COMMIT

The examples in this section are based a copy of the departments table. A copy is used because there are fewer blocking constraints on the table. The copy of the table is created as follows:

```
USE AdventureWorks2012;
GO
SELECT * INTO HumanResources.Department2
FROM HumanResources.Department;
```

With SQL server the auto COMMIT mode can be switched off by issuing the following command:

```
SET IMPLICIT_TRANSACTIONS OFF;
```

Once this command is executed subsequent DELETE, INSERT and UPDATE statements will require an explicit ROLLBACK or COMMIT to make any changes permanent. Note that these commands must be enclosed between a BEGIN TRANSACTION and a ROLLBACK or COMMIT. Transactions are treated in more detail in sections two of this book. In the next example, the sales department row from the Departments2 table is DELETED and ROLLBACK:

```
USE AdventureWorks2012;
GO
SET IMPLICIT_TRANSACTIONS OFF;
GO
```

—This switches off the auto commit database mode.

The row(s) to be deleted can be reviewed with the following statement:

```
SELECT * FROM HumanResources.Department2
WHERE
Name = 'Sales';
```

The query returns a single record as follows:

DepartmentID	Name	GroupName	ModifiedDate
3	Sales	Sales and Marketing	2002-06-01 00:00:00.000

Table 10.3

The record is now temporarily deleted with the folowing DELETE statement:

```
BEGIN TRANSACTION
DELETE FROM HumanResources.Department2
WHERE
Name = 'Sales';
GO
```

Once the Sales row is temporarily deleted, the following SELECT statement verifies that the row has indeed been temporarily deleted from the table:

```
SELECT * FROM HumanResources.Department2
WHERE
Name = 'Sales';
```

The output returns no data

DepartmentID	Name	GroupName	ModifiedDate

Table 10.4

The delete is then rolled back with the following statement:

ROLLBA5CK TRANSACTION;

The BEGIN TRANSACTION command is terminated with a ROLLBACK TRANSACTION command that restores the deleted sales row to the Department2 table. Issuing a COMMIT TRANSACTION at this point would have permenatly deleted the row.

The sales row has been restored to the table and can be seen by executing the following SELECT statement:

SELECT * FROM HumanResources.Department2
WHERE
name = 'Sales';

DepartmentID	Name	GroupName	ModifiedDate
3	Sales	Sales and Marketing	2002-06-01 00:00:00.000

Table 10.5

The restored sales row is displayed. Always remember to switch on the auto COMMIT mode once the DELETE tests are done. The command used is:

USE AdventureWorks2012;
GO
SET IMPLICIT_TRANSACTIONS ON;

DELETE and Database Constraints

As initially mentioned, DELETE statements are subjected to database constraints. If the statement violates a constraint, the statement will fail. For example, if an attempt is made to DELETE the sales row of the original department table, the statement fails as follows:

```
USE AdventureWorks2012;
GO
DELETE FROM HumanResources.Department
WHERE
Name = 'Sales';
```

The statement fails with the following error:

Msg 547, Level 16, State 0, Line 1

The DELETE statement conflicted with the REFERENCE constraint "FK_EmployeeDepartmentHistory_Department_DepartmentID". The conflict occurred in database "AdventureWorks2012", table "HumanResources.EmployeeDepartmentHistory", column 'DepartmentID'.

The statement has been terminated.

The failure is due to the violation of a foreign key constraint on the HumanResources.EmployeeDepartmentHistory table. The DepartmentID column on this table is a foreign key from the HumanResources.Department table. Thus the values in the EmployeeDepartmentHistory.DepartmentID column must also exist in the Department. DepartmentID column. Deleting any row from this table will cause a mismatch of values in the DepartmentID columns of the two tables.

Deleting Oracle Duplicate Rows

Duplicate rows are two or more rows where each column value is exactly the same in the same table. This leads to inaccurate query results. The objective is to delete all but one of the duplicates in the table. Duplicate rows can be mistakenly inserted into tables due to poor table and constraint (absent PRIMARY KEY) design. They can also occur as a result of failures in data extraction and load jobs where the table constraints have been disabled for performance.

However, it so happens that in Oracle tables, there is always an invisible pseudo-column called ROWID for each row. This column stores the unique physical address of each row in the table. This column can be used to distinguish between duplicate rows in tables. Once the row differences are determined, duplicate instances of the row can be deleted. For example, the following code creates a new table and INSERTS duplicate rows into it:

```
CREATE TABLE new_regions
( region_id NUMBER,
region_name VARCHAR2(25));
INSERT INTO new_regions (region_id,region_name) VALUES
    (1,'AUSTRALIA');
INSERT INTO new_regions (region_id,region_name) VALUES
    (1,'AUSTRALIA');
```

INSERT INTO new_regions (region_id,region_name) VALUES
    (5,'ASIA');

INSERT INTO new_regions (region_id,region_name) VALUES
    (5,'ASIA');

The following shows the duplicate rows and their assciated row_ids:

SELECT rowid,region_id,region_name FROM new_regions;

ROWID	REGION_ID	REGION_NAME
AAAE+DAAEAAAAGuAAA	1	AUSTRALIA
AAAE+DAAEAAAAGuAAB	1	AUSTRALIA
AAAE+DAAEAAAAGuAAC	5	ASIA
AAAE+DAAEAAAAGuAAD	5	ASIA

Table 10.6

To delete one of each duplicate row, the table is joined to itself and a MAX or MIN function is used to distinguish each instance of the duplicate based on their rowids. To see which rows will be deleted, the following subquery is used:

SELECT n.rowid, n.region_id,n.region_name
FROM new_regions n
WHERE n.rowid >
(SELECT MIN(r.rowid) FROM new_regions r
WHERE r.region_id = n.region_id
AND r.region_name = n.region_name);

This shows the rows that will be delated when this subquery is used as a condition for a DELETE statement:

ROWID	REGION_ID	REGION_NAME
AAAE+DAAEAAAAGuAAB	1	AUSTRALIA
AAAE+DAAEAAAAGuAAD	5	ASIA

Table 10.7

The DELETE statement can now be written as follows:

DELETE FROM new_regions n

WHERE n.rowid >

(SELECT MIN(r.rowid) FROM new_regions r

WHERE r.region_id = n.region_id

AND r.region_name = n.region_name);

The DELETE statement uses the subquery to identify the duplicate rows by comparing each column value to a mirror image of itself. The MIN function is then used to filter out just one occurrence of the duplicates for deletion. The final result is shown below.

SELECT rowid,region_id,region_name FROM new_regions;

ROWID	REGION_ID	REGION_NAME
AAAE+DAAEAAAAGuAAA	1	AUSTRALIA
AAAE+DAAEAAAAGuAAC	5	ASIA

Table 10.8

Two different rows are now left in the table.

Deleting SQL Server Duplicate Rows

The occurrence of duplicate rows in an SQL server table is also due to poor table and constraint (absent PRIMARY KEY) design. SQL server uses a different method. The following statement CREATES a new table and INSERTS three duplicate rows:

```
USE AdventureWorks2012;
GO
CREATE TABLE Person.AddressTypeS(
AddressTypeID int,
NameName nvarchar(50),
ModifiedDate datetime);
INSERT INTO Person.AddressTypeS (AddressTypeID,NameNa
    me,ModifiedDate)
VALUES (1,'Procurement',GETDATE()),
(1,'Procurement',GETDATE()),—Duplicate
(2,'Payment',GETDATE()),
(2,'Payment',GETDATE()),—duplicate
(2,'Payment',GETDATE());—Duplicate
```

To see the duplicates, the following statement is used:

```
SELECT * FROM Person.AddressTypeS ORDER BY
    AddressTypeID;
```

AddressTypeID	NameName	ModifiedDate
1	Procurement	2012-05-27 10:55:43.140
1	Procurement	2012-05-27 10:55:43.140
2	Payment	2012-05-27 10:55:43.140
2	Payment	2012-05-27 10:55:43.140
2	Payment	2012-05-27 10:55:43.140

Table 10.9

The ROW_NUMBER analytic function can be used to delete SQL server duplicate rows. The function works by numbering table rows based on the values of its columns specified in the partition clause. If the columns of the duplicate rows are analysed using this function, each duplicate row will have a different number. The first occurrence of the row will always be numbered as row 1. Thus, any row number greater than one will be a duplicate. The following statement demonstrates how the rows are numbered:

```
SELECT AddressTypeID, NameName,ModifiedDate,ROW_
    NUMBER() OVER(PARTITION BY AddressTypeID,NameNa
    me,ModifiedDate ORDER BY NameName)AS rownumbers
FROM Person.AddressTypeS;
```

This outputs the following table.

AddressTypeID	NameName	ModifiedDate	Rownumbers
1	Procurement	2012-05-27 10:55:43.140	1
1	Procurement	2012-05-27 10:55:43.140	2
2	Payment	2012-05-27 10:55:43.140	1
2	Payment	2012-05-27 10:55:43.140	2
2	Payment	2012-05-27 10:55:43.140	3

Table 10.10

Notice that the first occurrence of each duplicate is always numbered as 1. This analytic query can be used as a condition for a DELETE of duplicates. In order to concretise the calculated rownumbers column for use in the WHERE clause, a view or common table expression (CTE) is used. A CTE is a named query with columns that can only be referenced within the context of its creation. As opposed to views, it disappears after its creation and cannot be referenced by another query. There is more on CTEs in chapter twelve. The following statement deletes the duplicate rows having rownumbers greater than 1. Thus a single occurrence of the duplicate row is preserved.

```
WITH delete_CTE AS (
SELECT AddressTypeID, NameName,ModifiedDate,ROW_
    NUMBER() OVER(PARTITION BY AddressTypeID,NameNa
    me,ModifiedDate ORDER BY NameName)AS rownumbers
FROM Person.AddressTypeS)
```

```
DELETE FROM delete_CTE
WHERE rownumbers >1;
GO
```

The result of this statement is:

(3 row(s) affected)

The following statement returns the remaining rows.

```
SELECT * FROM Person.AddressTypeS ORDER BY
     AddressTypeID;
```

AddressTypeID	NameName	ModifiedDate
1	Procurement	2012-05-27 10:55:43.140
2	Payment	2012-05-27 10:55:43.140

Table 10.11

This shows that all the duplicates have been deleted and we are left with a single occurrence of each row.

TRUNCATE versus DELETE Table

Another way to delete all records from a table is to issue the TRUNCATE statement. This statement is faster than DELETE because system resources are not used to record the deleted rows. As a result, a truncated table cannot be rolled back. The WHERE clause cannot be defined for a TRUNCATE statement thus all table rows are always deleted.

The DELETE statement is slower because each row is deleted sequentially, and for each row deleted, system recourses are used to record them for future (ROLLBACK) restoration if the need occurs. The deleted rows are stored with database backups.

The generic syntax for the TRUNCATE statement is:

TRUNCATE TABLE table_name;

Conclusion

This chapter covered the deletion of data from tables. It also highlighted the impact of constraints and precautions to follow when business critical data is being deleted. Finally, it prescribed the use of the TRUNCATE statement to delete all rows in non-business-critical large tables.

Chapter Eleven

Overview

This chapter covers the use of data definition language (DDL) statements to create advanced database objects such as tables and constraints. It shows how the objects specified in the first chapter are created.

Creating Database Tables and Constraints

Constraints are rules imposed on database tables to enforce data integrity. They are there because the quality and correctness of table data is always threatened during data maintenance operations. Thus the constraints ensure that rogue INSERT, DELETE, and UPDATE statements do not corrupt the table data.

The constraints specified on a table are derived from business rules. For example, a business may devise a rule that a manager's salary should never exceed 30000 pounds. Another business rule could be that each employee must have a unique ID number and his or her last name must always be recorded. These rules are enforced with CONSTRAINTS. Some business requirement analysis is needed to determine which constraints are necessary for your tables.

Constraints should be used with caution because if they are overused, data maintenance becomes very restrictive. From a technical perspective, some CONSTRAINTS are used to maintain the logical relations between tables. They ensure that the joins in SELECT queries always return the correct result when several tables are queried. The CONSTRAINTS also improve the performance of the DBMS SQL optimiser.

Types of Constraints

CHECK constraint: The CHECK constraint ensures the values in a database column always comply with a business rule. For example, the business rule that states that a manager's salary should never exceed 30000 pounds can be enforced using this constraint.

UNIQUE constraint: This constraint ensures that all the values in a column are unique for each row. Duplicate values are rejected. A table can have several columns with the unique constraint. For example, this constrain can be used to enforce a business rule that states that all employees must register their external e-mail address. Obviously each address must be different.

The NOT NULL constraint: This constraint is used to ensure that a value is always present in a column for each row. The value can never be null. This constraint can be used to enforce the business rule that the last name of each employee must be recorded.

PRIMARY KEY constraint: This constraint combines the properties of the NOT NULL and UNIQUE constraints. It is used to ensure that the values in the primary key column are always unique and can never be null for each row. There can only be one primary key column in a table. The primary key can be a single column or a combination of columns. It is a best practice to delegate the automatic generation of integer primary key values to the database using the identity property or sequences. This constraint can be used to ensure that all employees in a company have a unique ID. Indexes are also automatically created on primary keys to speed up SELECT queries.

FOREIGN KEY constraint: This constraint establishes a logical relationship between two tables. It ensures that the values in the foreign key column in, for example table A, must be present in a reference column of table B. The table B-referenced column is generally the primary key or unique column of table B. This property is known as *referential integrity*. This is an explicit IT requirement that preserves the data correctness and integrity between normalised tables. Though it is an explicit IT requirement, it is also an implicit business requirement because it ensures business data is always consistent.

For example, in the SQL server HumanResources schema, the HumanResources.EmployeePayHistory table has a foreign key constraint on its BusinessEntityID column. This column references the BusinessEntityID column on the HumanResources.employee table. This ensures that no rows can be entered into the HumanResources. EmployeePayHistory table if the BusinessEntityID value is not present in the Employee.BusinessEntityID column. This is logical from a business perspective because you should not be able to pay anyone who is not an employee of the company. The FOREIGN KEY can also include an ON DELETE clause that specifies what to do with the foreign key values if the referenced column values are deleted. It can either set the values to null or simply delete all the rows that contain the deleted referenced values. If this clause is omitted, rows in the table can never be deleted if their values exist in the foreign key of another table.

Creating and Maintaining Tables

Tables and other relational objects are created and managed using SQL Data Definition Language (DDL) statements. They include CREATE, ALTER, and DROP statements. These statements are very similar in Oracle and SQL server. These database management systems (DBMS) also provide visual tools for table creation and management.

The CREATE statement always include a wide range of optional parameters used to specify how and where the table should be created. Most of these parameters can be ignored by the developer. Once the table has been created, the database administrator can fine tune the storage requirements.

The generic syntax for creating a table is:

CREATE TABLE table_name (column1_name data type,
    column2_name data type, column3_name data type);

It is always mandatory to state the name of the table, the name of each column, and their data types. The column names must be enclosed within brackets. Once the constraints on a table have been determined, these constraints can be included during table creation. Alternatively the constraints can be added using the ALTER command after the table has been created.

As a general database rule, two database object types in the same schema cannot have the same name. For example, two tables or two functions in the AdventureWorks2012.HumanResources schema cannot have the same name. When an attempt is made to create an object with a name that already exists, the code fails. You get around this in Oracle by using the CREATE or REPLACE command. T-SQL uses the OBJECT_ID function.

In T-SQL you need to check if the object already exists in the sys. objects view. If the object exists, drop it before recreating it. The generic syntax is:

```
USE AdventureWorks2012;
GO
IF OBJECT_ID ('schema_name.object_name','object_type')IS
    NOT NULL
DROP object_type schema_name.object_name;
GO
CREATE object_type schema_name.object_name;
```

Were object_type is the description of the object in the sys.objects view.

Creating Oracle Tables

There are some subtle differences in creating tables between the different databases. For the most part, the syntax is very similar in Oracle and SQL server. The following example creates a Trainee_Student table in the Oracle HR database. A row is then inserted and displayed. The table is created without constraints.

```
CREATE TABLE Trainee_Student (Student_id NUMBER(6,0),
Enrollment_date DATE,
Last_name VARCHAR2(25),
```

Email VARCHAR2(25),

Max_salary NUMBER(8,0),

Department_Id NUMBER(4,0));

The table is created.

Then the next statement inserts a row:

INSERT INTO Trainee_Student (Student_id, Enrollment_

    date,Last_name,Email,Max_salary,Department_Id)

VALUES(1,sysdate,'Ebai','vee2012@hotmail.com',3000,10);

The next statement displays the row.

SELECT * FROM Trainee_Student;

STUDENT _ID	ENROLLMENT _DATE	LAST _NAME	EMAIL	MAX _SALARY	DEPARTMENT _ID
1	02-MAY-12	Ebai	vee2012@ hotmail. com	3000	10

Table 11.1

The next example creates a table with constraints. The constraint name is defined with the CONSTRAINT keyword, and then the type of constraint is stated. The constraints are either defined in line with the column name or out of line, as a standalone statement. Once the constraints have been defined, they are either enabled or disabled. The following statements DROP and recreates the Trainee_Student table with constraints. Only the CHECK constraint is defined off line.

DROP TABLE Trainee_Student;

The table has been deleted. The following statement recreates the table with constraints:

```
CREATE TABLE Trainee_Student
(Student_id NUMBER(6,0) CONSTRAINT Stud_ID_PK
    PRIMARY KEY ENABLE,
Enrollment_date DATE,
Last_name VARCHAR2(25) CONSTRAINT Stud_Last_Name
    NOT NULL ENABLE,
Email VARCHAR2(25),
Max_salary NUMBER(8,0),
Department_Id NUMBER(4,0) CONSTRAINT Stud_Dep_FK
REFERENCES departments(department_id),
CONSTRAINT Salary_Range CHECK (Max_salary BETWEEN
    1000 AND 5000) ENABLE);
```

The PRIMARY KEY, NOT NULL, REFERENCES(FOREIGN KEY) and CHECK constraint have been created and enabled on the table. Notice that the FOREIGN KEY constraint has been created using the REFERENCES key word that identifies the reference table and column. In this case the Departments tables' department_id column is used. Any statement that violates any of these constraints will fail.

A row that does not violate any constraints is now inserted into the table. For example:

```
INSERT INTO Trainee_Student (Student_id, Enrollment_
    date,Last_name,Email,Max_salary,Department_Id)
```

VALUES(1,sysdate,'Jobs','jobs2012@hotmail.com',2000,300);

This inserts a single row into the table as shown

SELECT * FROM Trainee_Student;

STUDENT _ID	ENROLLMENT _DATE	LAST _NAME	EMAIL	MAX _SALARY	DEPARTMENT _ID
1	07/15/2012	Jobs	jobs2012@ hotmail. com	2000	300

Table 11.2

All attempts to insert illegal rows that violate any constraint will now fail. For example:

INSERT INTO Trainee_Student (Student_id, Enrollment_

date,Last_name,Email,Max_salary,Department_Id)

VALUES(2,sysdate,'Jones','jo2012@hotmail.com',7000,300);

The insert fails with the following error message: *ORA-02290: check constraint (HR.SALARY_RANGE) violated.*

This is because the CHECK constraint has been violated by trying to insert a salary of 7000, which is out of the 1000 to 5000 range stated by the CHECK constraint.

If an attempt is made to nullify the last_name of the student trainee in the table, the code fails with the following error message:

UPDATE Trainee_Student SET Last_Name = NULL;

ORA-01407: cannot update ("HR"."TRAINEE_STUDENT"."LAST_NAME") to NULL

To illustrate how the FOREIGN KEY constraint works with DELETE, an attempt is made to delete a row from the referenced departments table that has department_id values in the department_id foreign key column of the created Trainee_Student table:

DELETE FROM Departments WHERE Department_Id = 300;

The DELETE statement fails with the following error message: ORA-02292: integrity constraint (HR.STUD_DEP_FK) violated—child record found.

This is because Department_Id 300 exists in the foreign key of the Trainee_Student table.

The FOREIGN KEY constraint also prevents the insertion of values that do not exist in the referenced departments.department_id column into the foreign key column of the Trainee_Student table. For example:

INSERT INTO Trainee_Student (Student_id, Enrollment_date,Last_name,Email,Max_salary,Department_Id)
VALUES(3,sysdate,'King','KI2012@hotmail.com',2000,400);

This code fails with the following error: *ORA-02291: integrity constraint (HR.STUD_DEP_FK) violated—parent key not found.*

The failure is caused because there was an attempt to INSERT 400 into the Trainee_Student department_id foreign key. The 400 violates the FOREIGN KEY constraint because it is absent from the referenced departments.department_id column values.

Modifying Oracle Tables

As the business environment changes, there will be new requirements for table changes. These changes will typically affect the table columns and constraints. Once a table has been created, its structure and attributes can be modified using a database edition wizard or with SQL. The ALTER TABLE statement is used to modify tables. It is a best practice to create copies of tables before modifying them. Some ALTER commands might fail if the table contains data. This is because the data might not conform to the attempted new structure.

Renaming Tables

Trainee_Student table can be renamed by issuing the following statement:

```
ALTER TABLE Trainee_Student RENAME TO Student_Trainee;
```

The Trainee_Student table has been renamed to Student_Trainee. All the properties of Trainee_Student are inherited by Student_Trainee. However, all objects dependent on the Trainee_Student table must be checked for consistency.

Altering Table Columns

New columns can be added and deleted. Their properties can also be modified.

The following statement adds a new Login_id column to the Student_Trainee table. A default value of student_user is assigned to the new column. This value will be used to immediately populate the column and for future new rows when a value is absent for Login_id.

    ALTER TABLE Student_Trainee ADD (Login_id VARCHAR2(25)
        DEFAULT 'student_user');

The new Login_id column is created and populated with the student_user value.

Columns can also be deleted or modified. The following statement deletes the Login_id column.

    ALTER TABLE Student_Trainee DROP (Login_id) ;

The Login_id column is deleted. To modify the properties of a column, the following statement is used.

    ALTER TABLE Student_Trainee MODIFY (Email VARCHAR2
        (30));

This statement increases the size of the e-mail column from 25 to 30.

Altering CONSTRAINTS

Constraints can be added or modified once a table is created. They can be disabled once they become unnecessary. When a new constraint is added and enabled to a table that already contains data, the data must conform to the rules of the added constraint. If the data is not compliant the constraint will remain disabled. For example:

ALTER TABLE Student_Trainee ADD CONSTRAINT emp_email
    UNIQUE (Email) ENABLE;

The previous statement adds a new UNIQUE constraint to the e-mail column of the Student_Trainee. The constraint is enabled because the data in the column is unique for each row.

Enabling and Disabling Constraints

As business rules change it might become necessary to disable or enable existing constraints. For example, if the salary range limit of student employees is suspended, the following statement disables the CHECK constraint on the salary_range of the Student_Trainee table:

ALTER TABLE Student_Trainee DISABLE CONSTRAINT
    Salary_Range;

The salary constraint is disabled and now any student salary is permissible. Note that disabling a PRIMARY KEY constraint disables any associated FOREIGN KEY. If after some time the salary range requirement is needed, the following statement re-establishes the constraint:

ALTER TABLE Student_Trainee ENABLE VALIDATE
CONSTRAINT Salary_Range;

Note that while enabling this constraint, if any existing value in the Max_salary column for any row violates the constraint, the statement will fail and the constraint will remain disabled.

Constraints should be deleted when they become obsolete. Deleting some constraints has a direct impact on others—for example, a delete of a PRIMARY KEY constraint will only succeed if it is not referenced by a foreign key of another table. In this case, the FOREIGN KEY constraint must also be deleted. For example the following statement which tries to delete a PRIMARY KEY constraint fails:

ALTER TABLE Departments DROP PRIMARY KEY;

Error message: ORA-02273: this unique/primary key is referenced by some foreign keys

This PRIMARY KEY constraint can be dropped using the CASCADE option which drops the related FOREIGN KEY constraints as follows

ALTER TABLE Departments DROP PRIMARY KEY CASCADE;

The statement DROPs the PRIMARY KEY constraint on the departments table. The CASCADE option automatically DROPS any FOREIGN KEY that referenced the department table PRIMARY KEY.

Deleting Tables and Constraints

The DROP statement is used to permanently delete a table, including all its rows. Once a table is deleted, all of its dependent objects, such as user defined functions, views or procedures become invalid. In the professional world it is quite common to drop and recreate tables with corrupted data. In these cases most of these dependent objects will need to be recreated and granted new access privileges to the table.

To delete a copy of the employee table, the following code is used:

DROP TABLE Employee1;

The table and all its rows have been deleted.

DROP statements will fail if the table has been referenced by the FOREIGN KEY of another table. For example:

DROP TABLE Departments;

This statement fails with the following error message:

ORA-02449: unique/primary keys in table referenced by foreign keys.

The statement failed because the department_id PRIMARY KEY is referenced by the Student_Trainee table department_id FOREIGN KEY. To get around this, the CASCADE CONSTRAINTS option is used. This option drops both the table and the referencing FOREIGN KEY constraint. For example:

DROP TABLE Departments CASCADE CONSTRAINTS;

Both the departments table and the Stud_Dep_FK FOREIGN KEY constraint of the TRAINEE_STUDENT have now been deleted.

Creating and Maintaining SQL Server Tables

The rules for creating SQL server tables are very similar to the Oracle rules. This section will highlight the few deviations and new constraints used for SQL server tables. The tables can be created with table creation wizards or with the CREATE statement. The table constraints can be defined in the CREATE table statement or they can be defined after the table has been created using the ALTER table statement. The CREATE table statement must include the table name and a list of column names and their associated data types. For example:

```
Use AdventureWorks2012;
GO
CREATE TABLE HumanResources.Trainee_Student (Student_
     id int,
Enrollment_date DATE,
Last_name nvarchar(25),
Email nvarchar(25),
Max_salary money,
Department_Id int ) ;
```

The code creates a table called Trainee_Student. This is an ordinary table without constraints. With SQL server it is always prudent to test for the existence of an object before recreating it. If the object exists, it should be deleted before being recreated. The following example recreates the same table but includes constraints:

```
Use AdventureWorks2012;
GO
IF OBJECT_ID ('HumanResources.Trainee_Student','U')IS NOT
    NULL
DROP TABLE HumanResources.Trainee_Student;
GO
CREATE TABLE HumanResources.Trainee_Student (Student_
    id int PRIMARY KEY IDENTITY(1,1),
Enrollment_date DATE DEFAULT (getdate()),
Last_name nvarchar(25) NOT NULL,
Email nvarchar(25),
Max_salary money CHECK (Max_salary between 1000 and
    3000),
Department_Id smallint REFERENCES HumanResources.
    Department(DepartmentID));
```

The statement recreates the table and defines the PRIMARY KEY, CHECK, NOT NULL, and FOREIGN KEY constraints. Notice that the PRIMARY KEY constraint uses the IDENTITY property that automatically generates primary key values. The identity property is set with the fllowing syntax:

IDENTITY (S, I) where S stands for the starting value and I stands for the incremental value.

A single row can now be inserted by using the following statement:

INSERT INTO HumanResources.Trainee_Student (Enrollment_
 date,Last_name,Email,Max_salary,Department_Id)
VALUES(GETDATE(),'Jobs','jobs2012@hotmail.com',2000,2);

Notice that the student_id column is ommited by the INSERT statement. This is because the Identity property generates values for that column. To see the inserted row, the following statement is run:

SELECT * FROM HumanResources.Trainee_Student;

Which outputs

Student _id	Enrollment _date	Last _name	Email	Max _salary	Department _Id
1	2012-05-08	Jobs	jobs2012@ hotmail.com	2000.00	2

Table 11.3

The IDENTITY property has generated the first student_id primary key value of 1. All the constraints work exactly as they do with Oracle. The SQL server tables are also altered and deleted using the same Oracle syntax.

Refer to previous Oracle examples for specifics.

Conclusion

This chapter covered the creation and maintenance of tables in databases. The creation of constraints and their impact on subsequent SQL table queries was also covered. The main difference between the available table properties was highlighted as the SQL server IDENTITY property.

Chapter Twelve

Overview of Creating Advanced Database Objects

Advanced database objects are used to improve the usability of databases. Their implementation is similar in Oracle and SQL server.

Creating Synonyms

Synonyms are used to reduce programming complexity. They are specifically used to shorten the fully qualified names of database objects. Synonyms can be created for tables, views, and stored procedures. They are useful because fully qualified names tend to be very long, resulting in several opportunities for the programmer to introduce errors. For example, in the SQL server AdventureWorks2012 database, AdventureWorks2012.HumanResources.Employee is the fully qualified name of the employee table. This can be shorterned to Employee as follows:

```
USE AdventureWorks2012
GO
```

—Create a synonym for the Employee table in HumanResources schema database.

```
CREATE SYNONYM Employee
FOR AdventureWorks2012.HumanResources.Employee;
GO
```

The employee synonym is created. This synonym can now be used in queries as follows:

SELECT BusinessEntityID,HireDate FROM Employee WHERE
    BusinessEntityID = 50;

This returns:

BusinessEntityID	HireDate
50	2002-03-05

Table 12.1

The Oracle syntax is similar but includes the accessibility context that could be PUBLIC or PRIVATE. For example, the following statement creates an Oracle tracking synonym for the Hr.Job_history table:

CREATE PRIVATE SYNONYM Tracking FOR HR. JOB_HISTORY;

This private synonym can now be assigned to a specific user. Public synonyms are available to all users.

Creating Views

A view is stored SELECT query that presents a virtual table to users and other applications. The columns of a view are derived from one or more tables (base tables) or views in the SELECT query. A view is always empty until it gets populated when the query is run by a calling query or application. Views are generally used to improve table security by presenting only a set of restricted rows to the users. For example, a view containing only clerks could be created on the employees table. Any user accessing this view will have access only to clerk data. Views can generally be used like any ordinary table to SELECT, UPDATE, DELETE, and INSERT data. Changes to view data are propagated to the base tables.

The overriding use of views is to hide and reduce statement complexity and present more informative tables. Due to the normalised schema design of databases, information is scattered amongst different tables. There might be general business requirements that require information from several of these tables. Rather than always writing complex statements that join the required tables, a view can be created on these tables. Once the view is created, it is queried like a single table, avoiding the join complexity of the base tables.

T-SQL Views

For example, in the SQL server AdventureWorks2012 database, there might be reoccurring business requirements to retrieve employee details such as their salary, names, addresses, job titles, and hire dates. The issue for IT is that each of these details is stored in different tables, so each requirement will need a new complex query that joins the tables. A simple solution is to create a single view that will perform the joins. This view will then be queried as a single table to meet the business requirements. The view is created as follows:

```
USE AdventureWorks2012;
GO
CREATE VIEW HumanResources.emp_details_vw AS
```

```
SELECT h.BusinessEntityID,h.JobTitle,h.HireDate,n.
    FirstName,h.OrganizationLevel,p.Rate,a.AddressLine1,a.
    PostalCode
FROM HumanResources.Employee h,HumanResources.
    EmployeePayHistory p,Person.Address a,
Person.Person n,Person.BusinessEntityAddress e
WHERE h.BusinessEntityID = p.BusinessEntityID
AND a.AddressID = e.AddressID
AND e.BusinessEntityID = h.BusinessEntityID
AND n.BusinessEntityID = h.BusinessEntityID;
```

The HumanResources.emp_details_vw is created which retrieves data from the Employee, EmployeePayhistory, Person, and BusinessEntityAddress tables. All details of an employee can now be retrieved from the view without joining the base tables. For example, all the details of employee 100 can be retrieved by issuing the following statement:

```
SELECT JobTitle,Rate,FirstName,AddressLine1
    FROM HumanResources.emp_details_vw WHERE
    BusinessEntityID = 100;
```

This retrieves the following row:

JobTitle	Rate	FirstName	AddressLine1
Production Technician—WC50	11.00	Lolan	8152 Claudia Dr.

Table 12.2

Oracle Views

Oracle views share the same properties with SQL server views. A similar Oracle view returns employee details from the following four tables: employees, countries, locations, and departments. Once this view is created, reoccurring business requirements to return employee information can be simply resolved by querying this view and avoiding the complexity of joining the base tables.

```
CREATE VIEW emp_details_vw AS (
SELECT employee_id,first_name, last_name,department_
    name, city, salary
FROM employees e, countries c, locations l,departments d
WHERE e.department_id = d.department_id
AND l.location_id = d.location_id
AND l.country_id = c.country_id)
```

To now get the details of employee 200 the view is queried as follows:

```
SELECT * FROM emp_details_vw
WHERE employee_id = 200;
Output
```

EMPLOYEE _ID	FIRST _NAME	LAST _NAME	DEPARTMENT _NAME	CITY	SALARY
200	Jennifer	Whalen	Administration	Seattle	4400

Table 12.2

The details of employee 200 are obtained without having to write a complex query.

T-SQL Common Table Expressions (CTEs)

CTEs can be used as SQL server temporary views. Their definition is not stored in the database but can be used in a query within the context of its creation. This means the query using the CTE must appear before the end of the WITH statement (before GO). They are created by associating and naming a SELECT query using a WITH keyword. They are commonly used either when a permanent view is not required or when insufficient database privileges prohibit view creation. For example, the previous HumanResources.emp_details_vw can be recreated and used as a CTE as follows:

```
USE AdventureWorks2012;
GO
WITH emp_details_cte
AS
(SELECT h.BusinessEntityID,h.JobTitle,h.HireDate,n.
    FirstName,h.OrganizationLevel,p.Rate,a.AddressLine1,a.
    PostalCode
FROM HumanResources.Employee h,HumanResources.
    EmployeePayHistory p,Person.Address a,
Person.Person n,Person.BusinessEntityAddress e
WHERE h.BusinessEntityID = p.BusinessEntityID
AND a.AddressID = e.AddressID
AND e.BusinessEntityID = h.BusinessEntityID
AND n.BusinessEntityID = h.BusinessEntityID)
```

—An outer query is now used to reference the emp_details_cte

```
SELECT JobTitle,Rate,FirstName,AddressLine1 FROM
    emp_details_cte
WHERE BusinessEntityID = 100;
GO
Output
```

JobTitle	Rate	FirstName	AddressLine1
Production Technician—WC50	11.00	Lolan	8152 Claudia Dr.

Table 12.3

The second SELECT query uses the emp_details_cte CTE to retrieve employee details. The CTE disappears after the GO ends the CTE creation statement. Any statement that refers to the emp_details_cte will fail after this point. The only way to reuse this CTE is to save it to a script file or rebuild it as a View.

Using the Oracle WITH Clause to Replicate T-SQL CTEs

The new Oracle 11gWITH clause can be used to replicate T-SQL CTEs. A SELECT query is defined and named within a WITH clause, and then other queries within the query block can reference the columns specified within the WITH clause. This effectively creates a temporary view that can only be referenced within the context of the WITH clause. For example, the previous view created (emp_details_vw) can be defined and queried using the WITH clause as follows:

```
WITH emp_details AS (
SELECT employee_id,first_name, last_name,department_
    name, city, salary
FROM employees e, countries c, locations l,departments d
```

WHERE e.department_id = d.department_id

AND l.location_id = d.location_id

AND l.country_id = c.country_id)

SELECT * FROM emp_details

WHERE employee_id = 200;

Output

EMPLOYEE _ID	FIRST _NAME	LAST _NAME	DEPARTMENT _NAME	CITY	SALARY
200	Jennifer	Whalen	Administration	Seattle	4400

Table 12.4

Notice that the second query terminates the WITH clause with a semicolon. The same results are obtained.

Creating Sequences

Sequences are relational objects used to generate a mathematical series of numbers. They are generally used to populate numeric primary keys columns. Sequences are used to guarantee that primary key values are always unique and follow a defined arithmetic order. They are not tied to any table, so a single sequence can be used to populate several columns in several different tables. A sequence is created using the CREATE SEQUENCE statement. The sequence properties include name, increment (ascending or descending), start value, maximum value, and cycle. The cycle indicates whether the sequence should start again once the maximum value is reached. Obviously for primary key sequences, duplicates are rejected and thus its sequence cannot cycle.

Creating Oracle Sequences

A sequence could be used to help populate a new trainee_student table in the Oracle HR database. For example the business rule might decree that each trainee student student_id must be a number and every new student_id must be equal to the previous student_id number plus 2. The following code creates a Trainee_SEQ sequence used to populate the student_id primary key of the Trainee_Student table:

```
CREATE SEQUENCE Trainee_SEQ MINVALUE 1 MAXVALUE
    10000 INCREMENT BY 2 START WITH 2 NOCYCLE;
```

The sequence is created with a starting value of 2, increments by 2 and a maximum value of 10000.

Next a Trainee_Student table is created and two rows are inserted using the sequence.

```
CREATE TABLE Trainee_Student (Student_id NUMBER(6,0)
    CONSTRAINT train_ID_PK PRIMARY KEY ENABLE,
Enrollment_date DATE,
Last_name VARCHAR2(25),
Email VARCHAR2(25),
Max_salary NUMBER(8,0),
Department_Id NUMBER(4,0));
```

Table created. Two rows are then inserted into the table. The sequence_name.nextval function is used to automatically generate new Student_ids.

INSERT INTO Trainee_Student (Student_id, Enrollment_
date,Last_name,Email,Max_salary,Department_Id)
VALUES(Trainee_SEQ.nextval, sysdate,'Ebai','vee2012@
hotmail.com',3000,10);
INSERT INTO Trainee_Student (Student_id, Enrollment_
date,Last_name,Email,Max_salary,Department_Id)
VALUES(Trainee_SEQ.nextval, sysdate,'Jobs','Jobs2012@
hotmail.com',5000,20);

The inserted rows are then displayed.

SELECT * FROM Trainee_Student;

The output is:

STUDENT _ID	ENROLLMENT _DATE	LAST _NAME	E-MAIL	MAX _SALARY	DEPARTMENT _ID
2	10-MAY-12	Ebai	vee2012@ hotmail.com	3000	10
4	10-MAY-12	Jobs	Jobs2012@ hotmail.com	5000	20

Table 12.5

Notice the student_id values of 2 and 4, which have been generated by the Trainee_SEQ.nextval function.

Sequences are a new feature to SQL server 2012. The 2005 and 2008 versions relied on identity columns to generate automatic integer numbers. The statement to create an SQL server 2012 sequence is as follows:

CREATE SEQUENCE HumanResources.Test_seq
START WITH 1
INCREMENT BY 2

MINVALUE 1

MAXVALUE 10000

CYCLE;

The created sequence starts with 1 and increments by 2. The SQL server syntax is exactly like the Oracle syntax; however, to retrieve and insert the next sequence value the following function is used: NEXT VALUE FOR HumanResources.Test_seq. SQL server sequences are more flexible than identity columns because they are independent of any table. However, values generated by identity columns can never be updated thus they are more appropriate for primary keys. Careful analysis must be conducted to decide which method is required for a given system.

Indexes and ROWIDs

Indexes are relational objects used to speed up data retrieval in databases. The most common type of index is called a B-Tree index. Bitmap indexes are more common for data warehousing applications. Indexes can be created on one or more columns of a table. They are automatically created on primary key columns in tables. These primary key indexes are used for enforcing the unique/primary key constraint and cannot be deleted while the constraint is still in place. They can also be manually created on highly selective columns that are used in WHERE clause of queries.

ROWIDS are physical addresses of every row in the database. Indexes use ROWIDS to improve query retrieval performance. Every index entry stores the combination of the indexed column value and its physical address (ROWID) in the database for every row. Thus the index knows exactly where every row is physically stored in the database. These index entries are then broken up into address ranges. For example, an indexed table with one million rows could be broken up into one thousand address ranges such as Address range1 (ROWID 1 to 1000), range2 (ROWID 1001 to 2000), range3 (ROWID 2001 to 3000), etc. Once these ranges have been established, if a query is executed to retrieve data identified by an indexed column value, the database will go only to the address rage that contains the required row avoiding the rest. This effectively avoids full table scans, thus improving performance.

Indexes should be used with care as they reduce INSERT and UPDATE performance. This is because whenever an indexed row is updated system recourses are used to update the index value reducing performance. They can also exponentially increase the size of the database. Only one index can exist for a particular column, but a table can have an index on each column. They should be routinely recreated to improve efficiency.

To create an index on the phone_number column of the Oracle HR employee table the following statement is used (the syntax is the same for SQL server):

CREATE INDEX enp_phone_ix ON Employees (phone_number);

Triggers

Triggers are used to enable database auditing, enforce business rules, or maintain data history (managing slowly changing dimensions). Database triggers are compiled stored procedures that are used to automatically perform an action when a database event occurs. The events that might automatically fire a trigger include table level DML statements (INSERT, UPDATE, DELETE), database level DDL statements (CREATE, DROP, ALTER), and user events such as a user logging off. Table level triggers perform actions based on the events that affect the table data such as the update of a row. Database level trigger perform actions based on events that affect most relational structures themselves such as the deletion of a table or synonym. Error handlers can also be embedded in triggers to manage errors. Triggers can be programmed to automatically fire BEFORE the statement is issued, AFTER the statement is issued, and before or after each row is modified by a DML statement. The INSTEAD OF trigger executes the trigger code instead of the triggering event. The INSTEAD OF triggers are used to prevent inconsistent database actions while the AFTER triggers are used for logging events. Once triggers are created, they can be enabled and disabled as required.

Triggers should only be used to maintain data integrity for business rules that cannot be enforced using normal database constraints or user security privileges. For example, a trigger should not be created to prevent the data modification on a table by certain users. It is more practical to simply deny the users access privileges to the table.

Database Level DDL Triggers

Database Level triggers are fired by DDL statements such as CREATE, ALTER, or DROP.

Constraints enforcement takes a higher precedence over trigger enforcement. Thus, database triggers can serve as a second line of defence to prevent the dropping of independent tables that do not have any foreign key constraint. For example, to create a database level FOR trigger to prevent the deletion of tables in the SQL server database, the following code is used:

```
USE AdventureWorks2012;
GO
CREATE TRIGGER prevent
ON DATABASE
FOR DROP_TABLE
AS
RAISERROR ('Tables cannot be droped',10, 1)
ROLLBACK
GO
```

Once the trigger is created if a user attempts to drop a table with foreign key constraints, the constraint will be automatically used to prevent this instead of the trigger as follows:

```
DROP TABLE HumanResources.Employee;
Output
Msg 3726, Level 16, State 1, Line 1
```

Could not drop object 'HumanResources.Employee' because it is referenced by a FOREIGN KEY constraint.

The constraint prevents the dropping of the table. However, if an attempt is made to drop a standalone table without constraints, the trigger will be used to prevent the DROP statement as follows:

```
DROP TABLE HumanResources.shift1;
Tables cannot be droped
Msg 3609, Level 16, State 2, Line 1
```

The transaction ended in the trigger. The batch has been aborted.

The DROP was prevented by the trigger.

Table Level Triggers and Data History Maintenance

The history of data changes is very important for consistent reporting and trend analysis. For example, if an employee is transferred from one department to another during the year, the business is still interested in knowing the current and previous employee positions. The history of these employee position changes is required for end-of-year analysis. Table level triggers can be used to maintain this history by inserting the previous employee positions into a department history table. Thus every time an employee record is updated, the previous and updated rows will be available for analysis. Triggers can be written to fire if there is an update to any column of the table or only if a specified column of the table is updated. This special column monitoring is a feature used to manage slowly changing dimensions in data warehouse applications.

SQL Server AFTER UPDATE Triggers

SQL server AFTER UPDATE triggers are fired after a row has been updated. SQL server uses two internal tables called INSERTED and DELETED to store modified rows. Once a row is deleted or updated, its original values are transferred to the DELETED table. When a row is inserted, its new values are stored in the INSERTED table. T-SQL triggers are used to retrieve these DELETED rows and insert them into a history table. The rows in the history table are then used for data history preservation. For example, the following trigger is used to maintain employee department history:

```
USE AdventureWorks2012;
GO
IF OBJECT_ID ('HumanResources.DeptHistory', 'TR') IS NOT
    NULL
DROP TRIGGER HumanResources.DeptHistory;
GO
CREATE TRIGGER HumanResources.DeptHistory
ON HumanResources.EmployeeDepartmentHistory
AFTER UPDATE
AS
BEGIN
INSERT INTO HumanResources.EmployeeDepartmentHistory
SELECT deleted. BusinessEntityID, deleted.DepartmentID,
    deleted. ShiftID,
deleted.StartDate,GETDATE(),GETDATE() FROM DELETED;
END
GO
```

This trigger will insert the previous updated employee department row of into the HumanResources.EmployeeDepartmentHistory table. For example if the department of employee 30 is updated from 7 to 10, the trigger ensures that the initial row with department 7 is maintained as shown.

This statement returns the initial employee department history of employee 30:

```
SELECT * FROM HumanResources.EmployeeDepartmentHistory
WHERE BusinessEntityID = 30;
Outputs
```

Business EntityID	Department ID	Shift ID	Start Date	End Date	Modified Date
30	7	1	2003-03-02	NULL	2003-03-01 00:00:00.000

Table 12.6

The departmentid of employee 30 is now updated from 7 to 10 as follows:

```
UPDATE HumanResources.EmployeeDepartmentHistory
SET DepartmentID = 10 WHERE BusinessEntityID =30;
```

The trigger inserts the original row in to the HumanResources. EmployeeDepartmentHistory table. Thus the employee will now have two entries in the table, maintaining the history as required.

The table is now queried to see the row inserted by the trigger:

```
SELECT * FROM HumanResources.EmployeeDepartmentHistory
WHERE BusinessEntityID = 30;
```

This outputs the following table:

Business EntityID	Department ID	Shift ID	Start Date	End Date	Modified Date
30	7	1	2003-03-02	2012-05-16	2012-05-16 10:57:53.197
30	10	1	2003-03-02	NULL	2003-03-01 00:00:00.000

Table 12.7

The trigger inserted the second row where departmentid is 7 thus maintaining the employment history of the employee. Notice that the trigger fires for any column update on the table. To specify that the trigger should only fire after updates of the DepartmentID column the CREATE section of the trigger should be rewritten as follows:

```
CREATE TRIGGER HumanResources.DeptHistory
ON HumanResources.EmployeeDepartmentHistory
AFTER UPDATE
AS IF UPDATE(DepartmentID)
BEGIN
```

Oracle AFTER UPDATE Triggers

The principles of triggers are the same as in SQL server. The code and method are slightly different. Oracle maintains the original and new values of updated columns with correlated variables called :old and :new. For the employee table, the original and new values can be accessed in triggers using the variable.column name (for old values :old.employee_id, :old.department_id and for new values :new. employee_id, :new.department_id) for each column. For example, a trigger can be built on the employee table that updates the job_history table with a new row containing the original job_id values every time an employee's job_id changes. For this trigger to be successful, the in-built trigger called UPDATE_JOB_HISTORY should be disabled to avoid conflicts.

```
CREATE OR REPLACE TRIGGER emp_job_hist
AFTER UPDATE OF job_id ON employees
FOR EACH ROW
BEGIN
INSERT INTO job_history
VALUES (:old.employee_id,sysdate,sysdate + 365,:old.
    job_id,:old.department_id);
END;
```

The trigger is created. It is set to insert the old employee job details into the Job_history table every time an employee job_id changes. For example, the current job_id of employee 201 is displayed as follows:

```
SELECT * FROM employees WHERE employee_id = 201;
```
Output (subset of columns)

EMPLOYEE_ID	FIRST_NAME	LAST_NAME	JOB_ID	SALARY
201	Michael	Hartstein	MK_MAN	13000

Table 12.8

The output shows that the current job_id of employee 210 is MK_MAN. The following statement displays job history details of employee 201 is as follows:

```
SELECT * FROM Job_history WHERE employee_id = 201;
```

EMPLOYEE _ID	START_DATE	END_DATE	JOB_ID	DEPARTMENT _ID
201	17-FEB-96	19-DEC-99	MK_REP	20

Table 12.9

The output shows that employee 201 had a previous job_id of MK_REP. The employee job_id is now updated in the employees table as follows:

```
UPDATE employees SET job_id = 'SH_CLERK' WHERE
    employee_id = 201;
```

This UPDATE statement changes the job_id of employee 201 from MK_MAN to SH_CLERK in the employees table. The trigger then inserts the original job_id MK_MAN into the job_history table. The job_history table now contains a record of this change as shown below:

```
SELECT * FROM Job_history WHERE employee_id = 201;
```

EMPLOYEE _ID	START_DATE	END_DATE	JOB_ID	DEPARTMENT _ID
201	17-FEB-96	19-DEC-99	MK_REP	20
201	16-MAY-12	16-MAY-13	MK_MAN	20

Table 12.10

T-SQL Table Variables with the UPDATE OUTPUT Clause

T-SQL UPDATES have some interesting options. It is sometimes necessary to keep an audit trail of modified values. For example, in data warehousing applications the old values of slowly changing dimensions are needed for consistent reporting and analysis. Triggers can be used to record these changes, but another option in T-SQL is to use the OUTPUT clause with a table variable. This clause can be used to capture the old and new values for each modified row. This example explores programmable T-SQL, which is covered in the T-SQL procedural section of this book (see Part two). This example can be reviewed after the reader has gone through the SQL procedural section.

For example, the following code creates a table variable used to store the old and new values. The UPDATE statement is then used to update the rate of the first three employees in the HumanResources. EmployeePayHistory Table. The OUTPUT clause is used to capture these changes by automatically querying the internal DELETED and INSERTED tables. The values are then inserted into the @AuditTable variable. It uses the deleted.column_name function to capture the old column values and uses the inserted.column_name function to capture the new column values.

```
DECLARE @AuditTable table(
Business_id int,
Old_rate money,
New_rate money,
ModifiedDate datetime);
UPDATE TOP(3) HumanResources.EmployeePayHistory
SET Rate = Rate + 20, ModifiedDate = GETDATE()
OUTPUT inserted.BusinessEntityID,
deleted.Rate,--Records the old rate value
inserted.Rate,--Records the new rate vale
inserted.ModifiedDate
```

INTO @AuditTable;

SELECT * FROM @AuditTable;--Prints all the changed values

Output

Business_id	Old_rate	New_rate	ModifiedDate
1	125.50	145.50	2012-07-09 11:06:47.267
2	63.4615	83.4615	2012-07-09 11:06:47.267
3	43.2692	63.2692	2012-07-09 11:06:47.267

Table 12.11

The SELECT statement retrieves all the updated records stored in the @AuditTable variable. The UPDATE statement uses the TOP function to UPDATE only the TOP 3 rows of the HumanResources. EmployeePayHistory table. Also note that the UPDATE statement updates two columns. The output of this table variable could then be inserted into a history table for history preservation.

Conclusion

This chapter covered the creation of advanced objects in databases. The chapter also included new SQL server 2012 and Oracle 11gcomponents. This chapter should be reviewed once Part two of this book has been covered.

Chapter Thirteen

Overview

This chapter covers the tuning of SQL statements and databases. The bulk of the tuning activities will be performed by the database administrator. However, developers and business analysts can provide insight into what needs to be tuned. For example the business analyst could be aware of the most common business queries. This information can be used by the DBA to tune the source tables.

SQL Performance Tuning

The goal of performance tuning is to eliminate performance bottlenecks in your programs. This is manifested by long response times during program operation. Performance may degrade due to several issues, including system resources such as memory and CPU functioning overcapacity; overloaded input output network traffic; deadlocks where there are interdependent request for the same resources by competing programs; and poor system design. Note that performance tuning is an ongoing concern and should be executed throughout the life of an application.

The SQL developer should liaise with the owners of business processes and IT components in order to optimise overall performance. Most overcapacity performance bottlenecks can be resolved by scheduling resource intensive operations to run during off-peak periods. Another infrastructure strategy is to deploy a pervasive grid of on-demand computing, storage, and network resources with dynamic provisioning.

Tuning the Business Process

The business process is sometimes the biggest source of performance degradation. The developer should collaborate with business analysts to optimise the business process. For example, there might be too many unnecessary business reconciliations in an ETL application. These reconciliations can be eliminated by designating one system as the single source of truth. In OLTP systems, performance might degrade due to validations during data capture. For example, the business process might require names and addresses to be validated at the point of capture. This process can be reengineered so that the validations are performed using a faster batch ETL data quality job.

The Optimiser

Oracle and SQL server use a query optimiser to generate a set of plans detailing how a query is to be executed. The least expensive plan with the shortest data access path will be selected and used. These plans are generated based on the structure of the database, the query, available access paths, and previous execution statistics. SQL tuning is geared to influence how the optimiser generates these execution plans. The tuning bottom-line is that, since the developer understands the business logic and usage of queries, they can persuade the optimiser to generate better execution plans.

Schema Design for Performance OLAP or OLTP

Performance tuning begins with the database design. The database design should reflect its intended purpose. SQL statements perform differently on databases designed to support OLTP (Online Transaction Processing) and OLAP (Online Analytical Processing) systems. Generally, relational structures such as indexes, which improve data retrieval, have a detrimental effect on updates and inserts. These two contrasting interests must be carefully monitored during tuning. Ideally, these two types of database should be separated within the business environment.

OLTP system databases are designed to support very dynamic business activities with millions of daily transactions. These databases are usually normalised with many tables, B-tree indexes, and joins. Most queries in these databases should affect very few rows. SELECT queries will run faster using B-tree indexes that avoid full table scans. Since INSERT, UPDATE, and DELETE queries also manipulate a small number of rows, the performance degradation incurred because of the B-tree indexes on these tables is relatively small.

OLAP databases are designed to manipulate large chunks of data. They are used in business primarily to support management decisions through data analysis. They are typically denormalised data warehouses with fewer tables, joins, and indexes. This design reduces the number of joins required for SELECT queries implicitly improving their performance. The lack of B-tree indexes also encourages full table scans that can improve I/O of large SELECT queries. The reduced number of indexes also improves the bulk INSERT and UPDATE performance.

It is common practice to drop and recreate all indexes before and after bulk load batch jobs.

Constraints and Performance

Using constraints rather than triggers for referential integrity also improves performance. Defining all unique, check, not null, primary, and foreign key constraints assists the optimiser to produce optimal execution plans. They also reduce the occurrence of expensive SELECT DISTINCT and OUTER JOIN queries.

Choosing the correct data type for table columns also improves performance by optimising storage and eliminating expensive implicit and explicit data type conversions.

Denormalising OLTP Databases for Performance

If all the business reporting is performed on OLTP databases, some denormalisation can be used to source high load SELECT queries. This denormalisation is achieved by using materialised views in Oracle and indexed views in SQL server. These views store pre-computed complex data from several tables. They are generally updated when their base objects are updated thus any queries that require the complex data can just get it from the view without going through all the calculations and joins at execution time.

Tuning SQL Statements

SQL statements are also used by the optimiser to generate the execution plan, thus writing efficient relational queries that use efficient relational objects such as indexes will improve execution plan generation and thus performance. As a general rule, always return the least possible number of rows and columns. The optimiser uses both the conditions and column list to generate an execution plan, with the conditions taking a higher precedence. Fully qualifying column names in SQL statements will also help produce optimal execution plans.

Displaying Execution Plans

The execution plan is used to analyse how a certain statement is executed by the database. It can be used to verify that the statement is being executed in the best possible way. The execution plan for SQL server can be seen by setting the Include Actual Execution Plan option from the query context menu (Query→Include Actual Execution Plan) of the management studio or by setting the SHOWPLAN_TEXT ON optimiser property. For Oracle, the execution plan is available by default. The plans can be examined by clicking on the EXECUTION PLAN tab of the results window.

The execution plan displays the cost of each individual operation, number of affected rows, join order, indexes used, predicates, tables used, etc. The execution plans of Oracle and SQL server are presented differently but they relay approximately the same information. For example, the execution plan for the retrieval of an employee's details from the SQL server employees table is as follows:

```
USE AdventureWorks2012;
GO
SELECT FirstName,LastName,NationalIDNumber FROM
    HumanResources.Employee e, Person.Person p
```

WHERE e.BusinessEntityID = 205

AND p.BusinessEntityID =e.BusinessEntityID;

After the query is executed, clicking on the execution plan window displays the execution plan. Moving the mouse over the displayed elements of the execution plan shows the execution details.

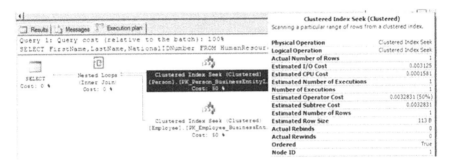

Fig 13.1

The second method is to use the SET SHOWPLAN_TEXT ON statement before the query as follows:

USE AdventureWorks2012;

GO

SET SHOWPLAN_TEXT ON;

SELECT FirstName,LastName,NationalIDNumber FROM

HumanResources.Employee e, Person.Person p

WHERE e.BusinessEntityID = 205

AND p.BusinessEntityID =e.BusinessEntityID;

The following plan is displayed:

StmtText

|--Nested LOOPs(Inner Join)

|--Clustered Index Seek(OBJECT:([AdventureWorks2012

].[Person].[Person].[PK_Person_BusinessEntityID] AS

[p]), SEEK:([p].[BusinessEntityID]=(205)) ORDERED
FORWARD)
|--Clustered Index Seek(OBJECT:([AdventureW
orks2012].[HumanResources].[Employee].
[PK_Employee_BusinessEntityID] AS [e]), SEEK:([e].
[BusinessEntityID]=(205)) ORDERED FORWARD)

Once the tuning is finished always remember to switch of the
SHOWPLAN_TEXT function with the following command.

SET SHOWPLAN_TEXT OFF;

Oracle Execution Plans

In Oracle, the execution plan can be retrieved by two methods. The
first method is to use the Explain plan of the query editor. The second
more detailed method is to retrieve the plan from a temporary table
called PLAN_TABLE. The first method uses the explain tab of the
query editor as follows:

```
SELECT e.first_name, e.last_name, e.job_id FROM employees
    e, jobs j
WHERE employee_id = 203
AND e.job_id = j.job_id;
```

Explain

Query Plan

Operation	Options	Object	Rows	Time	Cost	Bytes	Filter Predicates *	Access Predicates
SELECT STATEMENT			1	1	1	28		
TABLE ACCESS	BY INDEX ROWID	EMPLOYEES	1	1	1	28		
INDEX	UNIQUE SCAN	EMP_EMP_ID_PK	1	1	0			"EMPLOYEE_ID" = 203

* Unindexed columns are shown in red

Index Columns

Owner	Table Name	Index Name	Used in Plan	Columns	Uniqueness	Status	Index Type	Join Index
HR	EMPLOYEES	EMP_DEPARTMENT_IX		DEPARTMENT_ID	NONUNIQUE	VALID	NORMAL	NO
		EMP_MANAGER_IX		MANAGER_ID	NONUNIQUE	VALID	NORMAL	NO
		EMP_EMP_ID_PK	✓	EMPLOYEE_ID	UNIQUE	VALID	NORMAL	NO
		EMP_EMAIL_UK		EMAIL	UNIQUE	VALID	NORMAL	NO
		EMP_NAME_IX		LAST_NAME,FIRST_NAME	NONUNIQUE	VALID	NORMAL	NO
		EMP_JOB_IX		JOB_ID	NONUNIQUE	VALID	NORMAL	NO

Fig13.2

The Oracle Plan_table method uses the EXPLAIN PLAN FOR statement:

> EXPLAIN PLAN FOR SELECT e.first_name, e.last_name,
> e.job_id FROM employees e, jobs j
> WHERE employee_id = 203
> AND e.job_id = j.job_id;
> After the query is executed the plan table is queried as
> follows:
> SELECT * FROM PLAN_TABLE;

A subset of the resulting table is below:

Fig 13.3

There are automatic DBMS tools that can be used to identify and propose changes to poorly performing SQL statements. A careful examination of the execution plan can be informative about the reasons for poor performance such as high CPU or I/O costs. As a general guide, once these performance issues have been identified, restructure the statement and test for performance.

Restructuring SQL Statements for Performance

Since the developer understands the business requirements, poorly performing statements can be rearranged for better performance. As a general rule, always use an INNER JOIN where appropriate and always keep the statement simple with minimal nesting.

The following are tips of things to avoid in SQL statements.

It is always better to avoid SELECT DISTINCT and OUTER JOINS where appropriate. SELECT DISTINCTS can be avoided through the use of correct primary and foreign key relationships. OUTER JOINS can be avoided by defining a column in the joined table to handle the exempted event. For example in chapter four (table 4.10) an outer join was used to return reviewed products. This join could be avoided by creating a review flag column in the Production. ProductReview table. It is also quite costly to run SELECT * queries and they should be avoided as much as possible. Subqueries are also very expensive and should be substituted with inner joins where possible. Excessive I/O can also be avoided by using stored procedures and functions.

The root cause of most of the SQL inefficiencies will be in the WHERE clause conditions. Inner joins are the most efficient but they start losing their efficiency when they perform transformations such as implicit or explicit data type conversions and functional calculations. This is because the indexes on the tables will be ignored. For example, in the Oracle HR schema the following statement transforms the employee_ids into characters in the WHERE clause:

```
SELECT e.first_name, e.last_name, j.start_date, j.end_date
    FROM employees e, job_history j
WHERE TO_CHAR (e.employee_id) = '200'
AND TO_CHAR(e.employee_id) = TO_CHAR(j.employee_id);
```

Looking at the execution plan below it is obvious that the index on the employees table is ignored and a full table scan is initiated. The execution plan is also very complex and multilayered. This reduces the efficiency of the SQL as indicated by the high costs of (21). The cost is highlighted in red. The only way to overcome this is to use a function-based index.

Operation	Options	Object	Rows	Time	*Cost*	Bytes	Filter Predicates *	Access Predicates
SELECT STATEMENT			1	1	*6*	39		
HASH JOIN			1	1	*6*	39		TO_CHAR("E"."EMPLOYEE_ID") = TO_CHAR("J"."EMPLOYEE_ID")
VIEW		index$_join$_001	1	1	*3*	19		
HASH JOIN								ROWID = ROWID
INDEX	FAST FULL SCAN	EMP_NAME_IX	1	1	*1*	19		
INDEX	FAST FULL SCAN	EMP_EMP_ID_PK	1	1	*1*	19	TO_CHAR("E"."EMPLOYEE_ID") = '200'	
TABLE ACCESS	FULL	JOB_HISTORY	2	1	*3*	40	TO_CHAR("J"."EMPLOYEE_ID") = '200'	

Fig 13.4

If the data conversions are removed and the following statement is used:

```
SELECT e.first_name, e.last_name, j.start_date, j.end_date
    FROM employees e, job_history j
WHERE e.employee_id = 200
AND e.employee_id = j.employee_id;
```

The execution plan below shows that the indexes are used and a full table scan is avoided. The execution plan is also much simpler. Notice that the overall cost is reduced from 21 to 6.

Operation	Options	Object	Rows	Time	Cost	Bytes	Filter Predicates *	Access Predicates
SELECT STATEMENT			2	1	2	78		
NESTED LOOPS			2	1	2	78		
TABLE ACCESS	BY INDEX ROWID	EMPLOYEES	1	1	1	19		
INDEX	UNIQUE SCAN	EMP_EMP_ ID_PK	1	1	0			"E" . "EMPLOYEE_ ID" = 200
TABLE ACCESS	BY INDEX ROWID	JOB_HISTORY	2	1	1	40		
INDEX	RANGE SCAN	JHIST_ EMPLOYEE_IX	2	1	0			"J" . "EMPLOYEE_ ID" = 200

Fig 13.5

As a general rule, avoid the use of data conversions and functions in the WHERE clause of SQL statements.

Other negative operators such as the NOT LIKE and <> should also be avoided when possible. They can generally be replaced with an inner join, EXISTS, and IN operators.

Using SQL Hints to Influence the Optimiser

Since the developer understands the database schema and potential data profiles of the tables, he or she can instruct the optimiser about how to generate specific execution plans. The developer could know the number of rows in newly loaded tables or new structural table changes. Since this information is not yet available to the optimiser, execution tips could be used to influence the execution order at execution time. These optimiser execution tips are called hints. These hints should be constantly managed and updated in tune with database changes. The optimiser generally generates the most effective execution plans, so hints should be used as a last resort.

The classification of hints is not universal, but the three general types of hints include JOIN, QUERY, and TABLE hints. Hints in SQL server are very declarative while in Oracle they are inserted like comments.

JOIN Hints

Joint hits are used to instruct the optimiser on how it should perform a join between two tables. This is helpful in situations where many tables are being joined. The goal is to order the joins so the most restrictive joins returning the fewest rows are first executed. Use this hint only when you know something about the table that is unknown by the optimiser. For example, when the employees, department, and job_history tables are joined in the Oracle schema, the optimiser can be instructed to join the employees and job_history table first before joining the result to the departments table. Oracle uses the /*+ORDERED */or /*+LEADING*/ hint to force this join order as follows:

```
SELECT /*+ ORDERED */ first_name, last_name,
    department_name,j.job_id
FROM employees e, departments d,job_history j
WHERE e.employee_id = j.employee_id
AND e.department_id = d.department_id;
```

With SQL server, in order to force the join table order using a hint, the SET FORCEPLAN optimiser property should be used. When this property is switched ON, the optimiser will join the tables as they appear, and the HASH keyword is required to define the table order. For example:

```
SET FORCEPLAN ON;
GO
SELECT h.BusinessEntityID, e.NationalIDNumber,d.Name
FROM HumanResources.EmployeeDepartmentHistory h
    INNER HASH JOIN HumanResources.Employee e ON
h.BusinessEntityID=e.BusinessEntityID JOIN
HumanResources.Department d ON d.DepartmentID =
    h.DepartmentID
WHERE d.DepartmentID = 1;
```

In this example, the hashed h.BusinessEntityID=e.BusinessEntityID join is executed before any other join.

Table Hints

Table hits are used to instruct the optimiser about how to access tables. Like with all hints, this method should only be used if the developer knows details about the table that are unavailable to the optimiser. For example, the developer can instruct the optimiser to use a full table scan rather than an index scan for a query. For example, in the Oracle HR schema, the following statement forces the optimiser to do a full table scan when accessing the employee table. (Note that with Oracle hints, the table names must be aliased):

```
SELECT /*+ FULL(e) */ first_name, last_name
FROM employees e
WHERE e.employee_id = 100;
```

The SQL server version is uses the WITH statement. The following example instructs the optimiser to access the Person. Person table using an index called XI_Person_LastName_FirstName_MiddleName.

```
USE AdventureWorks2012;
GO
SELECT LastName,FirstName FROM Person.Person
WITH( INDEX (IX_Person_LastName_FirstName_MiddleName) )
WHERE BusinessEntityID = 67;
```

Query Hints

These are hints used to optimise a specific statement. They can be used to tell the optimiser what specific values are important for the query optimisation. They do not tell the optimiser how to generate the execution plans. For example, the following code instructs the Oracle optimiser to optimise the retreval of the first five rows for employees who work for department 50. Note that all the qualifying rows will be retrieved but the first five will be done faster.

```
SELECT /*+ FIRST_ROWS(5) */ e.first_name, e.last_name,e.
    department_id
FROM employees e
WHERE e.department_id = 50;
```

The optimiser optimises the retrieval of the first five rows using an index while the rest of the retrieved rows are retrieved at a slower rate.

SQL server uses the option clause. For example, the developer might know that the optimiser has sufficient optimisation statistics for marketing specialist jobtitles in the employee table. The following hint tells the optimiser to use the marketing specialist statistics to execute the query to find design engineers. Note that only the design engineers are returned, the marketing specialist hint is just there to provide the statistics.

```
DECLARE @Jtitle nvarchar(30)= 'Design Engineer';
SELECT NationalIDNumber, JobTitle FROM
    HumanResources.Employee e
WHERE E.JobTitle = @Jtitle
OPTION ( OPTIMIZE FOR (@Jtitle ='Marketing Specialist'));
```

Tuning the Database for Performance

Databases have automatic tuning capabilities that the database administrator (DBA) will be using throughout. The tuning will include optimising the database parameters, log files, data storage, and compression. Other tuning activities include deleting unused indexes, recreating disorganised indexes, and deleting unused triggers.

The DBA can also improve performance by partitioning large database tables. Partitions are used to logically break a table into smaller chunks. This reduces contention for table data because a query can manipulate an individual partition, leaving the other partitions free for other queries. Range and list partitions can also be used to target and improve query performance. For example, a year-range partition can be created that partitions a table data by year, so a query will use only use the stated year partition, avoiding a full table scan.

The DBA can also create index organised and clustered tables to improve performance. Clusters are groups of tables that are physically stored together. The developer can identify tables that are constantly being queried together. Once these tables are stored in a cluster, queries on these tables will naturally be faster. With index organised tables, the table data is stored in the index, and queries on the table become faster.

Tuning Transactions

With transactions, the weaker the isolation level, the faster the query will run. Thus, for all non-critical transactions, only table snapshots should be used. Note that the isolation level is totally dependent on business transaction requirements. The developer should work closely with the business analyst to find areas where transactions can be increasing isolated.

Conclusion

This chapter covered the key SQL performance issues. It should act as a guide for creating optimal database designs and SQL statements.

PART TWO

Overview

Part two focuses on the procedural extension of SQL. It provides the fundamental concepts of PL/SQL and programmable T-SQL. Relevant transactional and data warehousing concepts are fully covered.

PL /SQL Programmable T-SQL Overview

Oracle and SQL server have extended the functionality of SQL by introducing procedural programming constructs. The Oracle extension is called PL/SQL (Procedural Language SQL), while in SQL server it is called Programmable T-SQL. They are both powerful extensions with constructs such as cursors, flow control, conditional processing, user-defined functions, and stored procedures. These constructs are particularly important for complex transactional processing, where a set of mutually dependent SQL statements are executed together. There are several other advantages for this extension:

- Both languages are tightly integrated with SQL, the standard database language. Thus, most SQL constructs are available for use.

- Exception handling. Errors in PL/SQL statements can be caught and managed so that the application shuts down in a controlled and consistent manner.

- Code reuse: frequently used PL/SQL statements can be integrated into functions and procedures for reuse.

- The object-oriented-programming concept of encapsulation can be implemented with stored procedures and user-defined functions.

- Better performance: the use of stored procedures improves performance because one execution plan is used to execute several SQL statements on the database server, reducing the network overhead and improving throughput of individual SQL statements.

- Easy maintenance: once the code has been written and tested, several applications can start using them. Any changes required will only be made in the single stored procedure.

- Portability. Since the code is compiled and stored in the oracle database, it can be used by any application which connects to an oracle database.

Oracle PL/SQL

PL/SQL enables the use of procedural constructs available in other third generation languages. It combines powerful procedural processing language constructs such as conditional logic (IF THEN ELSE), sequence (GOTO), and iteration (LOOPS) with the powerful data manipulation capabilities of SQL. PL/SQL helps programmers group a collection of related SQL statements in blocks for repeated reuse. There are three types of blocks, including anonymous blocks, procedures, and functions. Anonymous blocks are unnamed and are not stored for re-execution and sharing within the database. They can only be reused by saving them in a script. Functions and procedures are stored and can be reused or shared with other applications. Functions and procedures are collectively called subprograms.

Anonymous Blocks

Anonymous blocks are made up of clearly defined sections. Each block section groups related declarations of variables and statements. Each block is made up of three sections:

- The DECLARATION section (optional) starts with reserved word (DECLARE).

- The EXECUTION section (mandatory) starts and ends with (BEGIN . . . END;).

- The EXCEPTION HANDLING section (optional) starts with (EXCEPTION).

The Declaration Section

This section is optional and starts with the DECLARE keyword. Variables and constants are declared and optionally assigned values. Each declaration must end with a semicolon. These variables can have any SQL data type such as DATE, NUMBER, VARCHAR, CHAR, and INTEGER. Composite PL/SQL data types such as RECORDS and CURSORS are also declared in this section. These variables and constants are used for data manipulation in the execution section. The declaration section ends implicitly when the execution section starts with the BEGIN keyword.

The Execution Section

This section is mandatory and starts with the BEGIN keyword. The BEGIN keyword implicitly terminates the DECLARE section. All of the required programming logic is written in this section. Only declared variables can be called in this section. Values are assigned to variables using the assignment symbol (:=). Each statement must end with a semicolon. Generally these values are retrieved from the database using SQL statements. Exception (error) handlers are also implemented within this section. The execution section ends with the END keyword that terminates the block with a semicolon.

The Exception Section

This section is optional and starts with the EXCEPTION keyword. There are two types of exception handlers: user-defined and predefined exception handlers. Exception handlers are used to 'gracefully' terminate programs when errors are encountered. Graceful error handling means returning an error message to the user describing what has gone wrong. Error handlers can also include cleaning up operations. These operations might include releasing tied up memory resources or dropping partially updated tables so your application can be rerun seamlessly. An example of an anonymous block is as follows:

```
DECLARE--Declare section (optional)
Variable_Name Data type;
EXCEPTION--(optional)
BEGIN--Execution section (mandatory)
Variable_Name := value
EXEPTION WHEN NO_DATA--Exception section (Optional)
```

THEN do something;

END;

General Guidelines

Comments are used to document and improve readability of PL/SQL code. Single-line comments begin with a double hyphen (--) anywhere on a line and extend to the end of the line. Multi-line comments begin with a slash-asterisk (/*) and end with an asterisk-slash (*/).During bug fixing it is necessary to display the changing values of your variables. Variable values are printed on screen using the DBMS_OUTPUT. PUT_LINE function.

PL/SQL Variables and Constants

Variables are used to temporarily store data during the execution of a PL/SQL block. Variables can be assigned any SQL or PL/SQL data type such as RECORD, DATE, NUMBER, VARCHAR, CHAR, INTEGER, etc. The main advantage of using variables is that their value can change during execution so they change the input calculation context. For example a payroll program can use variables to process different employee numbers. Constants are similar to variables, but their value cannot change during execution. You must assign a value to the constant during its declaration. The keyword CONSTANT must also be used to define a constant. Variables can be assigned to only a single value at a time. Cursors and records variables are used to handle composite value assignments. Identifiers are used to name variables. Most alphanumeric characters and symbols can be used to name identifiers except hyphens, slashes, and spaces.

Declaration of Variables and Constants

By default, variables are initialised to NULL on creation. Variables and constants are declared in the DECLARE section and have the following syntax:

```
DECLARE
Variable_Name Data type;
Constant_Name CONSTANT data type;
For example:
DECLARE
--Variable declaration.
Salary NUMBER;
Country VARCHAR2(28);
Salary_increase CONSTANT NUMBER := 1000;
```

Variable Value Assignment

The assignment of a value to a variable can be done either in the DECLARE or EXECUTION section. Note that you can only assign values to variables that have been declared. There are three methods of assigning values to variables. Including directly assigning a value to variables when they are being declared (:=), using SELECT INTO and stored procedures and functions:

The following example illustrated the direct method.

```
Variable_Name Data type: = value;
For example:
Salary NUMBER := 10000;.
```

This assigns the Value 10000 to the NUMBER variable called 'salary'.

Variables can also be assigned values with the SELECT INTO statement in the execution section of a block. This method is used to assign variable values with data from a database. The variable must have been declared for this method to be used. For example:

```
DECLARE
my_name VARCHAR2(128);
my_salary number(9);
my_id number(4) := 200;
BEGIN
SELECT salary, First_name
INTO my_salary, my_name FROM employees
WHERE employee_id = my_id ;
--Display current variable values
DBMS_OUTPUT.PUT_LINE ('The Salary of Employee' ||
    my_name || 'is '|| my_salary );
End;
Output
The Salary of Employee Jennifer is 4400
```

The example above selects the first name and the salary of an employee whose employee_id is equal to 200 (employee_id variable was declared and assigned the value 200 in the DECLARE section). These values are then assigned to the my_name and my_salary variables using the SELECT INTO statement. Note that these two variables have already been declared in the DECLARE section. The DBMS_ OUTPUT.PUT_LINE function displays the value of the variables.

The final method of assigning a value to a variable is by using subprograms (functions and procedures). With procedures a value can be assigned to a variable using an output parameter. The statements in the procedure will assign a value to the variable. For example the following procedure is used to assign a value to the my_salary parameter:

add_salary (my_id, **my_salary**);

Functions are the preferred method of assigning values to variables. They always return a value which can be assigned to the variable. The syntax for assigning a value to a variable using a function is as follows:

Variable_name := function_name (actual_parameter);

There is more on procedures and functions later.

Scope of Variables

It is sometimes necessary to nest PL/SQL blocks. In these cases, the visibility of variables declared in each block is determined by where it is declared.

The scope of a variable dictates where it can be used in nested PL/SQL blocks. Variables declared at the parent level block (outer) can be used by all the sub blocks (inner), while those declared in a sub block cannot be referenced by the outer block. For example:

DECLARE

--Start of outer block. The variables declared here are visible in all inner blocks

```
my_salary NUMBER(8);
emp_id NUMBER(6) := 200;
BEGIN
SELECT salary INTO my_salary FROM employees WHERE
    employee_id = emp_id;
DBMS_OUTPUT.PUT_LINE ('The outer block variables(
    my_salary) is '|| my_salary );
DECLARE
```

--Start of inner block. The outer block variable(my_salary and emp_id) are visible here. salary_increase NUMBER(8,2) :=100;

```
new_sal NUMBER(8,2):= 1000 ;
```

--new_sal is visible only within this inner block.

```
BEGIN
new_sal := my_salary + new_sal;
DBMS_OUTPUT.PUT_LINE ('my_salary is now added to
    new_sal and is = '|| new_sal );
END;--End of inner block.
END;--End of outer block.
Output
The outer block variables( my_salary) is 4400
my_salary is now added to new_sal and is = 5400
```

In this example the outer block variable called my_salary is visible throughout the blocks while the inner block variable new_sal is only visible within the inner block.

PL/SQL Control Constructs

They are the most useful PL/SQL extension to SQL. It grants SQL the access to critical procedural programming process flow control mechanisms such as iteration, conditional logic, and sequence control. These extensions facilitate the processing of very complex business data manipulation logic without using more complex and difficult languages such as c++, visual basic, and Java.

Conditional Control Statements

Conditional control statements permit the programmer to take alternative actions when certain conditions are true, false or null (unknown). It is very similar to the CASE expression. In PL/SQL it can be constructed with the following common IF-THEN-ELSE syntax:

```
IF condition
THEN
Action 1;
ELSE
Action 2;
END IF;
```

The IF clause checks the validity of a given condition, the THEN clause states the action to execute if the condition is true, and the ELSE clause states the action to take if condition is false or null. In a situation where you have to check for more than one condition, the ELSEIF clause is used to test the other conditions and provide an alternative action. The syntax for this is:

```
IF condition1 (a = b)
THEN
Action 1;
ELSIF condtion2 (a > b) THEN
Action 2;
ELSE
Action 3;
END IF
```

In this situation if condition1 (a = b) is true, Action 1 is executed. Alternatively if condition2 (a >b) is true, Action 2 is executed. However, if both conditions are false, then Action 3 is executed. For example:

```
DECLARE
a NUMBER(1):= 1;
b NUMBER(1):= 3;
BEGIN
IF a = b
THEN
DBMS_OUTPUT.PUT_LINE ('The number' ||a|| 'is equal to'||
    b );
ELSIF a > b
THEN
DBMS_OUTPUT.PUT_LINE ('The number' ||a|| 'is greater
    than' || b );
ELSE
```

DBMS_OUTPUT.PUT_LINE ('The number' ||a|| 'is less than'
   || b);
END IF;
END;
Output
The number 1 is less than 3

In the example the IF and ELSEIF statements return FALSE values, thus their THEN statements are not executed. Thus the ELSE statement executes and prints out the message using the DBMS_OUTPUT. PUT_LINE function.

Iterative Control Constructs

Iterative control statements are used to repeat the execution of one or more statements for a specified number of times. They generally repeat the statements while a given condition is true. LOOP statements are used for iteration. They terminate implicitly or explicitly when the condition becomes false. The status of the controlling condition is updated by an implicit or explicit counter within the LOOP. The counter must be initialised outside the LOOP. The counter itself is incremented or decremented within the LOOP until the EXIT condition becomes true. If the exit condition is not met, the LOOP will get into an infinite number of iterations.

There are three types of LOOP statements: (simple) LOOP, WHILE LOOP, and FOR LOOP.

The *simple LOOP* encloses the required statements between LOOP and END LOOP keywords. This statement is used when you need to execute a set of statements at least once. The LOOP stops when the EXIT condition is met. The general syntax is as follows:

```
DECLARE
b number(1)
BEGIN
LOOP
Execute statements;
EXIT;

--or use EXIT WHEN condition is true;

END LOOP;
END;
```

For example

```
DECLARE
counter NUMBER(1):=1;--Assign value to counter outside
    LOOP.
my_name Varchar(10);
my_id NUMBER(4):=100;
BEGIN
LOOP
SELECT First_name INTO my_name FROM employees
    WHERE employee_id =my_id ;
DBMS_OUTPUT.PUT_LINE('Employee number '||my_id||' is
    called '||my_name);
my_id := my_id + 1;--Change employee_id for next iteration of
    LOOP
```

counter := counter+1;--Increment counter for every iteration

EXIT WHEN counter = 4;--exit when counter gets to 4

END LOOP;

END;

Output

Employee number 100 is called Steven

Employee number 101 is called Neena

Employee number 102 is called Lex

In this example, a counter variable is assigned the value 1 outside the LOOP. The counter is then incremented by 1 inside the LOOP until it gets to 4, so the LOOP iterates and executes three times. The SELECT INTO statement and DBMS_OUTPUT.PUT_LINE print command are executed thrice. The LOOP exits when the counter equals 4. Notice that the my_id value is also incremented so that we have a different value for employee_id after each iteration. The result outputs three employee first_names.

The WHILE LOOP is used when you need to evaluate a condition before entering the LOOP. The iteration continues as long as the condition stays true. Once the condition becomes false the iteration stops. The exit condition can be implicit because the condition is tested before each iteration. Thus once the condition becomes false, the LOOP exits. It is optional to use the explicit EXIT WHEN clause. The general syntax is:

DECLARE

counter number(1):=0;

BEGIN

WHILE <condition>

```
LOOP statements;
END LOOP;
END;
```

We can obtain the same results from the previous example using the WHILE LOOP. In the next example, the counter is initialised outside the LOOP to 1. The counter is then incremented within the LOOP. The test condition is always evaluated after each LOOP iteration so it terminates when the counter variable becomes greater than 4. An explicit EXIT WHEN clause could be used, but it is rather unnecessary.

```
DECLARE
counter number(1):=1;
my_name Varchar(10);
my_id number(4):=100;
BEGIN
WHILE counter < 4
LOOP
SELECT First_name INTO my_name FROM employees where
    employee_id =my_id ;
DBMS_OUTPUT.PUT_LINE('Employee number '||my_id||' is
    called '||my_name);
my_id := my_id + 1;
counter := counter+1;
END LOOP;
END;
Output
Employee number 100 is called Steven
Employee number 101 is called Neena
Employee number 102 is called Lex
```

The same results are obtained using the while LOOP. The SELECT INTO statement and DBMS_OUTPUT.PUT_LINE print command are executed thrice.

The *FOR LOOP* is used when some statements are to be executed for a known or unknown number of times. The counter is automatically assigned to range/list of values until it exhausts the list of values. The range/list of values could be an explicit range/list of values or a set of values returned from a query. The LOOP implicitly exits when it has used all the values. The counter is also implicitly declared by the FOR statement. An explicit EXIT WHEN clause could be used but it is rather unnecessary because the LOOP exits when the list is exhausted. The generic syntax is:

```
DECLARE
BEGIN
FOR counter IN int1..int
LOOP statements;
END LOOP;
END;
```

The FOR LOOP is used to obtain the same results from the previous example.

```
DECLARE
my_name Varchar(10);
my_id number(4):=100;
BEGIN
FOR counter IN 2..4
LOOP
```

```
SELECT First_name INTO my_name FROM employees where
    employee_id =my_id ;
DBMS_OUTPUT.PUT_LINE('Employee number '||my_id||' is
    called '||my_name);
my_id := my_id + 1;
END LOOP;
END;
Output
Employee number 100 is called Steven
Employee number 101 is called Neena
Employee number 102 is called Lex
```

In this example, the counter variable was implicitly declared and initialised within the FOR LOOP. The counter was automatically incremented until the exit condition was attained when the counter value became 4. The counter can also be fed by a SELECT statement. For example, the following counter declaration would return the same results:

```
FOR counter IN (SELECT first_name FROM employees
    WHERE employee_id <103)
LOOP
```

Sequential Control with All Other Process Flow Controls

Sequential control constructs in PL/SQL are used to force the sequence of execution to jump to a named (labelled) section when a condition is met. Labels are not declared, they are identifiers enclosed by double angle brackets (<<>>). The GOTO command is used to execute the jump. Labels can be used to jump out of LOOPs when a certain condition is met. They are also very handy for error handling. They must precede an executable statement or a PL/SQL block. The executable statement sets the test condition that triggers the label execution. The following example uses labels in a simple search LOOP.

```
DECLARE
counter number(5):=0;
Phone_no VARCHAR2(20) ;
Counter_exit number(5);
my_name Varchar(20);
my_id number(4):=100;
search_for Varchar(50):='John';--Name to be searched.
BEGIN
```

/*assign the maximum number of LOOP iterations to the count of all employee records. This is set so that all employee records are potentially searched.*/

```
SELECT COUNT(*) INTO Counter_exit FROM employees;
LOOP
SELECT First_name, PHONE_NUMBER INTO my_name,
    Phone_no FROM employees where employee_id =my_id ;
my_id := my_id + 1;--Increment the employee_id after each
    iteration.
counter := counter+1;
```

--If the search name is found go to the label

```
IF my_name = search_for THEN GOTO Search_employees;
END IF;
```

```
EXIT WHEN counter = Counter_exit ;
END LOOP;
<<Search_employees>>--If employee found display details else
    not found.
my_id := my_id - 1;--calculate the previous employee number
    before it was incremented by the LOOP.
IF my_name = search_for THEN
DBMS_OUTPUT.PUT_LINE('The employee called '||my_
    name||' has employee_id '||my_id||'. His phone number
    is '||Phone_no);
ELSE
DBMS_OUTPUT.PUT_LINE ('There are no records '|| search_for);
END IF;
END;
```

Output:

The employee called John has employee_id 110. His phone number is 515.124.4269

The code above scrolls through each employee record and tests the retrieved name against the value of the search_for variable (john). If the name matches the variable value, then the GO TO sequential control fires and program control jumps to the stated label (<<Search_employees>>--). The LOOP is implicitly terminated. In the label, a CONDITIONAL control is used to test and print the employee name and phone number. If no match is found, the LOOP iterates until it terminates when all employee rows have been tested (the exit condition is the maximum number of employee rows). When the LOOP terminates the label <<Search_employees>>—executes and the conditional displays the 'not found' message. Cursors will be used to elegantly implement this search.

Cursors and Records

The standard variables can only contain a single value of a given type at a time. In the real world it is sometimes necessary to individually process several rows of data with different column data types. Cursors and records are used to achieve this goal. They are known as composite data types because their fields can have different scalar data types. The main functional difference between cursors and records is that cursors can store more than one row while records can only store a single row. Cursors and records are also declared in the DECLARE section. Cursors are used to store the results of queries that could be an arbitrary number of rows. Each of these cursor rows is then individually moved into records for individual processing.

Cursors

Cursors are named SELECT statements. They are specific temporary private SQL areas created in memory when an SQL query is executed. Cursors retain both the processing information and returned data of a specific SQL statement. There are two main types of PL/SQL cursors: implicit and explicit cursors. Both types have attributes that are used to track and manage them.

Records

Records are composite data types whose fields can have a combination of different data types. A record can be described as a set of individual variables assigned to a single identifier name, which is the record name. Records are generally used to store a row from a table with each record field (variable) containing a column of the row. Once a record has been declared, it becomes available for use as the data type of a record variable. The individual variables within a record can be assigned values using the assignment operator (:=) or the SELECT INTO statement. The fields in records can contain any SQL table data type. Whereas cursors can hold several rows of data, records can only contain a single row of data. Records are generally used to move cursor rows into a subprogram as a single parameter. Records are declared using the TYPE keyword. They are declared in the DECLARE section. Only declared records can be referenced. The general syntax of records is:

```
DECLARE
TYPE Record_name IS RECORD
(col_name1 col_data type, col_name2 col_data type,..);
Rec_name Record_name;
BEGIN
```

Record_name is the identifier name of the record. col_name1 and col_name2 are the identifier names of the records columns (variables). The col_datatype is the data type of each column in the record. Rec_name is the declared record variable that has a user defined data type of Record_name. The record variable is used to reference each record column within a program; the column names are qualified with the record name. The general syntax in this case will be:

```
Rec_name.col_name1 and Rec_name.col_name2
```

Declaring Record Data Types

There are two other method of declaring record column data types. The first method as previously seen is to explicitly declare the data type in line with its declaration. The second method is to align them to database table columns. In this way the record column inherits the data type of the database table columns. This second method is achieved by using the %TYPE and %ROWTYPE keywords. For example:

The %TYPE keyword is used to declare a record by aligning each record column with a table column name as follows.

```
DECLARE
TYPE emp_record IS RECORD
(emp_id employees.employee_id%type, emp_hireDate
    employees.hire_date%type, Emp_firstname employees.
    first_name%type, emp_lastname employees.
    last_name%type);
emp_rec emp_record;
BEGIN
```

In this example, the data type definition is replaced with the employees table column names followed by the %TYPE keyword. All the record columns will inherit the data type and size of the aligned employees table columns. For example, the emp_hireDate record column will inherit the employees table hire_date column DATE data type. This method is recommended because it avoids data type declaration errors and code maintenance is simpler when the table structure changes.

The final method of record declaration uses the %ROWTYPE keyword. With this method the TYPE declaration is omitted. The %ROWTYPE keyword implicitly declares a record containing all the columns of a table or cursor. This method should only be used when all the columns in a table are needed in a record. Their general syntax is:

```
DECLARE
Record_name table_name%ROWTYPE;
BEGIN
For example:
DECLARE
emp_record employees.%ROWTYPE;
BEGIN
```

In this case, emp_record will implicitly contain all the employee table columns. Each record column can be referenced by using the record name as the table qualifying name. A record variable is not required to reference each of the record columns. The general syntax for referencing each record column name is:

```
record_name.column_name;
```

For example, the employees table has employee_id, first_name, last_name, hire_date . . . columns

Thus the emp_record columns can be referenced as emp_record. employee_id, emp_record. first_name, emp_record.last_name, emp_record.hire_date. The main advantage of this type of declaration is that structural changes to the base table are dynamically propagated to the code with minimal changes.

Assigning Values to Records

Once the record has been declared, values can now be assigned to the individual columns. Just like common variables, the record columns are null after declaration. Records are initialised using either the assignment operator (:=) or the SELECT INTO statements. For example:

```
DECLARE
TYPE emp_record IS RECORD
(emp_id number(6,0), emp_hireDate DATE,
emp_firstname varchar2(25),emp_lastname varchar2(25));
emp_rec emp_record;--declare record variable.
BEGIN

--assign the value 200 to emp_id using the assignment operator.

emp_rec.emp_id := 200;

--assign values to Emp_firstname, emp_lastname,emp_hireDate
with SELECT INTO.

SELECT First_name, last_name,hire_date INTO emp_rec.emp_
    firstname, emp_rec.emp_lastname, emp_rec.emp_hireDate
FROM employees where employee_id =emp_rec.emp_id ;

--Display assigned values.

DBMS_OUTPUT.PUT_LINE('The employee called '|| emp_rec.
    emp_firstname ||' '|| emp_rec.emp_lastname ||' WAS
    Hired on '|| emp_rec.emp_hireDate);
```

END;

Output

The employee called Jennifer Whalen was hired on 09/17/2003.

In this example a record called emp_record is declared with four columns. This record data type is then assigned to a record variable called emp_rec. The emp_id column of the record variable is then assigned the value 200 using the assignment operator. The rest of the record columns are assigned values from the employee table using the SELECT INTO statement. The output displays the names and hiredate of an employee whose employee_id is equal to 200. The same results can be achieved using the %ROWTYPE keyword. The main difference here is that a record variable is not required to access the record fields.

```
DECLARE
emp_record employees%ROWTYPE;
```

--The emp_record record contains all the columns of the employees table.

```
BEGIN
```

--assign the value 200 to emp_id using the assignment operator.

```
emp_record.employee_id := 200;
```

--assign values to Emp_firstname, emp_lastname,emp_hireDate with SELECT INTO.

```
SELECT First_name, last_name, hire_date INTO emp_record.
    First_name, emp_record.last_name, emp_record.hire_date
FROM employees where employee_id =emp_record.
    employee_id;

--Display assigned values.

DBMS_OUTPUT.PUT_LINE('The employee called '|| emp_
    record.First_name ||' '|| emp_record.last_name ||' WAS
    Hired on '|| emp_record.hire_date );
END;
Output:
```

The employee called Jennifer Whalen WAS Hired on 09/17/2003.

Implicit Cursors

Implicit cursors are automatically created whenever any DML (SELECT, INSERT, UPDATE, and DELETE) statement is executed. They are also created when queries that return a single row are executed. Implicit cursors are automatically managed by PL/SQL, so no coding is required to manage them. However, informative messages can be retrieved from them using their attributes such as %FOUND, %ISOPEN, %NOTFOUND, and %ROWCOUNT. These attributes are used in a similar manner with explicit cursors.

Explicit Cursors

Explicit Cursors must be declared and associated with a specific query. The cursor name must also be a valid identifier name. The three main commands used to control a cursor are OPEN, FETCH, and CLOSE. Once the cursor is declared, the OPEN command initialises the cursor by running the associated query. The set of rows returned by the OPEN command is called the result set. The FETCH command is then used to repeatedly move each row into a set of variables or a record. Once all the rows have been moved and processed, the cursor is closed with the CLOSE command. The general declaration syntax of a cursor is:

```
DECLARE
CURSOR employee_cur IS SELECT * FROM employees;
```

The above cursor called employee_cur is associated with a query that returns all employee records from the employee table.

Opening the Cursor

The declared cursor is opened in the execution section. The OPEN command executes the associated query and identifies the qualifying rows from the query. If the FOR UPDATE clause is specified the cursor rows become locked in the database. By default, the logical pointer identifies the first row as the current row available for a fetch. The general syntax is:

```
DECLARE
CURSOR employee_cur IS SELECT * FROM employees;
BEGIN
OPEN employee_cur;
```

Fetching the Cursor

The cursor rows can either be fetched into a record or into a list of variables. Once a row has been fetched, the logical pointer moves to the next row till it gets to the last row of the cursor. This repetitive search is usually achieved using iterative LOOPS. The general syntax to move a cursor row into a list of variables is:

```
FETCH cursor_name INTO var1, var2, var3, var4;
```

In this method the variables (var1 to var4) must have been declared. The data type and scale of the variables must match the data type and scale of the cursor's associated query columns. The general syntax to search a cursor row into a record is:

```
FETCH employee_cur INTO record_name;
```

Fetching cursor rows into a record is the better way of processing cursors because it is easier to manage the data type associations between the record and the cursor. The destination record is generally declared using the %ROWTYPE keyword, using the cursor as the source table. Thus the data type of each cursor column will be the same as the data type of the record columns.

Closing the Cursor

Cursors are closed using the CLOSE command. Once the cursor is closed, the cursor rows become undefined. Memory and processing resources are released. All operations referencing the closed cursor will fail and raise the predefined exception called INVALID_CURSOR.

Trying to open an open cursor will also fail. Thus, all cursors must be explicitly closed at the end of a program.

Explicit Cursor Attributes

Explicit cursor attributes are used to manage the processing of cursors. They return useful information about the status of cursors and its result set (rows returned by the associated cursor query). These cursor attributes can only be used by procedural statements. They are called by appending them to the cursor name. They include:

Attributes	Return values
Cursor_Name%ISOPEN	TRUE if cursor is already open. FALSE otherwise
Cursor_Name%NOTFOUND	TRUE if FETCH statement returns zero rows. FALSE otherwise
Cursor_Name%ROWCOUNT	Returns the number of rows fetched so far
Cursor_Name%FOUND	TRUE if FETCH statement returns at least one row. FALSE otherwise

Table 13.1

An example is an alteration of the simple employee search program. The program searches through the employee table to find and display the details of an input employee name assigned to a variable called search_name.

```
DECLARE
CURSOR search_cursor IS SELECT * FROM employees;
search_record search_cursor%ROWTYPE;--Implicitly declare a
    record with the cursor data type.
```

```
search_name varchar2(30):='Alexander';--Name to be searched.
BEGIN
IF search_cursor%ISOPEN = FALSE THEN--check cursor
    status
OPEN search_cursor;
END IF;
LOOP
FETCH search_cursor INTO search_record;
DBMS_OUTPUT.PUT_LINE('The current name being searched
    is '||search_record.first_name );
```

--increment counter and then test if the current name is the name being searched. If so go to the label.

```
IF search_record.first_name = search_name THEN GOTO
    Search_employees;
END IF;
```

--Exit when cursor attribute search_cursor%NOTFOUND is TRUE

```
EXIT WHEN search_cursor%NOTFOUND OR search_
    cursor%NOTFOUND IS NULL;
END LOOP;
CLOSE search_cursor;
```

```
<<Search_employees>>--If employee found display details else not
found.
```

```
IF search_record.first_name = search_name THEN
DBMS_OUTPUT.PUT_LINE('The employee called '||search_
    record.first_name||' has employee_id '||search_record.
    employee_id||'. His phone number is '||search_record.
    Phone_number||' and his salary is '||search_record.
    salary);
ELSE
DBMS_OUTPUT.PUT_LINE('There are no records for
    '||search_name);
END IF;
END;
```

Output

The current name being searched is Steven

The current name being searched is Neena

The current name being searched is Lex

The current name being searched is Alexander

The employee called Alexander has employee_id 103. His phone number is 555.423.4567 and his salary is 9000.

The code declares a cursor (search_cursor) that contains all the fields from the employees table. The cursor is then used to declare a record (search_record). The record now contains all the cursor elements. The code then checks if the cursor is open before opening it. The fetching process is done inside the LOOP. Successive cursor rows are fetched into the record. The code displays and compares the current fetched employee first_name with the name specified in the search. If a match is found the execution jumps to the Search_employees label that displays the employee details. If no match is found the LOOP will terminate when search_cursor%NOTFOUND attribute becomes TRUE (this happens when there are no more cursor rows to be searched). Note: a counter is not required for the exit condition. The cursor attribute search_cursor%NOTFOUND will determine when all rows have been processed, signalling the exit condition. If a match is not found the LOOP terminates and the cursor is closed and then the Search_employees label displays the not found message.

Oracle REF CURSOR And Dynamic SQL

Cursor variables are pointers to memory locations. Thus cursor variable do not contain any data, they only point to a location where the data is stored. PL/SQL cursor variable have REF CURSOR data type. The Oracle REF CURSOR is a special type of cursor. Unlike normal explicit cursors, they are not tied to a specific SELECT statement. They can be assigned to more than one SELECT statement. This property of REF CURSORs makes them capable of executing dynamic SQL. This is because the REF CURSOR only points to the memory location of data returned by the SELECT statement. The SELECT statements are assigned to the REF CURSOR with string variables using the OPEN FOR command. This use of character string variables to feed REF CURSORS with unknown SQL statements is known as dynamic SQL. This greatly improves the flexibility of PL/SQL applications. The following example uses a single REF CURSOR to process two different but equivalent SELECT result sets.

```
DECLARE
TYPE ref_cursor IS REF CURSOR;
ref_record ref_cursor;
counter NUMBER;
```

```
emp_record employees%ROWTYPE;
Select_1 Varchar(100):='SELECT * FROM employees WHERE
    employee_id BETWEEN 100 AND 101';
Select_2 Varchar(100):='SELECT * FROM employees WHERE
    employee_id BETWEEN 125 AND 126';
BEGIN
OPEN ref_record FOR Select_1;
FOR Counter IN (SELECT employee_id FROM employees
    WHERE employee_id BETWEEN 100 AND 101)
LOOP
FETCH ref_record INTO emp_record;
DBMS_OUTPUT.PUT_LINE('The current name being processed
    is '||emp_record.employee_id||' '||emp_record.first_
    name||' '||emp_record.last_name );
END LOOP;
CLOSE ref_record ;
DBMS_OUTPUT.PUT_LINE('THE FIRST CURSOUR IS NOW
    CLOSED!! THE SECOND CURSOR BEGINS');
OPEN ref_record FOR Select_2;
FOR Counter IN (SELECT employee_id FROM employees
    WHERE employee_id BETWEEN 125 AND 126)
LOOP
FETCH ref_record INTO emp_record;
DBMS_OUTPUT.PUT_LINE('The current name being processed
    is '||emp_record.employee_id||' '||emp_record.first_
    name||' '||emp_record.last_name );
END LOOP;
CLOSE ref_record ;
END;
Output
```

The current name being processed is 100 Steven King.

The current name being processed is 101 Neena Kochhar.

THE FIRST CURSOR IS NOW CLOSED! THE SECOND
CURSOR BEGINS

The current name being processed is 125 Julia Nayer.

The current name being processed is 126 Irene Mikkilineni.

A ref cursor called ref_cursor is declared. Then a cursor variable called ref_record is created using the ref_cursor data type. Two SELECT statements are then assigned to two variables (Select_1 and Select_2). The cursor variable is then opened using the OPEN FOR keyword. The first SELECT statement is assigned to the cursor variable using variable Select_1. This prints out the names of employee 100 and 101. The cursor is then closed. The second SELECT statement is assigned to the cursor variable using the second variable called Select_2. This prints out the names of employees 125 and 126.

Subprograms, Procedures, Functions, and Parameters

Subprograms are the most important feature of PL/SQL. All of the PL/SQL blocks we have seen so far are anonymous (unnamed) blocks. They cannot be used by another application. Subprograms are named PL/SQL blocks. They are used to automate repeatable business processes. For example, a payroll subprogram can be used to run the monthly payroll process. They are also used to decompose complex processing programs into simple maintainable units. For example, a payroll application might combine both salary calculation and post-payment reporting. Subprograms can be used to decouple the program into two separate manageable programs. They are reusable and sharable, thus facilitating code maintenance and reduce code variation. This is because once written they are compiled and stored on the server, and then reused several times for data processing.

The two main types of subprograms are functions and procedures. They are structurally similar in that both have a declarative section, an execution section, and an optional error handling section. The declarative section is called the specification (spec) while the execution section is called the body. They use parameters to manage the processing within the subprogram. However, they differ functionally because procedures are used to execute a specific task while functions are always used to execute a specific task and return a value. For example, a procedure might be used to increase employee salaries without returning any value while a function can be used to update an employee salary and return the new value to another application.

Subprogram Parameters

Parameters are used to pass variables and constants into and out of subprograms. Their usage depends on their declared mode. There are three possible modes to declare a parameter, including IN, OUT, and IN OUT.

Parameters declared as IN are basically constants. They are used to pass parameters whose value cannot change within the subprogram. If the parameter mode is not specified, the default IN mode is used.

Parameters declared as OUT are used to return computed values from subprograms. They must be assigned values only within the subprogram. OUT parameters cannot be initialised with values when the subprogram is executed.

Parameters declared as IN OUT are used to pass variables into and out of a subprogram. Their value can be changed within the subprogram. As opposed to OUT parameters, IN OUT parameters must be initialised with values when the subprogram is executed.

Stored Procedures

Procedures are used to perform a specific task and can take zero or more parameters. They have a specification and a body. The specification (spec) begins with the keyword PROCEDURE and ends with the parameter list. For procedures without parameters, the spec ends with the procedure name. The procedure body starts with the IS or AS keyword and ends with the END keyword. The body of the procedure is similar to an anonymous block. It has three sections: the optional declarative, execution, and optional error handling section. Unlike anonymous blocks, the DECLARE keyword is not used. The general structure of a stored procedure is as follows:

```
CREATE [OR REPLACE] PROCEDURE procedure_name
    (optional list of parameters)
AS
```

This is the optional declaration section where local variables and cursors are declared. The declare keyword is not used.

```
BEGIN
```

The execution section is where tasks are performed.

```
EXCEPTION
```

Optional exception section

END;

For example, the following procedure is used to update employee salaries. The procedure will accept an employee_id through the input parameter called emp_id. The salary of the employee will be increased by the value entered for the amount input parameter.

```
CREATE OR REPLACE PROCEDURE Update_salary (emp_id
    IN NUMBER,amount NUMBER)--Formal parameters are
    declared.
AS
Original_sal NUMBER;--declare local variables
Current_sal NUMBER;
BEGIN
SELECT salary INTO Original_sal from employees WHERE
    employee_id = emp_id;
UPDATE employees SET salary = (salary + amount) WHERE
    employee_id = emp_id;
SELECT salary INTO Current_sal from employees WHERE
    employee_id = emp_id;
DBMS_OUTPUT.PUT_LINE(The original salary was '||Original_
    sal||'while the current salary is '||Current_sal);
END;
```

The OR REPLACE clause in the creation statement is optional and is used to avoid errors when the procedure is being updated. The code creates a procedure named Update_salary, which is compiled and stored in the database. When executed, the procedure updates and displays the previous and the updated salary. Notice that the mode of the amount parameter is not specified, thus the default IN mode is used. This procedure is now ready for reuse to update any employee salary. The procedure is executed either by using the EXEC command from the SQL command prompt or by calling it from another program. To execute the procedure from another program, the following code is used:

```
BEGIN
update_salary(100,50);
END;
Output
```

The original salary was 24000 while the current salary is 24050

To execute from the SQL prompt the general syntax is : EXEC procedure_name(parameters);

```
EXEC Update_salary(200,50);
```

User-Defined Functions

As discussed, functions are structurally similar to procedures. They also have a specification (spec) and a body. Their main structural difference is inspired by the difference in their usage. Functions are always used to return a computed value while procedures may or may not return a value. In order for functions to return a value, a mandatory RETURN clause has been introduced. The specification of a function begins with the FUNCTION keyword and terminates with the RETURN clause. The RETURN clause simply defines the data type of the computed value. Parameters are optional and are handled like in procedures. The body of the function also starts with the IS or AS keyword and ends with the END keyword. The structure of the body has the optional declarative section, mandatory executive section, and the optional error handling section. The DECLARE keyword is not used. The declaration section implicitly begins after the IS /AS keywords. Functions must also include a RETURN statement that assigns the computed value to the function identifier and ends the execution. The general syntax of a function is:

```
CREATE OR REPLACE FUNCTION function_name
    (parameters)
RETURN return_data type;
AS
Declaration_section
Variable_name data type;
BEGIN
Execution_section
RETURN return_variable;
EXCEPTION
exception section
Return return_variable;
END;
```

For example, the following simple function will compute and return the first name of an employee whose employee ID will be specified when the function is called.

```
CREATE or REPLACE FUNCTION employee_name (emp_id
    NUMBER, emp_name OUT varchar2)
RETURN varchar2
```

```
IS
BEGIN
SELECT first_name INTO emp_name FROM employees
    WHERE employee_id = emp_id;
RETURN emp_name;
END;
```

The function returns the emp_name parameter, which is declared as OUT. The function uses the emp_id input parameter to determine the value of returned first_name. The data type of the OUT parameter must be the same as the RETURN data type. As a result, they are both specified as varchar2. This function can be called from another subprogram to assign a value to a parameter as follows:

```
DECLARE
f_name VARCHAR2(30);
emp_id NUMBER:= 150;
BEGIN
f_name:= employee_name(emp_id,f_name);
dbms_output.put_line('The first name of the employee is' | |
    f_name);
END;
Output
```

The first name of the employee is Peter.

The employee ID is initialised to 150 thus the function returns the first name of which is Peter. Notice that the function is used to assign a value to the f_name variable and a value is never specified for an OUT parameter.

Error Handling

Exception handlers are optionally used to manage runtime errors in subprograms. They ensure that the subprogram fails gracefully. They are generally used to exit the subprogram with an informative error message. Exceptions consist of a name, error code, and error message. They can also be used to perform a corrective measure or log errors when they occur. Exceptions are generally designed to handle anticipated errors. There can be several WHEN clauses in an exception handler to trap several anticipated exceptions. The THEN clause is used to specify statements which should be executed when an exception is caught. When an unanticipated error occurs, the WHEN OTHER clause is used to handle it. There are three types of exceptions, including unnamed predefined, named predefined and user-defined exceptions. Their main difference is how their names are derived. The names of the exceptions are used to catch the identified exception in the WHEN clause of the exception. The general syntax for an exception handler is:

```
DECLARE
Declaration section

--User defined exceptions can be declared here.

BEGIN
Exception section
EXCEPTION
WHEN exception_name1 THEN
--Exception handling and corrective statements
WHEN exception_name2 OR exception_name3 THEN
--Error handling and corrective statements
```

WHEN Others THEN

--Generic exception handling statements

END;

Named Predefined Exceptions

These are exceptions that have been identified, named, and handled by the Oracle database. It is optional to rewrite them. They are automatically triggered when the code violates an Oracle database rule. They can also be explicitly handled by using the exception name in the WHEN clause. For example, the NO_DATA_FOUND exception is (implicitly) automatically raised when a SELECT INTO query returns no data:

```
DECLARE
emp_name varchar2(30);
emp_id number:=13;
BEGIN
SELECT first_name INTO emp_name FROM employees
    WHERE employee_id = emp_id;
END;
Output
ORA-01403: no data found
```

The NO_DATA_FOUND exception is automatically raised because there isn't any employee with an employee id of 13. Thus the SELECT INTO query returns no data. This exception can be explicitly handled so that the predefined message is more specific and informative. For example:

```
DECLARE
emp_name varchar2(30);
emp_id number:=13;
tab_name varchar2(30):='Employees table.';
BEGIN
SELECT first_name INTO emp_name FROM employees
    WHERE employee_id = emp_id;
EXCEPTION
WHEN NO_DATA_FOUND THEN
DBMS_OUTPUT.PUT_LINE ('There is no record of employee_id'
    || emp_id|| 'in the' || tab_name);
WHEN OTHERS THEN--This handles all other undefined
    errors that might occur
DBMS_OUTPUT.PUT_LINE('An undefined error occurred.');
END;
Output
```

There is no record of employee_id 13 in the Employees table.

The explicit exception handler catches the error and returns a more descriptive error message:

'There is no record of employee_id 13 in the Employees table'. The WHEN OTHERS section is used to catch any undefined exceptions.

Unnamed Predefined Exceptions

These are similar to named predefined exceptions. They can be raised implicitly and explicitly. Unnamed predefined exceptions do not have an Oracle name. They have a code and a message. They are used by assigning a user-defined name to the predefined Oracle exception code. Once the name has been assigned, the exception's new name can be used to trap and handle the exception. The exception name is defined in the DECLARE section with a data type of EXCEPTION. Then the PRAGMA EXCEPTION_INIT expression is used to associate the error code to the defined name. The name is then used to explicitly handle the exception. For example:

```
DECLARE
Constraint_exception EXCEPTION;
PRAGMA EXCEPTION_INIT (Constraint_exception, -1407);
BEGIN
UPDATE employees SET last_name = NULL where employee_
    id =200;
EXCEPTION
WHEN Constraint_exception THEN
DBMS_OUTPUT.PUT_LINE('Error occurred because you tried
    to insert a NULL into the last_name field of employees
    table.');
END;
Output
```

Error occurred because you tried to insert a NULL into the last_ name field of employees table.

In this example, Oracle error code -1407 is assigned to the declared exception name Constraint_exception. The exception is raised when an attempt is made to insert a NULL into the last name field of the employees table. This is because there is a NOT NULL constraint that has been enabled for that field. The informative error message 'Error occurred because you tried to insert a NULL into the last_name field of employees table' is displayed when the error occurs.

User-Defined Exceptions

User-defined exceptions are used to explicitly flag deviations from desired business objectives. For example, there might be a business rule that states no programmer should have a salary greater than 8000. The user-defined exception will be used to identify any programmer whose salary is greater than 8000.

The RAISE keyword is used to force a user-defined exception. The name of the exception must be explicitly declared in the DECLARE section with a data type of EXCEPTION. Once the exception has been declared, it must be explicitly tested and RAISED within the execution section. The name is then used to trap and handle the exception in the EXCEPTION section. Using the salary example, the following code can be used:

```
DECLARE
High_salary EXCEPTION;
salary_amount Number;
emp_name Varchar(30);
BEGIN
```

```
SELECT salary, first_name INTO salary_amount, emp_name
    FROM employees WHERE JOB_ID = 'IT_PROG' AND salary
    > 8000;
IF salary_amount > 8000 THEN RAISE High_salary;--Raise
    the exception.
END IF;
EXCEPTION
WHEN High_salary THEN
DBMS_OUTPUT.PUT_LINE('The programmer called '||emp_
    name||' Has a salary of '||salary_amount|| 'Which is
    greater than 8000');
END;
Output:
```

The programmer called Alexander has a salary of 9000, which is greater than 8000.

In this example, the EXCEPTION high_salary is declared. Then the code selects the programmer whose salary is 9000. Thus the exception is raised and the following error message is returned: 'The programmer called Alexander has a salary of 9000, which is greater than 8000'.

PL/SQL Transaction Processing

A transaction is a set of mutually dependent individual actions. In order for a transaction to be complete, all of these actions must either fail or succeed as a group. Transaction controls in PL/SQL are used to create recovery units so that any time a complex operation fails, you can fully recover and re-execute the transaction without any data or process corruption. These controls are only relevant for statements that permanently change the data, such as DELETE, UPDATE, and INSERT.

The main keywords used to control transactions are SET TRANSACTION, ROLLBACK, SAVEPOINT, and COMMIT.

SET TRANSACTION

It is optionally used to set the mode of a transaction. The modes are READ ONLY or READ WRITE mode. The transaction mode is useful for performance optimisation. For example, in very busy environments where the data is constantly being updated, the READ ONLY mode will force transaction queries to ignore all future data changes. The current snapshot of the database is used for all transaction queries, so performance is improved by reducing resource contention due to table and row locks.

COMMIT

The COMMIT keyword is used to explicitly end a transaction. Once the commit keyword is encountered all the data changes made by the previous SQL statements are permanently saved to the database. It is worth noting that most databases are set up to implicitly commit once an SQL statement terminates. Logically, COMMIT is used to ensure the success of a set of transaction statements that must succeed together.

For example, to switch the job positions between employee 100 and 101, a transaction must accomplish this switch instantly so that both positions are filled without a gap. To ensure that both statements fail or succeed together, the COMMIT must be used with an error handler and a ROLLBACK as shown in the ROLLBACK section. With a COMMIT without an error handler, one statement could fail while the other succeeds. For example the current job_ids of employee 100 and 101 are displayed as follows:

```
SELECT employee_id, first_name, last_name, job_id FROM
    employee1
WHERE employee_id IN(100,101);
Output
```

EMPLOYEE_ID	FIRST_NAME	LAST_NAME	JOB_ID
100	Steven	King	AD_PRES
101	Neena	Kochhar	AD_VP

Table 13.2

The output shows the respective job_ids. The following transaction is used to switch the job_ids:

```
DECLARE
BEGIN
UPDATE employee1 SET job_id = 'AD_VP' WHERE employee_
    id = 100;
UPDATE employee1 SET job_id = 'AD_PRES' WHERE
    employee_id = 101;
COMMIT COMMENT 'Employee 101 and 100 have switched
    jobs' WRITE IMMEDIATE NOWAIT;
END;
```

The transaction saves the changes to the database as shown next.

Output

SELECT employee_id, first_name, last_name, job_id FROM
   employee1
WHERE employee_id IN(100,101);

EMPLOYEE_ID	FIRST_NAME	LAST_NAME	JOB_ID
100	Steven	King	AD_VP
101	Neena	Kochhar	AD_PRES

Table 13.3

In this transaction the jobs of employee 100 has been switched from AD_PRES to AD_VP while employee 101s job_id has been switched from AD_VP to AD_PRES. The optional COMMENT is used to document the transaction in the data dictionary for future analysis.

ROLLBACK Using EXCEPTIONS

The ROLLBACK explicitly ends a transaction. It is used to undo data changes made by the preceding SQL transaction statements. ROLLBACK is used to restore data when errors are detected within the transaction. Logically, ROLLBACK is used to ensure the failure of a set of transaction statements that must fail together. In the following example, the two employee IDs needed for the job switch are retrieved using their first and last names. The ID of the first employee, Steven King, is retrieved successfully. However, the second retrieval fails because Neen Kochhar is not a valid name. This triggers the NO_DATA_FOUND exception that uses a ROLLBACK to undo both updates. The following statement shows the current job_ids:

SELECT employee_id,last_name, job_id FROM employee1

WHERE employee_id IN(100,101);

Output

EMPLOYEE_ID	LAST_NAME	JOB_ID
100	King	AD_PRES
101	Kochhar	AD_VP

Table 13.4

The following transaction tries to switch the job_ids.

DECLARE

emp_id1 Number;

emp_id2 Number;

BEGIN

SELECT employee_id INTO emp_id1 FROM employee1

    WHERE last_name = 'King' AND first_name ='Steven' ;

SELECT employee_id INTO emp_id2 FROM employee1

    WHERE last_name = 'Kochhar' AND first_name ='Neen' ;

--The second SELECT INTO fails, thus the exception is raised
rolling back both updates

UPDATE employee1 SET job_id = 'AD_VP' WHERE employee_

    id = emp_id1;

UPDATE employee1 SET job_id = 'AD_PRES' WHERE

    employee_id = emp_id2;

EXCEPTION

WHEN NO_DATA_FOUND THEN ROLLBACK;

DBMS_OUTPUT.PUT_LINE ('An error occurred, thus this
    transaction has been rolled back');
END;
Output

An error occurred thus this transaction has been rolled back

The following statement confirms that the transaction did not
succeed.

SELECT employee_id,last_name, job_id FROM employee1
WHERE employee_id IN(100,101);
Output

EMPLOYEE_ID	LAST_NAME	JOB_ID
100	King	AD_PRES
101	Kochhar	AD_VP

Table 13.5

The job_ids have not changed.

SAVEPOINT Using COMMIT, EXCEPTIONS, and ROLLBACK

The SAVEPOINT keyword is used to mark and name the current
processing point of a transaction. Once a SAVEPOINT has been
declared, a ROLLBACK can be executed to undo all changes issued after
the SAVEPOINT. SAVEPOINTS are used to break up a transaction
into manageable independent units where the failure of the unit after
the SAVEPOINT does not impact the other unit. Logically they act
as recovery units. When a transaction fails after the SAVEPOINT all

the changes made before the SAVEPOINT are safe. For example, the following query returns the data for the two employees whose data is to be updated:

```
SELECT first_name,last_name,job_id,salary FROM employee1
    WHERE employee_id IN (100,101);
```

Output

FIRST_NAME	LAST_NAME	JOB_ID	SALARY
Steven	King	AD_PRES	24000
Neena	Kochhar	AD_VP	17000

Table 13.6

Then the following transactions are executed.

```
DECLARE
emp_id1 Number;
emp_id2 Number;
BEGIN
SELECT employee_id INTO emp_id1 FROM employee1
    WHERE last_name = 'King' AND first_name ='Steven' ;
SELECT employee_id INTO emp_id2 FROM employee1
    WHERE last_name = 'Kochhar' AND first_name ='Neena' ;
UPDATE employee1 SET job_id = 'AD_VP' WHERE employee_
    id = emp_id1;
UPDATE employee1 SET job_id = 'AD_PRES' WHERE
    employee_id = emp_id2;
DBMS_OUTPUT.PUT_LINE ('Good, employee jobs have been
    switched');
```

SAVEPOINT switch_employees;--All changes at this point are safe.

UPDATE employee1 SET salary = (salary + 1000) WHERE employee_id = emp_id2;

DBMS_OUTPUT.PUT_LINE ('Good, the salary of employee '| | emp_id2 | |' has been updated');

SELECT employee_id INTO emp_id2 FROM employee1 WHERE last_name = 'Kochhar' AND first_name ='Neen' ;

EXCEPTION

WHEN NO_DATA_FOUND THEN ROLLBACK TO switch_employees;

DBMS_OUTPUT.PUT_LINE ('Error!! this transaction has been rolled back to SAVEPOINT switch_employees');

END;

Output

Good, employee jobs have been switched.

Good, the salary of employee 101 has been updated.

Error!! this transaction has been rolled back to SAVEPOINT switch_employees.

The results of the transactions are:

SELECT first_name,last_name,job_id,salary FROM employee1 WHERE employee_id IN (100,101);

FIRST_NAME	LAST_NAME	JOB_ID	SALARY
Steven	King	AD_VP	24000
Neena	Kochhar	AD_PRES	17000

Table 13.7

In this example, all the updates before the SAVEPOINT (switch_employees) succeed, so they are committed to the database. The result shows that employees King and Kochhar have switched jobs but their salaries are still the same. This is because the next statement updates the salary of employee Neena and then prints out a confirmation message. However, the SELECT INTO after the salary UPDATE fails triggering the NO_DATA_FOUND exception. This exception rolls back all transactions after the SAVEPOINT so the salary update (for Neena) after the SAVEPOINT is rolled back.

Oracle Table Functions and User-Defined Types

Most functions only return scalar values such as a date or a number. Table value functions are used to return multiple rows from special tables called collections. These collections can be queried using the TABLE clause in a SELECT statement. The data type of collections is created by the programmer and can be based on the structure of a table. Collections are manipulated using in-built functions that include EXTEND, DELETE, LAST, and FIRST. The first step of collection creation is to declare a collection object. The second step is creating a collection table based on the created collection object. For example, a new employee_departments table is created that identifies the department name of each employee as follows:

```
CREATE TABLE employee_departments AS
SELECT e.employee_id, first_name, last_name, department_
    name,d.department_id
FROM employees e, departments d
WHERE e.department_id = d.department_id;
```

This table will be used by a table function to insert data into the collection table.

Now a collection object is created. The new collection object is called employee_dept. The AS OBJECT declaration is used as follows.

```
CREATE OR REPLACE TYPE employee_dept AS OBJECT
(employee_id NUMBER(6,0), first_name VARCHAR2(30),
last_name VARCHAR2(35), department_name VARCHAR2(30),
    department_id NUMBER (4,0));
```

A schema level collection table called emp_dep_table is now created and is assigned the employee_dept data type.

```
CREATE TYPE emp_dep_table IS TABLE OF employee_dept;
```

A function is now created that returns ranges of employees based on their employee_id numbers. It uses the EXTEND method to load ROWS into the collection as follows. The values from the created table are first assigned to individual variables, and then the variables are sequentially inserted into the collection using a FOR LOOP.

```
CREATE OR REPLACE FUNCTION get_emp_dept (emp_id1
    NUMBER,emp_id2 NUMBER)
RETURN emp_dep_table AS
Emp_depts emp_dep_table:=emp_dep_table();
dept_number NUMBER(6,0);
emp_id NUMBER(6,0);
fname VARCHAR2(30);
lname VARCHAR2(30);
```

```
dept_name VARCHAR2(30);

depts_id NUMBER(5,0);

i NUMBER(6,0);

BEGIN

FOR i IN emp_id1..emp_id2 LOOP

SELECT employee_id, first_name, last_name, department_
    name,department_id INTO emp_id, fname,lname,dept_
    name, depts_id FROM employee_departments WHERE
    employee_id = i;

Emp_depts.extend ;

Emp_depts(Emp_depts.last) :=employee_dept(emp_id,
    fname,lname,dept_name,depts_id);

END LOOP;

RETURN Emp_depts;

END;
```

The function can now be used to return employee ranges by using a SELECT statement as follows:

```
SELECT * FROM TABLE(get_emp_dept(119,121));
Output
```

EMPLOYEE _ID	FIRST _NAME	LAST _NAME	DEPARTMENT _NAME	DEPARTMENT _ID
119	Karen	Colmenares	Purchasing	30
120	Matthew	Weiss	Shipping	50
121	Adam	Fripp	Shipping	50

Table 13.8

The employees whose employee_id are between 119 and 121 have been returned from the employee_departments table.

Programmable T—SQL

All the constructs we have seen so far in PL/SQL are also available in programmable-SQL. It is the Microsoft SQL server procedural extension of SQL. Just as in PL/SQLs, this procedural language helps programmers group a collection of related SQL statements for repeated use. The language also combines the powerful program flow control constructs of procedural programming with the data manipulation capabilities of SQL. Transaction management constructs are also used to execute complex transactions. The following section will highlight the few significant structural differences between the two languages. Key constructs such as anonymous blocks, cursors, stored procedures, and functions will be explored. The PRINT keyword is used to print messages to the PC screen.

T-SQL OBJECT_ID Function

As a general database rule, two database objects types in the same schema cannot have the same name. For example, two tables or functions in the AdventureWorks2012R2.HumanResources schema cannot have the same name, so when an attempt is made to create an object with a name that already exists, the code fails. To get around this in Oracle, the CREATE or REPLACE command is used. T-SQL uses the OBJECT_ID function.

In T-SQL a check for the object's existence is executed in the sys. objects view. If the object exists, drop it before recreating it. The general syntax is:

```
USE AdventureWorks2012;
GO
IF OBJECT_ID ('schema_name.object_name','object_type')IS
    NOT NULL
DROP object_type schema_name.object_name;
GO
CREATE object_type schema_name.object_name;
```

T-SQL Anonymous Block

Anonymous blocks are used to group and execute related T-SQL statements (batch). These blocks can be tested and converted into functions and stored procedures for reuse. The blocks are made up of the following sections:

- The DECLARATION section (optional). Starts with reserved word (DECLARE).

- The EXECUTION section (mandatory). Starts and ends with (BEGIN . . . END).

- The EXCEPTION HANDLING section (optional). Starts with (TRY..CATCH).

T-SQL DECLARE

The DECLARE keyword is used to start the variable declaration section. The BEGIN keyword is used to explicitly end the declaration section and start the execution section. All local variables must be prefixed with the @ symbol, while global variables are prefixed with @@. All declared variables are initialised to null until a value is assigned to them. Values are assigned using the equal sign (=), SET, or SELECT keywords. The SELECT command is also used to output the values of variables. Value assignment using the equal sign is the most efficient method. The general declaration syntax is:

DECLARE variable1_name data type, variable2_name data type;

Assigning values to variables using the equal sign (=).

USE AdventureWorks2012

GO

DECLARE @myjob char(20) = 'Software Designer', @myname
    char(20) = 'Victor';

PRINT 'The value of variable @myjob = '+ @myjob + 'and the
    value of variable @myname = '+@myname;

Output

The value of variable @myjob = Software Designer and the
    value of variable @myname = Victor

In this example, the two variables @myjob and @myname are DECLAREed and initialised using the equal sign. The PRINT statement is used to print their values, which are 'software designer' and 'Victor', respectively. The SELECT keyword can also be used to display the values of the variable as follows:

USE AdventureWorks2012

GO

DECLARE @myjob char(20) = 'Software Designer', @myname
    char(20) = 'Victor';

```
SELECT 'the value of variable @myjob = '+ @myjob + 'and the
    value of variable @myname = '+@myname;
Output
the value of variable @myjob = Software Designer and the
    value of variable @myname = Victor
```

Assigning Values to Variables Using the SET Keyword

```
USE AdventureWorks2012
GO
DECLARE @myname char(10),@mycity char(20);
SET @myname ='Victor';
SET @mycity = 'Victoria';
PRINT 'the value of variable @myname = '+@myname+ 'and
    the value of variable @mycity = '+@mycity;
Output
the value of variable @myname = Victor and the value of
    variable @mycity = Victoria
```

In this example, the two variables @myname and @mycity are first DECLAREed and then initialised using the SET keyword. The PRINT statement is used to print their values, which are Victor and Victoria, respectively.

Assigning Values to Variables Using the SELECT Keyword

```
USE AdventureWorks2012
GO
DECLARE @mycity char(20);
SELECT @mycity = 'Victoria';
```

PRINT 'the value of variable @mycity = '+@mycity;

Output

the value of variable @mycity = Victoria

The variable @mycity is first declared. Then it is assigned the value Victoria using the SELECT keyword. The print statement is then used to print the value.

T-SQL Execution Section

The execution section of a T-SQL anonymous block begins with the BEGIN keyword and ends with the END keyword. Just like in PL/SQL, a series of related T-SQL statements can be enclosed and executed within these keywords. For example, the general syntax is:

```
BEGIN
--Statement1
--Statement2 . . .
END
Here is an example of a T-SQL anonymous block.
USE AdventureWorks2012
GO
DECLARE @empname nvarchar(20),@empid int =3,@empjob
    nvarchar(50);
BEGIN
SELECT @empname = firstname FROM Person.Person
WHERE BusinessEntityID = @empid;
SELECT @empjob = JobTitle FROM HumanResources.Employee
WHERE BusinessEntityID = @empid;
```

PRINT 'Employee 3 is called '+@empname+ 'and his jobtitle is

'+@empjob;

END

Output

Employee 3 is called Roberto and his jobtitle is engineering manager.

In this example, an employee's name and job title are retrieved using two SQL statements between the BEGIN and END keywords in the block. The first SELECT statement retrieves the first name while the second retrieves the job title. Notice that while Oracle uses the INTO keyword to assign a table column value to a variable, T-SQL uses the equal sign.

T-SQL Exception Handling (Try . . . CATCH)

Just like in PL/SQL, exceptions can be used to terminate programs gracefully with an error message.

To handle execution errors, you must enclose all the code between TRY and CATCH blocks. The TRY block is used to enclose the actual code while the CATCH block is used to handle the error. The TRY block begins with the keywords BEGIN TRY and ends with END TRY. The CATCH block begins with BEGIN CATCH and ends with END CATCH. All error messages are stored in the sys.message table. The error attributes can be individually retrieved using error attribute functions within the CATCH block. Some of the functions include:

The ERROR_LINE() function is used to return the line number of your script where the error was detected.

The ERROR_NUMBER() function is used to return the error number.

The ERROR_MESSAGE() function is used to return the error message.

The ERROR_SEVERITY() function is used to return the error severity.

Rather than retrieving individual error attributes it is more effective to handling errors by using the built in dbo.uspPrintError prcedure. The following example handles a data integrity error with individual error attributes:

```
DECLARE @empid int =3;
BEGIN TRY
BEGIN


--This delete statement will fail thus trigering the catch.

DELETE FROM Person.Person
WHERE BusinessEntityID = @empid;
PRINT 'Empolyee 3 deleted'
END
END TRY
```

--The CATCH block must immidiately follow the end of the TRY block.

```
BEGIN CATCH
```

--Error message functions are being used to handle the error.

```
SELECT ERROR_MESSAGE() AS Error_Message_Text,
ERROR_LINE() as Error_Line_number,
ERROR_NUMBER() AS System_error_number;
END CATCH;
```

Output

Error_Message_Text	Error_Line _number	System_error _number
The DELETE statement conflicted with the REFERENCE constraint "FK_EmailAddress_Person_ BusinessEntityID". The conflict occurred in database "AdventureWorks2012", table "Person.EmailAddress", column 'BusinessEntityID'.	5	547

Table 13.9

The delete fails because it violates FOREIGN key constraints on the Person.Person table, triggering the CATCH. The error message, line number, and error number are returned by the error functions. An easier way to return all the error attributes in a better format is to replace the individual error functions with the dbo.uspPrintError prcedure. For example:

```
USE AdventureWorks2012
GO
DECLARE @empid int =3;
BEGIN TRY
BEGIN
```

--This delete statement will fail, thus triggering the catch.

```
DELETE FROM Person.Person
WHERE BusinessEntityID = @empid;
PRINT 'Empolyee 3 deleted'
END
END TRY
```

--The CATCH block must immediately follow the end of the TRY block.

```
BEGIN CATCH
```

--dbo.uspPrintError procedure is used to handle the error.

```
EXECUTE dbo.uspPrintError;
END CATCH;
Output
(0 row(s) affected)
Error 547, Severity 16, State 0, Procedure—, Line 5
```

The DELETE statement conflicted with the REFERENCE constraint "FK_EmailAddress_Person_BusinessEntityID". The conflict occurred in database "AdventureWorks2012", table "Person. EmailAddress", column 'BusinessEntityID'.

The dbo.uspPrintError procedure has been used in this case to handle the same FOREIGN key violation error with minimal coding.

T-SQL Flow Control

Flow control constructs in T-SQL are also similar to their equivalent PL/SQL constructs. They are used to control the processing order of your T-SQL statements. They introduce powerful procedural programming constructs into T-SQL. They include conditional logic (IF THEN ELSE), sequence (GOTO), and iteration (WHILE). These constructs can be combined to resolve most programming difficulties.

T-SQL Conditional Logic

Conditional logic is used to introduce decision-making capabilities into T-SQL. Alternative execution paths are selected based on the validity of certain tested conditions. The Boolean IF ELSE construct is used. The condition is tested in the IF clause, and if the condition is TRUE the next section is executed. If the condition is FALSE the optional ELSE section is executed.

```
USE AdventureWorks2012
DECLARE @empname1 nvarchar(20),@empid1 int =3,@
    empsal int ;
BEGIN
SELECT @empname1 = firstname FROM Person.Person
WHERE BusinessEntityID = @empid1;
SELECT @empsal = rate FROM HumanResources.
    EmployeePayHistory
WHERE BusinessEntityID = @empid1;
IF @empsal > 20
```

```
PRINT 'The Employee '+@empname1+' Has an hour rate of
    £'+Convert(nvarchar,@empsal)+ 'which is > £20';
ELSE
PRINT 'The Employee '+@empname1+' Has an hour rate of
    £'+Convert(nvarchar,@empsal)+ 'which is < £20';
END;
Output
```

The employee Roberto has an hourly rate of £43, which is > £20.

In the previous example the name and hourly rate of an employee are selected. The IF ELSE construct is used to compare the rate against 20. Since the rate is 43, which is greater than 20, the IF statement evaluates to TRUE and the PRINT statement following the IF is executed.

T-SQL Iteration

Iteration is used to execute T-SQL statement(s) for an arbitrary amount of time. The WHILE LOOP is used to execute iteration in T-SQL. A test condition is set at the start of the WHILE LOOP. The enclosed T-SQL statements will be repeatedly executed as long as the test condition stays true. This test condition is being progressively altered within the LOOP until it becomes false.

```
USE AdventureWorks2012;
GO
DECLARE @empname1 nvarchar(20),@empid1 int,@empsal
    int, @empname2 nvarchar(20);
SET @empid1 = 1;--Initialise the test condition outside LOOP.
```

--This variable is used to control the LOOP and change the value of the BusinessEntityID for each iteration.

```
WHILE @empid1 < 4
BEGIN
SELECT @empname1 = firstname,@empname2 = lastname
    FROM Person.Person
WHERE BusinessEntityID = @empid1;
PRINT 'Employee ID '+convert (nvarchar, @empid1)+' is called
    '+@empname2+' '+@empname1;
SET @empid1 = @empid1+1;--Test condition is being
    incremented till it gets to 4 and the LOOP exits.
END
Output
Employee ID 1 is called Sánchez Ken
Employee ID 2 is called Duffy Terri
Employee ID 3 is called Tamburello Roberto
```

The first and last names of employees 1 to 3 are displayed. A variable called @empid1 is declared and initialised to 1 outside the LOOP. This variable is used to control the LOOP and change the selection criteria of the query. This is done by incrementing the variable by 1 inside the LOOP until it gets to 4 and thus the LOOP terminates because the test condition @empid1 < 4 becomes false.

T-SQL Sequential Control

Sequential control statements are used to branch from one section of code to another, ignoring everything in between. They are typically used to jump out of LOOPs before the LOOP naturally terminates.

They are implemented by using the GOTO statement to jump to a label within the code. The label must be declared within the code. Labels are terminated with a colon. For example, the following code searches for a specified employee called Christopher Hill:

```
USE AdventureWorks2012;
GO
DECLARE @empname1 nvarchar(20),@empid1 int,@
    empcounter int, @empname2 nvarchar(20),
@fname nvarchar(20)='Christopher', @lname
    nvarchar(20)='Hill';
SET @empid1 = 1;
SELECT @empcounter = COUNT (*)FROM Person.Person;
WHILE @empid1 < @empcounter
```

--test the counter to the number of people in the person.person table so that everybody is searched.

```
BEGIN
SELECT @empname1 = firstname,@empname2 = lastname
    FROM Person.Person
WHERE BusinessEntityID = @empid1;
IF @empname1 = @fname AND @empname2 = @lname GOTO
    Employee_found
```

--Jump out of LOOP if you find the employee

```
SET @empid1 = @empid1+1;--Test condition is being
    incremented till it gets to the value of @empcounter and
    the LOOP exits.
```

END

Employee_found:

IF @empname1 = @fname AND @empname2 = @lname

--Test the label because if the employee is not found the label is not ignored

PRINT 'THE Employee called '+@fname+' '+@lname+ 'Has been
    found';

ELSE

PRINT 'THE Employee called '+@fname+' '+@lname+ 'Could
    not found';

Output

The employee called Christopher Hill has been found.

The code scrolls through all the records in the person.person table looking for an employee called Christopher Hill. Notice that the LOOP counter exit condition variable @empcounter has been set to the total number of all records in the person.person table. Thus, all records will be searched until a match is found or the LOOP terminates if a match is not found. When the match is found, the GOTO Employee_found label is triggered. The execution then jumps into the label. A test condition is executed in the label to handle situations where a match is not found. In such a case, the 'could not be found' message will be the output. In this case, the 'has been found' message is triggered.

Cursors in T-SQL

Cursors are composite data types. Cursors are creating by associating an SQL query to a variable. Once the cursor is opened, the SQL query runs and populates the cursor with its result set. Cursors in T-SQL and PL/SQL have similar properties, but their syntax is slightly different. Cursors help programmers process a returned dataset one row at a time. Unlike in PL/SQL, T-SQL explicit cursors do not require a record variable to process the cursor rows individually. The FETCH NEXT from cursor_name command is used. The following commands are used to manage T-SQL cursors:

Cursors are declared like any other variable in the DECLARE section of a block.

CURSOR FOR SELECT is used to associate the declared cursor with an SQL query.

OPEN: the command runs the associated cursor query and initialises the cursor.

FETCH NEXT FROM cursor INTO is used to select successive column values into variables.

CLOSE is used to close the cursor.

Note that the cursor will still be in memory until the DEALLOCATE command is used to flush it out. For example, the following program uses a cursor to scroll through the names of three employees:

```
USE AdventureWorks2012;
GO
DECLARE @fname Varchar(50),@lname Varchar(50), @
    counter int =1;--initialise counter
DECLARE First_name1 CURSOR
FOR SELECT firstName, lastname FROM person.person;
OPEN First_name1;
WHILE @counter < 4--Test for LOOP exit condition.
BEGIN
FETCH NEXT FROM First_name1 INTO @fname, @
    lname;--Successively select each row into the variables.
PRINT'The employee is called' +' '+@fname+' '+@lname;
SET @counter = @counter +1;--increment counter
END
CLOSE First_name1;
DEALLOCATE First_name1;
Output
The employee is called Ken Sánchez.
The employee is called Terri Duffy.
The employee is called Roberto Tamburello.
```

In this example, the first and last name of the first three employees are displayed using a declared cursor called First_name1. The cursor selects the first and last names of employees from the person.person table when the OPEN cmmand is issued. A variable called @counter is declared and initialised to one outside the WHILE LOOP. The LOOP then uses the FETCH NEXT FROM comand to assign the first row of cursor values to the two declared variables @lname and @fname. The variable names are then printed. The counter is then incremented to two, and the LOOP iterates and assigns the second row of the cursor to the variables. This process continues until the @counter variable gets to four and the LOOP terminates.

T-SQL Functions and Procedures

T-SQL functions and procedures are similar to PL/SQL functions and procedures. They are used to enclose T-SQL statements for repeated use. They also use input and output parameters to process variables within the subprogram. They share the following benefits:

Reuse: Frequently used business processes can be implemented and reused using functions and procedures.

Performance: Since compiled functions and procedures reside in the database, using them saves network input/output overheads inherent with client server applications.

Maintenance: Most client business applications are complex and have interdependent components. So when the database structure changes, changing these interdependent components becomes problematic. Stored functions and procedures can be used to decouple these interdependent components, in which case changes are applied only to individual units.

T-SQL Stored Procedures

Stored procedures are used to perform a given task in the database. They use parameters to introduce variables into the processing T-SQL statements within the stored procedure. Procedures also indicate their success status after execution.

Output parameters can also be used to return single values. The procedure creation begins with the CREATE PROCEDURE procedure_name statement. The parameters are then declared followed by the AS keyword. An example of procedure creation is:

```
USE AdventureWorks2012;
GO
IF OBJECT_ID ('Person.DisplayName', 'P') IS NOT NULL
DROP PROCEDURE Person.DisplayName;
GO
CREATE PROCEDURE Person.DisplayName
@empid1 int--This is an input parameter
AS
DECLARE
@empname1 nvarchar(20),@empname2 nvarchar(20)--Local
    variables within the procedure.
BEGIN
SELECT @empname1 = firstname,@empname2 = lastname
    FROM Person.Person--Populate local parameters
WHERE BusinessEntityID = @empid1;
PRINT 'Employee ID '+convert (nvarchar, @empid1)+' is called
    '+@empname2+' '+@empname1;
END;
```

In this procedure, the OBJECT_ID function is used to check the existence of the procedure. If it exists, it will be dropped and recreated. There is a single input parameter called @empid1. This parameter is set when the procedure is run. The procedure then populates the two local variables called @empname1 and @empname2 with the first and last names of the employee specified by the @empid1 parameter. The name is then printed with the PRINT comand. To run this procedure, use the following code:

```
EXECUTE Person.DisplayName 20;
Output
Employee ID 20 is called Benshoof Wanida
Or
EXECUTE Person.DisplayName @empid1 = 20;
Employee ID 20 is called Benshoof Wanida.
```

T-SQL Functions

Programmable T-SQL functions are also similar to PL/SQL functions. They also accept parameters and always return a computed value. They can either return a single value (scalar functions) or a table. The CREATE FUNCTION statement then used to create the function. Optional parameters are then declared. Just like T-SQL variables, the name of parameters always begins with the @ symbol. The RETURN keyword is used to declare the data type of the returned computed value. It could be a single value. An example of a T-SQL scalar function is as follows:

```
USE AdventureWorks2012;
GO
IF OBJECT_ID ('HumanResources.Increase_Salary', 'FN') IS
    NOT NULL
DROP FUNCTION HumanResources.Increase_Salary;
GO
CREATE FUNCTION HumanResources.Increase_Salary (@
    empid1 int,@amount int )
```

```
RETURNS money
AS
BEGIN
DECLARE
@newsalary money
SELECT @newsalary = (Rate+@amount) FROM
    HumanResources.EmployeePayHistory
WHERE BusinessEntityID = @empid1;
RETURN (@newsalary);
END;
GO
```

This function is used to display a projected salary increase for any specified employee ID. The function uses the input parameters @empid1 and @amount to introduce the employee ID and rate increase respectively. The local variable @newsalary is then used to return the rate plus specified amount for the selected employee.

This functon can be executed as follows.

```
SELECT HumanResources.Increase_Salary (3,20)AS 'Projected
    Salary';
```

Output

Projected Salary
63.2692

Table 13.10

The rate of employee 3 is thus increased by 20.

The function can also be used to assign a value to a declared variable as follows:

```
DECLARE @increase money;
SELECT @increase = HumanResources.Increase_Salary (3,20);
PRINT @increase;
Output
63.27
```

T-SQL Table Functions

Programable T-SQL functions can also be used to return tables. The return data type of the function is table. This can be useful in ETL applications where data separation is required. For example, there can be a requirement to extract and load employee details for each department in a separate table. This can be done using a table function:

```
USE AdventureWorks2012;
GO
IF OBJECT_ID ('HumanResources.Department_list', 'IF') IS
    NOT NULL
DROP FUNCTION HumanResources.Department_list;
GO
CREATE FUNCTION HumanResources.Department_list (@
    dept_id int)
RETURNS TABLE
AS
RETURN
```

```
(SELECT p.FirstName,p.lastname, h.name FROM
    HumanResources.EmployeeDepartmentHistory d,Person.
    person p,HumanResources.Department h
WHERE p.BusinessEntityID = d.BusinessEntityID
AND d.DepartmentID = h.DepartmentID
AND d.EndDate IS NULL
AND h.DepartmentID = @dept_id);
GO
```

The created inline table-value function is used to return a table listing all the current employees of a selected department. The input parametre @dept_id is used to specify the number of the required department. For example, to display all the members of the executive department (department ID = 16), the following command is issued:

```
SELECT * FROM HumanResources.Department_list (16);
Output
```

FirstName	lastname	name
Ken	Sánchez	Executive
Laura	Norman	Executive

Table 13.11

The two executive members are listed in the table.

T-SQL Transactions Processing

Transactions statements in T-SQL are used to manage a set of logically related T-SQL statements. They are used to ensure process and data consistency during database transaction processing. For example, when money is moved from one account to another, the first statement debits the source account while the second credits the destination account. Transaction statements ensure that both statements either fail or succeed to complete the transaction.

Transactions are explicitly declared using the BEGIN TRANSACTION statement. They are explicitly terminated with either the COMMIT or ROLLBACK statement. SAVE transaction statements are also used to create named save points that protect all the work done before this point in case of a ROLLBACK

T-SQL SET TRANSACTION Isolation Level

The isolation level is similar to the Oracle SET TRANSACTION. It is optionally used to set the mode of a transaction. Some of the modes are READ COMMITTED, SNAPSHOT, REPEATABLE READ, SNAPSHOT, READ COMMITTED, or READ UNCOMMITTED mode. The READ COMMITTED is the default mode. The transaction mode is useful for performance optimisation by defining how tables and are going to be locked during the transaction. The lower the lock level, the faster the transaction will run. The default isolation level is acceptable for most transactions; however, business requirements should dictate the level.

T-SQL BEGIN and COMMIT TRANSACTION

The BEGIN TRANSACTION statement is used to begin and name a transaction. Once the transaction statements have been issued, the COMMIT TRANSACTION statement is used to terminate the transaction and permanently save any data changes. The following statement displays the rows that are about to be updated with the transaction:

```
USE AdventureWorks2012;
GO
SELECT BusinessEntityID, firstname,lastname
FROM Person.Person
WHERE BusinessEntityID= 12;
Output
```

BusinessEntityID	firstname	lastname
12	Thierry	D'Hers

Table 13.12

The lastname of employee 12 in the Person.Person table is shown.

BusinessEntityID	rate
12	25.00

Table 13.13

Employee 12's rate is shown.

The following transaction updates the rate and lastname of employee 12.

```
USE AdventureWorks2012;
GO
DECLARE @T_Name VARCHAR(20);
BEGIN TRANSACTION @T_Name;
UPDATE Person.Person SET LastName ='Ebai'
```

```
WHERE BusinessEntityID = 12;
UPDATE HumanResources.EmployeePayHistory SET Rate = 40
WHERE BusinessEntityID = 12;
COMMIT TRANSACTION @T_Name;
```

In the previous example, the transaction is decleared as @T_name. The transaction then updates employee 12's lastname and rate from D'Hers to Ebai and 25.00 to 40 respectively. The COMMIT then explicitly saves the changes and terminates the transaction.

The new values are shown below.

```
USE AdventureWorks2012;
GO
SELECT p.BusinessEntityID, firstname,lastname,h.Rate
FROM Person.Person p,HumanResources.EmployeePayHistory h
WHERE p.BusinessEntityID= h.BusinessEntityID
AND p.BusinessEntityID = 12;
Output
```

BusinessEntityID	firstname	lastname	Rate
12	Thierry	Ebai	40.00

Table 13.14

T-SQL BEGIN, ROLLBACK TRANSACTION

The ROLLBACK TRANSACTION is used to undo any changes made to the data from the start of the transaction to the ROLLBACK. If a SAVEPOINT is declared before the ROLLBACK, only changes made after the SAVEPOINT will be undone. The next example updates and rolls back a transaction (the following statement displays the rows to be updated):

```
USE AdventureWorks2012;
GO
SELECT p.BusinessEntityID, firstname,lastname,rate
FROM Person.Person p,HumanResources.EmployeePayHistory h
WHERE p.BusinessEntityID= h.BusinessEntityID
AND p.BusinessEntityID = 9;
Output
```

BusinessEntityID	firstname	lastname	rate
9	Gigi	Matthew	40.8654

Table 13.15

The output shows that employee 9's lastname is Matthew and her rate is 40.8654. The following transaction changes and then undoes the changes to employee 9's lastname and rate.

```
USE AdventureWorks2012;
GO
DECLARE @T_Name VARCHAR(20)= 'update_name_sal';
BEGIN TRANSACTION @T_Name;
UPDATE Person.Person SET LastName ='Kelly'
WHERE BusinessEntityID = 9;
UPDATE HumanResources.EmployeePayHistory SET Rate = 90
WHERE BusinessEntityID = 9;
ROLLBACK TRANSACTION @T_Name;
```

The lastname and rate have been changed then restored to their previous values as shown.

```
USE AdventureWorks2012;
GO
SELECT p.BusinessEntityID, firstname,lastname,rate
FROM Person.Person p,HumanResources.EmployeePayHistory h
WHERE p.BusinessEntityID= h.BusinessEntityID
AND p.BusinessEntityID = 9;
Output
```

BusinessEntityID	firstname	lastname	rate
9	Gigi	Matthew	40.8654

Table 13.16

In this example, the last name and rate of employee 9 are first updated, and then the ROLLBACK TRANSACTION restores the lastname and the rate to the previous values.

T-SQL SAVE Transaction and ROLLBACK Using TRY CATCH Error Handlers

The SAVE TRANSACTION creates a recovery point where changes before this point are not lost if an error occurs after it. All changes after the SAVE TRANSACTION will be restored to their original values.

Using the previous example, a SAVE TRANSACTION is issued after the first UPDATE statement. A primary key update error is then introduced after the SAVE TRANSACTION. A second update is then issued. Only the changes made by the transactions after the SAVE TRANSACTION will be undone. For example:

```
USE AdventureWorks2012;
GO
BEGIN TRY
DECLARE @T_Name VARCHAR(20)= 'update_name_sal';
BEGIN TRANSACTION @T_Name;
UPDATE Person.Person SET LastName ='Kelly'
WHERE BusinessEntityID = 9;
SAVE TRANSACTION @T_Name;
UPDATE HumanResources.Employee SET BusinessEntityID = 40
WHERE BusinessEntityID = 11;
UPDATE HumanResources.EmployeePayHistory SET Rate = 40
WHERE BusinessEntityID = 9;
END TRY
BEGIN CATCH
EXECUTE dbo.uspPrintError;
```

ROLLBACK TRANSACTION @T_Name;

PRINT 'The transactions has been rollbacked @T_Name'

END CATCH

Output

(1 row(s) affected)

(0 row(s) affected)

Error 2627, Severity 14, State 1, Procedure—, Line 7

Violation of PRIMARY KEY constraint 'PK_Employee_

BusinessEntityID'. Cannot insert duplicate key in object

'HumanResources.Employee'. The duplicate key value is (40).

The transactions has been rollbacked @T_Name

In the previous example, the transactions are enclosed within TRY CATCH blocks. A SAVE TRANSACTION @T_Name ensures that only the second transaction after the savepoint are undone. The UPDATE after the SAVE TRANSACTION triggers an error because it tries to UPDATE the primary key of the employee table. This error is caught by the catch bock that executes the ROLLBACK TO the SAVE TRANSACTION point. As a result, only the changes made by the first transaction are saved while those by the second transaction are erased, as shown below:

```
USE AdventureWorks2012;
GO
SELECT p.BusinessEntityID, firstname,lastname,rate
FROM Person.Person p,HumanResources.EmployeePayHistory h
WHERE p.BusinessEntityID= h.BusinessEntityID
AND p.BusinessEntityID = 9;
Output
```

BusinessEntityID	firstname	lastname	rate
9	Gigi	Kelly	40.8654

Table 13.17

The lastname has been changed from Matthew to Kelly by the first transaction while the rate stays the same.

Transaction Control and Data Warehousing Dimension Loads

In data warehousing applications, the details of the fact tables are totally dependent on the details of the dimension tables. Both tables are loaded periodically with the same transaction (ETL job) say, daily. If the loading of one dimension table fails and the job continues, the fact table will become corrupted. Thus, transaction controls are used to ROLLBACK all the fully and partially loaded dimension tables if an error occurs on one table. The job is also terminated and the fact table is not loaded. This protects the fact table because each fact table row must contain all dimension foreign keys. It also ensures that a recovery ETL load job reloads all dimensions and fact tables in the same context.

In the next example, a simple data warehouse containing two dimension tables and a fact table are created. The facts are obtained from a point of sales (POS) extract file. Transaction controls are used to ensure that all dimensions are successfully loaded before the fact table is loaded. The tables are created as follows:

```
USE AdventureWorks2012;
GO
```

```
CREATE TABLE Sales.POS_Sales_fact (Surrogate_fact_id int
    PRIMARY KEY IDENTITY(1,1),Date_id int,
shop_id int,Sales_gross_amount money );
CREATE TABLE Sales.Shop_dimension (Shop_id int,Shop_
    name nvarchar(30),
Town nvarchar(30));
CREATE TABLE Sales.date_dimension (Date_id int,
Full_date DATE, Month_name nvarchar(30),
Day_name nvarchar(30));
CREATE TABLE Sales.POS_File (POS_date DATE, POS_
    Amount money,
POS_Shop_id int);
```

Two dimensions, one fact, and a POS table are created. Data is now loaded into the data warehouse. Transaction controls are used to separate the dimension-loading statements from the fact-loading statements creating two logical loading units. In the dimension-loading unit, all statements must either fail or succeed as a group. In the following example, all the dimension and POS file-loading statements have been grouped into a logical unit between TRY CATCH blocks, so any load failure will trigger the CATCH that will ROLLBACK the transaction and terminate the execution. This protects the fact table load in the same batch. An error is introduced in the loading of the Sales.POS_File in the third set of values (('202',400,2)). The string 202 cannot be inserted into the POS_Date column, triggering the error.

```
USE AdventureWorks2012;
GO
BEGIN TRY
DECLARE @Load_dimensions VARCHAR(20) ;
```

```
BEGIN TRANSACTION @Load_dimensions;
INSERT INTO Sales.Shop_dimension
    (Shop_id,Shop_name,Town)
VALUES(1,'Tati','Douala'),(2,'H & M','London'),(3,'Jimmy
    C','New York');
INSERT INTO Sales.date_dimension(Date_id,Full_date,Month_
    name, Day_name)
VALUES (1,'2012/01/01',DATENAME(MONTH,'2012/01/01'),
    DATENAME(WEEKDAY,'2012/01/01')),
(2,'2012/01/02',DATENAME(MONTH,'2012/01/02'),DATENA
    ME(WEEKDAY,'2012/01/02')),
(3,'2012/01/03',DATENAME(MONTH,'2012/01/03'),DATENA
    ME(WEEKDAY,'2012/01/03'));
INSERT INTO Sales.
    POS_File(POS_date,POS_Amount,POS_Shop_id)
VALUES('2012/01/01',40,1),('2012/01/01',130,1), ('202',400,
    2),('2012/01/02',250,3),
('2012/01/03',250,3);
END TRY
BEGIN CATCH
EXECUTE dbo.uspPrintError;
ROLLBACK TRANSACTION @Load_dimensions;
PRINT 'The Dimensions have been rollbacked'
END CATCH
SAVE TRANSACTION @Load_dimensions;
BEGIN TRY
INSERT INTO Sales.
    POS_Sales_fact(Date_id,shop_id,Sales_gross_amount)
SELECT d.Date_id,s.Shop_id,p.POS_Amount
```

```
FROM Sales.POS_File p,Sales.date_dimension d,Sales.
    Shop_dimension s
WHERE p.POS_date=d.Full_date
AND p.POS_Shop_id = s.Shop_id;
END TRY
BEGIN CATCH
EXECUTE dbo.uspPrintError;
ROLLBACK TRANSACTION @Load_dimensions;
PRINT 'The Facts have been rollbacked'
END CATCH
Output
(3 row(s) affected)
(3 row(s) affected)
(0 row(s) affected)
Error 241, Severity 16, State 1, Procedure—, Line 10
```

Conversion failed when converting date and/or time from character string.

The dimensions have been ROLLBACKED.

Msg 628, Level 16, State 0, Line 19 Cannot issue SAVE TRANSACTION when there is no active transaction.

The load failed and all the inserted dimension rows have been deleted. Once the error is eliminated in the next section, the load is going to succeed.

Transaction Control and Data Warehousing Fact Table Loads

The rows in fact tables are made up of foreign keys from all dimensions tables and facts from a business transaction source such as a POS (point of sale) file. For each transaction fact value, there must be a corresponding dimension values in the business source file. Thus the dimension values are matched (look ups) against source values, and for each match found the dimension keys from the dimension tables and the fact values from the source file are loaded into the fact table. These look ups can be performed using joins in INSERT SELECT statements.

The following code corrects the error from the previous section and loads the dimension and fact tables. Each dimension is matched to the source which ensures that each fact row contains all dimension foreign keys. Rows where only partial matches are not found are implicitly rejected by the join.

```
USE AdventureWorks2012;
GO
BEGIN TRY
DECLARE @Load_dimensions VARCHAR(20) ;
BEGIN TRANSACTION @Load_dimensions;
INSERT INTO Sales.Shop_dimension
    (Shop_id,Shop_name,Town)
VALUES(1,'Tati','Douala'),(2,'H & M','London'),(3,'Jimmy
    C','New York');
INSERT INTO Sales.date_dimension(Date_id,Full_date,Month_
    name, Day_name)
```

```
VALUES (1,'2012/01/01',DATENAME(MONTH,'2012/01/01'),
    DATENAME(WEEKDAY,'2012/01/01')),
(2,'2012/01/02',DATENAME(MONTH,'2012/01/02'),DATENA
    ME(WEEKDAY,'2012/01/02')),
(3,'2012/01/03',DATENAME(MONTH,'2012/01/03'),DATENA
    ME(WEEKDAY,'2012/01/03'));
INSERT INTO Sales.
    POS_File(POS_date,POS_Amount,POS_Shop_id)
VALUES('2012/01/01',40,1),('2012/01/01',130,1), ('2012/01/
    02',400,2),('2012/01/02',250,3),
('2012/01/03',250,3);
END TRY
BEGIN CATCH
EXECUTE dbo.uspPrintError;
ROLLBACK TRANSACTION @Load_dimensions;
PRINT 'The Dimensions have been rollbacked'
END CATCH
SAVE TRANSACTION @Load_dimensions;
BEGIN TRY--Insert data into fact table.
INSERT INTO Sales.
    POS_Sales_fact(Date_id,shop_id,Sales_gross_amount)
SELECT d.Date_id,s.Shop_id,p.POS_Amount
FROM Sales.POS_File p,Sales.date_dimension d,Sales.
    Shop_dimension s
WHERE p.POS_date=d.Full_date
AND p.POS_Shop_id = s.Shop_id;
END TRY
BEGIN CATCH
EXECUTE dbo.uspPrintError;
ROLLBACK TRANSACTION @Load_dimensions;
```

PRINT 'The Facts have been rollbacked to Load_dimensions'

END CATCH

Output

(3 row(s) affected)

(3 row(s) affected)

(5 row(s) affected)

(5 row(s) affected)

The dimension and fact tables have been loaded. The following listing shows an analytic report which queries the related tables.

```
SELECT Shop_name,Town,Month_name, Day_name,
    SUM(Sales_gross_amount) AS "total sales"
FROM Sales.POS_Sales_fact f,Sales.Shop_dimension s,Sales.
    date_dimension d
WHERE f.shop_id = s.shop_id
AND f.date_id = d.date_id
GROUP BY Shop_name,Town,Month_name,Day_name;
```

Output

Shop_name	Town	Month_name	Day_name	total sales
H & M	London	January	Monday	400.00
Jimmy C	New York	January	Monday	250.00
Jimmy C	New York	January	Tuesday	250.00
Tati	Douala	January	Sunday	170.00

Table 13.18

The output shows that all the tables where correctly loaded.

Data Standardization, Validation, and Correction Using Programmable Objects

Data is captured in organisations from several sources. Generally, the validity of the data cannot be guaranteed at the source of capture. Database constraints and triggers should prevent this, but sometimes they are disabled when partial data is more important than its accuracy and formatting. For example, data captured over the phone or Internet may contain spelling or formatting errors. This data can be standardized, validated, and corrected to corporate data quality policies using SQL programmable objects and functions. For example, the following table is created and populated with three erroneous rows that do not meet the data quality standards of the company.

```
USE AdventureWorks2012;
GO
CREATE TABLE Person.names (person_id int, title
    nvarchar(8), firstname nvarchar(30),
middlename nvarchar(30),lastname nvarchar(30), Sex
    nvarchar(3));
INSERT INTO Person.names (person_id,Title,FirstName,Middle
    Name,LastName,Sex)
VALUES(1,NULL,'Tiger',NULL,'Mury','M'),
(2,NULL,'Emma','Law','Hewit','F'),
(3,Null,'Sanjay','Kip','Simpson','M');
SELECT * FROM Person.names;
Output
```

person_id	title	firstname	middlename	lastname	Sex
1	NULL	Tiger	NULL	Mury	M
2	NULL	Emma	Law	Hewit	F
3	NULL	Sanjay	Kip	Simpson	M

Table 13.19

The data quality standards may state that every name record must have correct data for the title, firstname, middlename, and lastname columns. Furthermore, a null title can be replaced with derived values while the null middlenames must be removed from the table and sent to an error table for reprocessing. The following error table is created:

```
SELECT * INTO Person.errors
FROM Person.names WHERE person_id = 0;
```

In the created Person.names table the first record has a missing middlename and must be sent to the error table for reprocessing. The other two records have missing titles. Their titles can be derived using a CASE statement that assigns the titles Mr or Mrs based on the sex of the person. The following code is used to cleanse the table to the required data quality standard.

```
USE AdventureWorks2012;
GO
DECLARE @title Varchar(5),@fname Varchar(50),@
    middlename Varchar(50),@emp_sex Varchar(5);
DECLARE @p_id int,@lname Varchar(50),@counter int =0;
DECLARE data_cleanse CURSOR
```

```
FOR SELECT person_id,Title,FirstName,MiddleName,LastNam
    e,Sex
FROM Person.names WHERE person_id <4;
OPEN data_cleanse;
WHILE @counter < 4
BEGIN
FETCH NEXT FROM data_cleanse INTO @p_id,@title,@
    fname,@middlename,@lname,@emp_sex
IF @middlename IS NULL
BEGIN
INSERT INTO Person.errors SELECT * FROM Person.names
    WHERE person_id = @p_id;
DELETE FROM Person.names WHERE person_id = @p_id;
PRINT'The row '+CAST(@p_id AS NCHAR)+' '+@fname+' '+@
    lname+'has been moved to the error table';
END
IF @title IS NULL
BEGIN
UPDATE Person.names SET Title =
( CASE Sex WHEN 'M' THEN 'Mr'
WHEN 'F' THEN 'Mrs' ELSE 'Minor'
END)
WHERE person_id = @p_id;
END
SET @counter = @counter +1;--increment counter
END
CLOSE data_cleanse;
DEALLOCATE data_cleanse;
```

The code uses a cursor to scroll through all employee records. It moves the first record where the middlename is null from the names table to the error table for reprocessing. The titles of the other two records are corrected using the UPDATE CASE statement. The result is as follows:

SELECT * FROM Person.names

Output

person_id	title	firstname	middlename	lastname	Sex
2	Mrs	Emma	Law	Hewit	F
3	Mr	Sanjay	Kip	Simpson	M

Table 13.20

The titles have been derived and corrected and the first record has been moved to the error file. The contents of the error file are shown below.

SELECT * FROM Person.errors:

Output

person_id	title	firstname	middlename	lastname	Sex
1	NULL	Tiger	NULL	Mury	M

Table 13.21

The table contains the erroneous row that will be reprocessed.

Conclusion

This section covered the most important components of the procedural SQL extension. Important business problems were also resolved using the extensions. Though all constructs were not covered, the reader should be able to build powerful applications with programmable T-SQL and PL/SQL.

Appendix

Getting Started with Oracle

Oracle Database 11g Express download and installation: Download from the following link.

http://www.Oracle.com/technetwork/database/enterprise-edition/downloads/index.html?ssSourceSiteId=ocomen

Installing Oracle 11g Express

Double click on the downloaded executable file and accept all the default options. The main input for the installation is the specification of the SYSTEM account password, which is specified in the following screen: Remember this password because you will need it later to login to oracle.

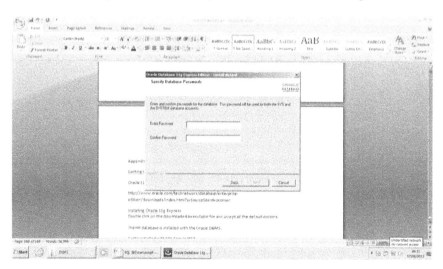

Fig a1

The HR database is installed with the Oracle DBMS.

Opening the Oracle Query Editor

Double click on the Get Started With Oracle Database 11g Express Edition icon on the desktop or go to Start→ All programs→Oracle Database 11g Express Edition→Get started.

The Oracle database homepage is displayed. Now click on application express button.

Fig a2

The following login screen is displayed:

Fig a3

Log in with username SYSTEM. The password is the one specified during installation.

The create workspace screen now appears. Create an application express login and password for the installed HR database as follows:

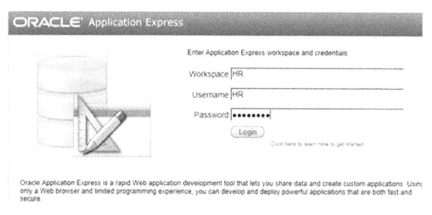

Fig a4

Once the information is complete, click on the create workspace button on the top right corner of the screen. The workspace is created, and the following message appears in the window:

'Successfully created workspace HR. To begin, click here to login'. Click on the 'click here' to login to the HR database on the following screen.

Fig a5

To get to the SQL editor, click on SQL Workshop→SQL Commands. Then type in and run a query as follows:

Fig a6

Execution Using SQL Plus to Access the Oracle 11g Hr database

The first order of business is to unlock the HR account and execute a query as follows:

Start→ All programs→Oracle Database11g Express edition →Run SQL command line

The SQL plus interface appears. Then connect to the database with the system account as follows:

SQL> conn system as sysdba

Enter Password: enter the password you specified during installation.

Now unlock the oracle hr account so that the procedure can be executed directly from the hr schema. Use the following statement:

SQL>ALTER USER hr IDENTIFIED BY manager ACCOUNT
UNLOCK;

Now connect with the unlocked account credentials as follows:

SQL> conn hr

Enter Password: Enter the password you specified when the account was unlocked.

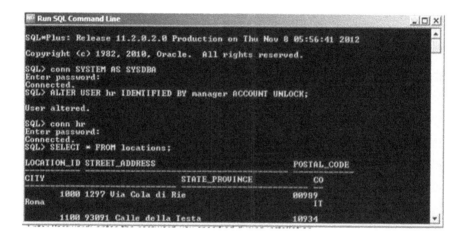

Getting Started with SQL Server 2012

Download Microsoft® SQL Server® 2012 Express with advanced services from the following site:

http://www.microsoft.com/en-us/download/details. aspx?id=29062

Choose the package appropriate to your operating system.

Installing SQL Server 2012 Express with Advanced Services

Verify that your computer meets the minimum system requirements stated on the website and then double click the downloaded executable file.

The installation centre is displayed after a few minutes. Choose the first option that installs a new SQL server stand-alone installation.

Fig a7

Accept all the default options and licence conditions and click next. The installation continues until the instance creation stage. The following screen is displayed:

Fig a8

Select the named instance option and enter the instance name and then click next. Accept the sever configuration options and click next. Then the database configuration screen appears as follows:

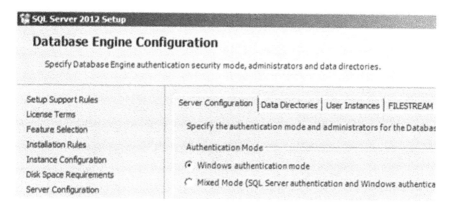

Fig a9

Accept the windows authentication mode option and then click on the FILESTREAM tab and enable the following options: Enable FILESTREAM for Transact-SQL access and Enable FILESTREAM for file I/O access.

Fig a10

Once the FILESTREAM options have been enabled, accept all the default options and click next. The installation package installs and configures the new SQL server 2012.

Now download and install the AdventureWorks2012 database:

http://msftdbprodsamples.codeplex.com/releases/view/55330

Once the database has been downloaded, launch the Microsoft SQL server management studio from the following sequence: Start→ All programs→Microsoft SQL server 2012→SQL server Management Studio. The following login screen appears:

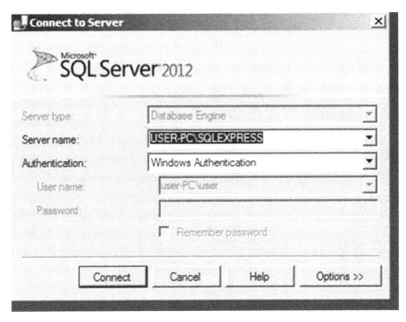

Fig a11

Click connect.

Opening the SQL Server Management Studio and Attaching the AdventureWorks2012 Database

Once the management studio is installed, right click the databases tree in the object explorer and select attach as follows:

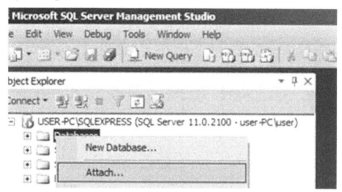

Fig a12

Click the add button and navigate to the location of the stored adventureworks2012 database. On the adventureworks 2012 details window, remove the log file specified and click OK as shown on the figure below.

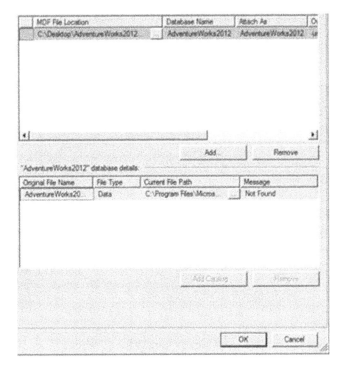

Fig a13

Writing and Executing the First T-SQL Query

Click the new query button and write a query as follows:

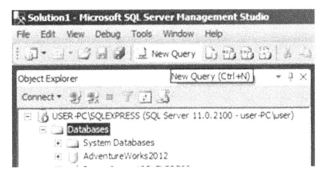

Fig a14

The query window opens and the adventureworks database can be queried as follows. Once the query is written, click the red execute button.

Fig a15

About the Author

Victor Ebai is an independent Business Intelligence consultant with twelve years' experience in the business intelligence industry, covering database, report, data warehouse, and SQL query development. SQL performance tuning is a passion of Victor's, and he's helped several FTSE 100 companies attain their BI interests. He was educated in Coventry University, United Kingdom, where he currently works and resides.

About the Book

What Is SQL? Guides beginners, intermediate and expert readers through the most important aspects of declarative and procedural SQL for oracle 11g and SQL server 2012.

With *What Is SQL?* You will learn or better understand how to

- Design, build, and query relational databases in the latest versions of Oracle and SQL server;

- Become an expert in standard SQL statements;

- Build advanced objects which simplify database queries;

- Answer complex business questions with simple SQL queries;

- Perform data quality operations that eliminate corrupted data from databases;

- Extend the functionality of SQL using PL/SQL and programmable T-SQL;

- Build and load data warehouses without using an expensive ETL tool;

- Troubleshoot and tune SQL code and database designs;

- Extensively use built-functions to retrieve and transform data;

- Translate complex business rules into database constraints;

- Create advanced queries that answer complex business questions;

- Manipulate data within tables;

- Create recoverable business transactions;

- Perform non-standard SQL operations such as deleting duplicate rows;

- Obtain free samples of Oracle11g and SQL server 2012 databases.

- Create your own business focused functions.

www.ingramcontent.com/pod-product-compliance
Lightning Source LLC
LaVergne TN
LVHW042331060326
832902LV00006B/97